In Memory Of

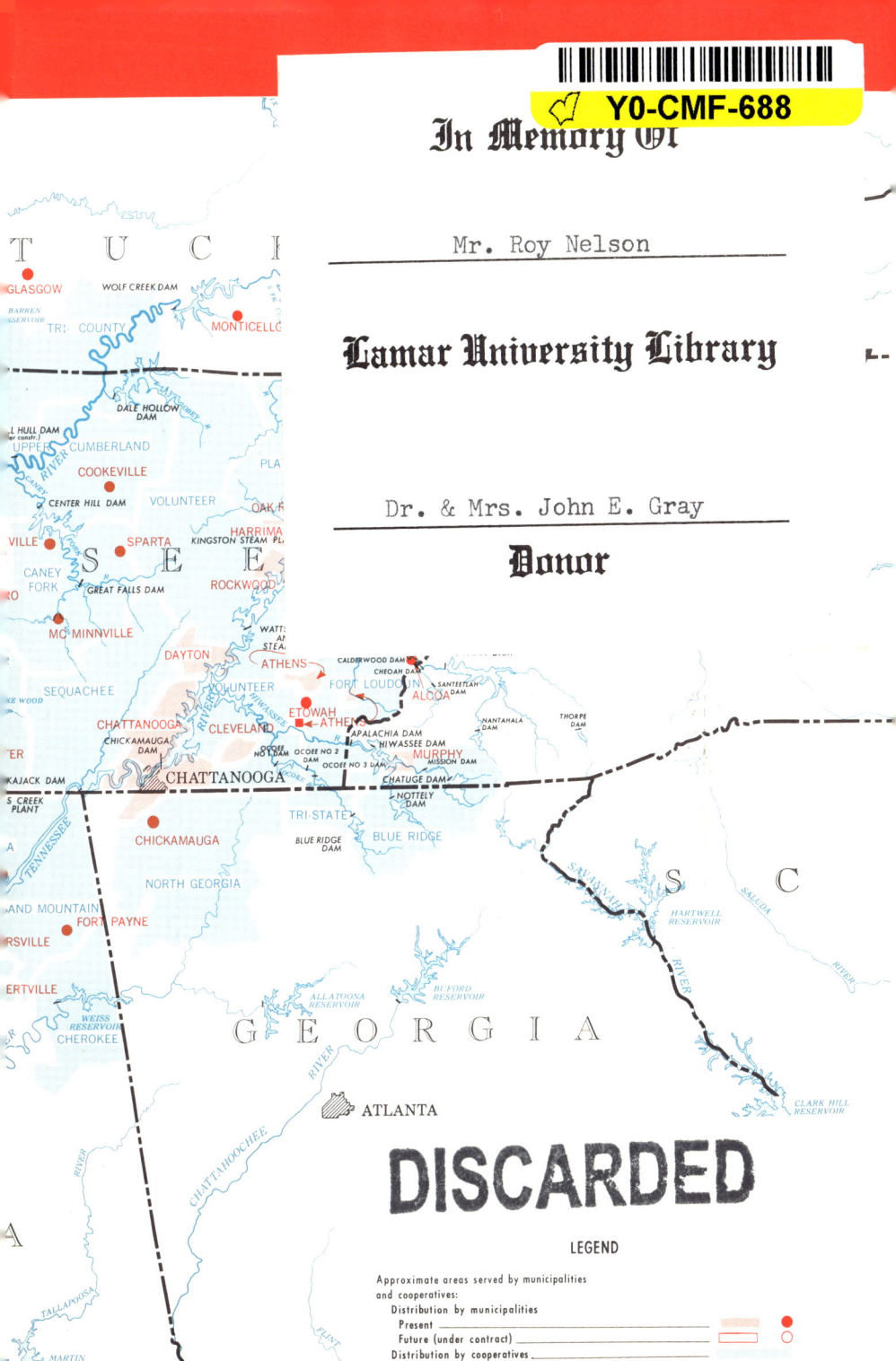

Mr. Roy Nelson

Lamar University Library

Dr. & Mrs. John E. Gray

Donor

DISCARDED

SPARKS AT THE GRASSROOTS

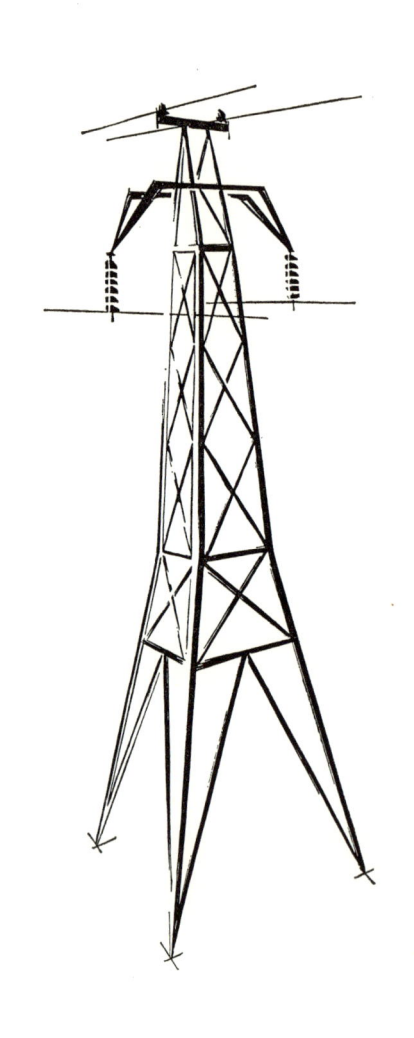

SPARKS

AT THE GRASSROOTS

MUNICIPAL DISTRIBUTION OF TVA
ELECTRICITY IN TENNESSEE

By Victor C. Hobday

THE UNIVERSITY OF TENNESSEE PRESS
KNOXVILLE

LIBRARY OF CONGRESS CATALOG CARD NUMBER 70-77845
STANDARD BOOK NUMBER 87049-099-0

Copyright © 1969 by The University of Tennessee Press
Manufactured in the United States of America
All Rights Reserved. First edition

FOREWORD

THE DEVELOPMENT of the federal system in the United States has been a source of controversy since the colonies managed to shake off the rule of the British. In recent years the pressures exerted on states and their subdivisions by the national system of grants-in-aid have excited acrimonious discussion and assiduous investigation, not to mention promises and hopes of further decentralization. Less attention has been given to that aspect of federal-state-local involvement that arises from contracts made between governmental units.

The Tennessee Valley Authority, long an object of interest, study, and publication by The University of Tennessee Bureau of Public Administration and The University of Tennessee Press, pursues its policy goals in the field of electrical power production and distribution by means of contracts made with municipalities and electric cooperatives. These contracts furnish not only a legal framework for the distribution and sale of electric power, but are, in addition, the means whereby the Authority pursues certain social and economic objectives which seem appropriate to it and which municipalities might or might not follow in the absence of the contracts. They are attended by certain problems arising from payments in lieu of taxes.

Dr. Hobday has undertaken to study TVA-municipal relations in depth, and we believe this volume represents the first such intensive study made available to the public. The University and the Bureau of Public Administration naturally take no position on the issues here examined, but we are happy to have the opportunity to present Dr. Hobday's findings.

> LEE S. GREENE
> Director
> The Bureau of Public Administration

PREFACE

AMONG TVA'S MANY FUNCTIONS, the generation and distribution of electric power are certainly the largest and possibly the most important. This book deals with the relationship between the Authority and the cities of Tennessee to which it supplies electric power and with the problems that have grown out of TVA's contractual arrangements with these cities for retail power distribution.

Ever since its inception, TVA has been the subject of continuing controversy, and its officials have been quite concerned about the Authority's public image in the Valley. The persistence of such concern is one of the reasons that a close analysis of TVA's relations with Valley cities becomes so very interesting. Strangely enough, this subject has not been fully explored until now.

My study began in 1953 after I had attended a meeting of TVA and municipal officials, who were attempting a broad review of contractual arrangements between the authority and the cities with an eye to improving an imperfect situation. It was my intention to make the study collaterally with my duties as executive director of the Municipal Technical Advisory Service, a part of the Division of University Extension of The University of Tennessee, but the study languished until a leave of absence provided me with the opportunity to complete the work as a project of the University's Bureau of Public Administration.

In 1965 I sent questionnaires to officials of the fifty-nine Tennessee municipalities that distribute TVA electricity: incumbent and former mayors, councilmen and aldermen with relatively long tenure in office, city managers, city recorders (city clerks), members of power boards, and managers of municipal power systems. The numbers distributed and returned were as follows (one was sent to a retired manager, and both he and the incumbent manager made a return):

Category	Number dispatched	Number returned	Per cent returned
Mayors	149	59	40%
Other members of governing bodies	103	35	34%
Other city officials	59	22	37%
Members of power boards	187	120	64%
Power system managers	60	46	77%
Totals	558	282	50%

After receiving and tabulating the questionnaire returns, I conducted supplementary personal interviews with thirty-two power board members (nine of these were also members of the cities' governing bodies), three power system managers, and four mayors. (Having worked closely with mayors and other officials of general municipal governments over the past fifteen years, I felt that it was unnecessary to interview many in this category.) Although the comments of the interviewees represented a range of views approximating those reported on the questionnaire, my impression was that greater frankness, especially in voicing views unfavorable to TVA, was evident in the personal interviews. Based on this sampling, I would say that the questionnaire returns were probably more pro-TVA than the true feelings of the respondents, at least with respect to administrative arrangements under the power contracts.

My other sources of information are varied. As part of my official duties, I have served as an adviser to many cities on power contracts and related problems and have participated in conferences and negotiations between TVA, representatives of the Tennessee Municipal League, and municipal officials. Congressional documents that might reasonably be expected to contain pertinent information have been scanned. Several books and a large number of periodical articles have been read. I have relied quite heavily on newspaper accounts in the tremendous collection (over 300,000 clippings covering the whole period of TVA's history) in the TVA Technical Library. The public speeches of high-ranking TVA officials were reviewed for pertinent comments, and indications of TVA policies were gleaned from various other sources. Materials in the files of the Tennessee Municipal League and the Tennessee Valley Public Power Association were examined. All power contracts between TVA and Tennessee municipalities that had any policy implications, from 1933 to mid-1964, were read, and a spot check of subsequent contracts indicated no significant changes. A few TVA officials were interviewed, and my notes of conferences in past years were re-examined.

Although I do not claim that this is a definitive study, my presentation should give the reader a good comprehension of the major problems and friction points that have developed during the period of TVA power service in Tennessee. Judged in its entirety, the TVA record in the Valley must be pronounced a tremendous success, but there have been sufficient sparks to make this story possible. And we should bear in mind that sparks only come from live wires!

No effort will be made to express my gratitude to the many people to whom I am indebted for helpful advice and assistance in pursuing this study. They have been thanked personally, and I am fearful that a listing of their names would result in some omissions. However, a special word of appreciation should be directed to the individuals in TVA who provided access to file materials and freely supplied all information that was requested, though at times they must have realized that my presentation of the information might not be as favorable as they would like.

V. C. H.

CONTENTS

1 THE FOUNDATIONS OF THE TVA POWER PROGRAM	3
The Beginnings	3
The Effect of World War I	5
A Decade of Indecision and the Birth of TVA	6
The Creation of a Market	9
Challenge in the Courts: Round One	12
The System that TVA Built	14
The Dominance of the Power Program	16
The Question of State Control	19
TVA Influence on Tennessee Legislation	21
Challenge in the Courts: Round Two	24
Governor Browning's Proposal for State Operation	27
Valley States Relinquish Power	29
2 PARTNERSHIP: A QUESTION OF BALANCE	32
The Basic Policy: Local Autonomy Through Local Distribution	32
TVA Organization and District Offices	35
Local Power Boards and Local Democracy	38
Autonomy of Power Boards	44
The View from the Municipal Side	50
TVA's Influence on Local Government	55
Power Contracts	60
3 POWER RATES: AN OVERHEATED ISSUE	74
Lowest Possible Rates: Mandate or Policy?	74
Wholesale Rates	78
TVA Control of Retail Rates	86
Retail Rate Reductions	91
Rates in Rural Areas	99
Promotion of Power Sales	102
Street Lighting Rates	104

4 CONFLICTS OVER SERVICE AREAS	110
TVA Selection of Distributors	110
Rural Service by Municipal Systems	117
Conflicts Beyond City Limits	119
Direct TVA Service to Large Industries	132
5 FINANCE: THE PROBLEM OF PROFITS	145
TVA Control of Revenues	145
Priorities in Use of Revenues	148
Prohibition of Charitable Contributions	153
Debt Service on General Obligation Bonds	156
Joint Operations with Other City Agencies	158
Return on Municipal Investment	165
Accounting Standards Prescribed by TVA	167
The Role of the Field Accountant	169
6 CONTROVERSY OVER TAX EQUIVALENTS	172
Early Policy	172
The Section 13 Amendment	178
TVA Opposition to Taxes on Its Power	180
Comparative Tax Data	186
Municipal Tax Equivalents	189
Tax Equivalents for Counties	210
A New Tax-Equivalent Formula	218
7 SUMMING UP	231
The United Front and Municipal Autonomy	232
Power Boards and Local Democracy	236
Is TVA Too Inflexible?	239
Tax Equivalents	240
A Final Word	243

APPENDIXES:

1 Power Sales by TVA and Distributors, in Millions of Kilowatt-Hours and Percentages of Totals, by Major Categories, 1950–1968	245
2 Years in Which Various Provisions of Street Lighting Rate Schedules Became Effective for Tennessee Owner-Cities	246
3 TVA Wholesale Power Rate—Schedule A	249
4 Functions of the TVA Distributors Accounting Section	252
INDEX	257

LIST OF TABLES AND FIGURES

1 Estimation by Two Groups of Municipal Officials of Degree of TVA's Influence	54
2 Estimation by Two Groups of Municipal Officials of Degree of Pressure Exerted by TVA	55
3 Questionnaire Response of General City Government Officials: The Effects of TVA Electric Systems on General City Governments	59
4 Tennessee Municipal Officials Executing TVA Power Contracts, 1933–1964	70
5 Monthly Commercial and Industrial Electric Bills: National Averages, Chattanooga, and Nine Selected Cities, 1940 and 1968	78
6 TVA Wholesale Power Rates	80
7 Number of TVA Municipal Distributors Applying Various Retail Rate Schedules, 1957, 1966, 1967, and 1969	98
8 Questionnaire Response: Attitudes of City and Power System Officials Toward Joint Use of Buildings	164
9 Questionnaire Response: Propriety of Exempting Electricity Sales from Local Option Sales Tax	186
10 Relation of Book Values to Original Costs for 42 TVA Municipal Distributors in Tennessee, 1940, 1945, 1953, and 1963	199
11 Distribution of Tennessee Municipal Systems by Percentages of Standard Maximum Tax Equivalents Paid, 1962–1968	205

FIGURES

1 Total power operating expenses and gross expenses of nonpower programs of TVA, fiscal years 1939–1967   18
2 Relative percentage allocations of TVA administrative and general expenses to power and nonpower programs, fiscal years 1939–1967   19

SPARKS AT THE GRASSROOTS

1 THE FOUNDATIONS OF THE TVA POWER PROGRAM

The Tennessee Valley Authority is the result of more than a century of concern over the problems and possibilities posed by the Tennessee River, which drains parts of seven states—Tennessee, Virginia, North Carolina, Alabama, Georgia, Mississippi, and Kentucky. It is not surprising that interest should have continued for so long, for the Tennessee Valley covers a wide geographical area which altogether represents a significant portion of the southeastern United States. But perhaps the very scope of the problem made the controversies, the false starts, and the pattern of trial and error over a period of many years inevitable. In fact, the problem was not singular, but many-faceted; navigation, conservation, and public power were the primary but not the only concerns of those who helped set the stage for the Authority's formation. Finally, it took the twin disasters of war followed by severe economic depression to stimulate enactment of legislation for the multiple-purpose program which TVA was commissioned to carry out.

The Authority's founders anticipated that power production would be secondary to navigation, flood control, rehabilitation and conservation of agricultural lands, and regional planning for proper use and development of the area's natural resources, but power has gradually become the primary program. Tennessee, because of its geographic location in relation to the river, enjoys more benefits from TVA's multiple-purpose programs than all of the other six Valley states combined.

THE BEGINNINGS[1]

As early as 1816 the federal government was studying how

[1] Good accounts of these early developments may be found in Elliott

to get boats around Muscle Shoals, a 37-mile strip of rapids, pools, and exposed rocks where the Tennessee River drops 134 feet. In 1818 the House of Representatives passed a resolution declaring that Congress had the authority to appropriate money for building roads and canals and for improving natural water courses (perhaps the beginning of pork-barrel legislation). An act of Congress in 1824 authorized the President to have the necessary plans, surveys, and estimates made of routes for such roads and canals as he might deem of national importance and necessary for transportation of mail. In the same year, the Secretary of War, reporting on nationwide surveys to be made by a board of engineers, identified the Muscle Shoals section of the Tennessee River as one of the projects of most importance.

Congress in 1828 made a grant of 400,000 acres of public lands to Alabama to finance a 6-foot canal around the Shoals. Following approval of plans by President Jackson in 1831, the state finally completed the canal in 1836 at a cost of about $650,000, but it was abandoned one year later because the structures were inadequate.

In 1852 Congress appropriated $50,000 to provide a minimum navigable depth of 2 feet from Knoxville downstream to Kelly's Ferry, 22 miles below Chattanooga. The work carried out under this appropriation produced nothing of permanence. A federal project started in 1875 and finished in 1890 produced two canals, with minimum 5-foot depths, around the Elk River Shoals and Big Muscle Shoals. In 1899 Congress gave its consent to construction of a dam at the Shoals for a private power development, but no action was taken under this authorization.

A bill passed by Congress authorizing private development for power purposes was vetoed by President Theodore Roose-

---

Roberts, *One River—Seven States*, The University of Tennessee *Record*, Extension Series, Vol. XXXI, No. 1 (Knoxville: The Bureau of Public Administration, June, 1955), and in C. Herman Pritchett, *The Tennessee Valley Authority: A Study in Public Administration* (Chapel Hill: The University of North Carolina Press, 1943), pp. 3–30. For a detailed study of the political and economic background in the period following World War I, see Preston J. Hubbard, *Origins of the TVA: The Muscle Shoals Controversy, 1920–1932* (Nashville: Vanderbilt University Press, 1961).

velt in 1903 on the grounds that it was not "right or just that this element of local value should be given away to private individuals." He expressed a view that when "the government is or may be called upon to improve a stream, the improvement should be made to pay for itself, so far as practicable." In 1907 Roosevelt signed legislation authorizing development "for power and other purposes," but no funds were appropriated.

Congress in 1904 granted a 99-year franchise to the Tennessee Electric Power Company for construction of a hydroelectric dam at Hales Bar, 33 miles below Chattanooga, with navigation locks to be provided by the federal government. After the city of Chattanooga, for want of statutory authority, failed to exercise its prior rights written into the authorizing act by conservationists in Congress, construction was started in 1905, but foundation difficulties delayed completion until 1913. This dual-purpose structure provided a minimum 6-foot navigation depth from Hales Bar to Chattanooga and had a power capacity of 51,000 kilowatts through fourteen hydroelectric units.

THE EFFECT OF WORLD WAR I

The great push at Muscle Shoals grew out of the wartime need for nitrates and anxiety over dependence upon Chile as a source of supply. Since at that time the only two known processes for fixing atmospheric nitrogen required large amounts of power, the National Defense Act of 1916 authorized the President to construct dams and other types of power plants, to be operated only by the government, to furnish power for nitrate plants. Acting under this authority, President Wilson in 1917 directed construction of two nitrate plants at Muscle Shoals and a dam to supply power to the plants. The first nitrate plant, costing almost $13 million, was not successful; the second plant, with appurtenances including two steam-generating plants, was completed after the end of the war at an estimated cost of $69 million and was placed on a standby status after a test run in 1919. Construction of the dam (Wilson Dam) commenced in 1917, and it was only 35 per cent completed when funds ran out in 1921. A supplemental appropriation in 1922 allowed its completion by 1925, at a total estimated cost of $47 million. Administration of these facilities was lodged in the War Department.

Secretary of War Newton D. Baker tried unsuccessfully to turn the plants over to private enterprise for peacetime production of fertilizer. This effort failing, a bill was introduced in Congress in 1919 to create a government corporation for this purpose; after considerable revision, it finally passed the Senate in 1921 but never reached the floor of the House.

The Harding administration in March, 1921, invited proposals from private concerns for acquisition of the plants; none was received. The chief of engineers then advertised for bids on the properties, and in July, 1921, Henry Ford made an offer to buy the two nitrate plants and accompanying steam plants for $5 million and to complete Wilson Dam and a second dam at cost, these to be leased to him for 100 years. Associated power companies in the area, also bidding for the power properties, modified their proposal to include fertilizer production. Ford's proposal was the only one to receive serious consideration, and in March, 1924, a majority of the House approved it. Senator George W. Norris was primarily responsible for its rejection by the Senate.

A DECADE OF INDECISION AND THE BIRTH OF TVA

Senator Norris' first bill, introduced in 1921, would have created a government corporation to take over the Muscle Shoals properties and operate them for fertilizer and power production. His subsequent investigations created some doubt as to the practicability of commercial fertilizer production, and in 1924 he introduced another bill which would have turned the nitrate plants over to the Department of Agriculture and would have created a federally owned corporation to operate the power plants; this bill was substituted for the House-approved bill accepting Ford's proposal, whereupon Ford withdrew his offer.

Senator Oscar W. Underwood sponsored a measure opposed in principle to the stand taken by Senator Norris. His bill would have authorized sale of power only at the Muscle Shoals switchboard, with transmission facilities to be supplied by the purchasers, thus effectively limiting the customers to the existing private power companies in the area. This bill was passed by the Senate in 1925 in preference to the Norris bill.

A Muscle Shoals Inquiry Commission, appointed by President Coolidge, in 1925 recommended that the properties be leased for not more than fifty years to a private operator, to be used for their original purposes of fertilizer production and purely incidental power generation. There followed halfhearted congressional efforts to secure a fertilizer lessee, but all bids were too unfavorable to be seriously considered. The House Committee on Military Affairs announced that if the situation was unchanged by the time of convening the 70th Congress it would give "full and careful consideration" to operation of the properties by a government corporation. The committee made good its threat by introducing a bill to create such a corporation to engage in fertilizer experimentation, production of fixed nitrogen, and sale of surplus power. After revision to incorporate several of Senator Norris' ideas, this bill was passed by both houses in May, 1928, but it was given a pocket veto by President Coolidge.

After Congress failed to adopt any of his bills, which he had introduced in three successive sessions, Senator Norris in 1927 sponsored a measure which would have authorized the Secretary of War to sell the power produced at Wilson Dam on a more firm basis. As it was, the secretary could only make short-term contracts, subject to congressional action and terminable on short notice, and the power could only be sold at the power plant to the Alabama Power Company because it owned the only transmission line to the plant. Senator Norris' bill would have empowered the secretary to lease or construct transmission lines from the dam and to make contracts up to ten years, with preference given to public agencies. This bill was adopted by the Senate in March, 1928, but it never reached the House—instead, some of its provisions were incorporated into the bill that received President Coolidge's pocket veto.

Pursuant to congressional directives in five acts adopted in the period 1922–28, the Corps of Engineers made several studies of the river, comparing the alternatives of low dams for navigation only and high dams for multiple purposes, based on development by private interests and the government. To carry out this policy, the Rivers and Harbors Act of 1930 provided for construction of high dams by private interests in cooperation with the government, but no private interest responded to the opportunity.[2]

In May, 1930, the House passed a bill proposed by the Military Affairs Committee which reverted to the theory of private operation; it would have empowered the President to establish a board to appraise the properties and undertake to secure leases, but the bill was unacceptable to the Senate. Nine months later the two houses agreed on a compromise bill which provided for leasing the nitrate plants and for governmental operation of the power plant. President Hoover vetoed the bill on March 3, 1931, primarily on grounds that the government should not compete with private enterprise in the power field.

Following his veto, President Hoover appointed a Muscle Shoals Commission which recommended that the properties be used for the production of commercial fertilizer, agricultural experimentation, and manufacture of chemicals, under a fifty-year lease preferably with a farmer-controlled corporation. A leasing bill subsequently passed the House in 1932, but no further action along this line was taken.

Data compiled by the Corps of Engineers indicated the waste of power: of a total of 7,566,626,000 kilowatt-hours available at Wilson Dam in the five years 1928 through 1932, only 1,296,135,000, or 17 per cent, were delivered to the single transmission line owned by the Alabama Power Company. A spokesman for the company testified that the sale of power at Wilson Dam was subject to termination "on 30 days' notice [and] . . . we cannot sell power to our customers on 30 days' notice."[3]

During this period there had developed a congressional determination to keep the Muscle Shoals properties in government ownership; the principal issue was whether the power should be sold at the switchboard or transmitted over government-owned lines. The "power trust" was also being heavily criticized because of corruption in holding companies and monopolistic

[2] *Tennessee Electric Power Co.* v. *T.V.A.*, 21 F. Supp. 947, 952–53 (1938).
[3] U. S., Congress, House, Committee on Military Affairs, *Hearings, Muscle Shoals*, 73d Cong., 1st Sess., 1933, pp. 103, 198.

practices such as inflated rate bases, high rates, and failure to undertake rural electrification. Advocates of public power were talking about the need for a "yardstick" of public operation to replace unsatisfactory regulation by state agencies and about the social and economic benefits that would flow from cheap electricity.

The Great Depression of the thirties and the political climate of the New Deal furnished a setting favorable to the governmental operation of the Muscle Shoals properties and public development of the entire Tennessee River as a natural resource. An act of 1933 created the Tennessee Valley Authority, a federal corporation with the directors appointed by the President and charged with broad responsibilities for river valley development, including the generating and marketing of electric power.[4] The Muscle Shoals properties were transferred to this Authority, now to be referred to as TVA. In line with the federal government's general power policy, TVA was directed to give preference to states, counties, cities, and nonprofit cooperative agencies in the sale of electricity.

THE CREATION OF A MARKET

A period of stalling and litigation by the private power companies was to delay the time when TVA power would become available to most people in the Valley. The Authority's most immediate problem was developing a market. It had power to sell but where could it be sold? The Alabama Power Company owned the only transmission line from Muscle Shoals, and at the end of TVA's first year of operation this company was taking 98 per cent of the total power output. Only five municipal and cooperative systems—with about 6,500 customers—were being served at that time.

In that day of virtually no rural electrification, cities were the only readily available markets. The few already operating their own power systems were TVA's first targets, but these were scattered and transmission facilities had to be constructed before a system could be established. In 1933 sixteen municipally owned systems in Tennessee were serving about 14,000 custom-

[4] U. S., *Statutes at Large*, XLVIII, 58.

ers; by 1937 seven had contracted to enter the TVA system (Pulaski and Dayton in 1935, Bolivar, Dickson, Milan, and Somerville in 1936, and Trenton in 1937). (Acquisitions of private power companies in the twenties had substantially reduced this market; Abbott and Greene reported that in 1922 there were forty-four municipal systems in Tennessee and by 1927 the number had shrunk to eighteen.[5]) The other nine municipally owned systems took longer to ponder the pros and cons of buying TVA power but gradually they fell into line: Lawrenceburg in 1939, Springfield in 1940, Lebanon in 1941, Cookeville in 1944, Morristown and Tullahoma in 1947, Union City in 1950, Dyersburg in 1956, and the last—Covington—in 1958. Those that postponed entry did so primarily because they were reluctant to give up the revenues that had been realized for general municipal purposes, but the pull of substantially lower TVA rates, especially when the time came for capital expansions of municipal generating plants, finally persuaded the holdouts.

Obviously, municipally owned systems were a small part of TVA's potential market. TVA's prime targets were the privately owned utilities that served the bulk of the Tennessee Valley area, and in 1934 the Authority initiated negotiations to purchase their power lines and facilities. The Authority adopted a policy declaring that "adverse economic effects upon a privately owned utility should be a matter for serious consideration . . . but not the determining factor." Primary considerations were to be "furthering of the public interest in making power available at the lowest rate consistent with sound fiscal policy and the accomplishment of the social objectives which low-cost power makes possible."[6] The companies were naturally reluctant to dispose of profitable markets. TVA was a patient negotiator, and some said that the agency sometimes paid excessive prices in order to attain its goal.

TVA asserted that each community had the "undeniable right

[5] Lyndon E. Abbott and Lee S. Greene, *Municipal Government and Administration in Tennessee*, The University of Tennessee *Record, Extension Series*, Vol. XV, No. 1 (Knoxville: The Bureau of Research, School of Business Administration, Feb., 1939), pp. 117–18.

[6] *TVA Annual Report for the Fiscal Year Ended June 30, 1934* (Washington, D. C.: U. S. Government Printing Office, 1935), pp. 22–23.

... to own and operate its own electric plant ... [as] one of the measures which the people may properly take to protect themselves against unreasonable rates" and this right could be realized by "acquiring the existing plant or setting up competing plants, as circumstances may dictate."[7] Several cities, including Memphis, Chattanooga, and Knoxville, undertook the latter course of action, which proved to be a most effective means of bringing the private companies to terms. Generally the threat —and some action—was sufficient; in only three cities—Fayetteville, Newbern, and Lewisburg—were duplicate systems substantially completed.

An indication of TVA's activities in encouraging municipal ownership was the charge by the *Knoxville Journal* that it "is deliberately endeavoring to influence all cities and towns in the Valley to establish municipal distributing systems."[8] There was some direct action, such as public appearances by Director David Lilienthal prior to the unsuccessful referendum in Birmingham, Alabama, on October 9, 1933, but TVA's participation principally took the form of advice and counsel to local proponents, aid in obtaining federal loans and grants (the Authority itself made a few loans), and sponsorship of state enabling legislation. The results were extremely favorable in Tennessee; referenda were held in nearly all of the cities served by private companies and municipal ownership won in every case but one, usually by lopsided majorities. The lone exception was the city of Bells, where the people voted 134 to 53 against public ownership in a referendum held in 1938; local ownership of the company in that city was the decisive factor.

Knoxville was the first Tennessee city to try to acquire a privately owned system.[9] Soon after approval by the voters of a bond issue for "construction or purchase" of a distribution system, the city initiated negotiations with the Tennessee

[7] *Ibid.*
[8] Oct. 8, 1933.
[9] On Nov. 25, 1933, the voters of Knoxville approved a bond issue of $3,225,000 for construction of a new distribution system. At mid-January, 1934, the Federal Public Works Administration approved a loan of $2 million and a grant of $600,000 to the city for such construction. The threat and partial execution of this plan, and the failure of the courts to rescue the company, finally brought it to terms about mid-1938.

Public Service Company to buy the properties within its corporate boundaries. The company served a much larger territory than Knoxville's urbanized area, including several cities in nearby counties; although the city possessed charter authority to operate beyond its boundaries, acquisition of such a far-flung system in its entirety was given no consideration. The company was not interested in selling any of its properties, especially those in its most profitable market, and it soon became apparent that Knoxville alone could not do the job.

A few months later TVA entered the picture as a negotiator representing Knoxville and other prospective buyers of parts of the company's utility system. This became the pattern of negotiations with the private companies. TVA's leadership was generally welcomed, and its decisions as to prices to be paid, allocation of these prices among participating cities, territories to be taken over by cities and cooperatives, and other details of the contracts were accepted by the cities with very little dissent. Nashville appears to have been the only city to register strong objection, asserting that its allocated part of the purchase price was too high. The city finally agreed to the purchase, but only after Governor Prentice Cooper threatened intervention by the state to acquire the Nashville properties in order to avoid jeopardizing the entire package. Time was short, the pressures were great, and, as one TVA official said, "many little fires had to be put out." The Authority ultimately succeeded in bringing together, under complicated contracts, a large number of municipal purchasers and private companies to build an integrated public power system.

CHALLENGE IN THE COURTS: ROUND ONE

In spite of high hopes and optimistic statements that TVA power would soon displace private power, little progress was made until the private companies realized that the courts would not protect them from competition. In a suit brought in September, 1934, by preferred stockholders of the Alabama Power Company seeking to block a sale of transmission lines to TVA, a federal district court held the TVA Act to be unconstitutional. After a reversal of this decision by a circuit court of appeals, the case, *Ashwander* v. *T.V.A.*,[10] was finally decided by the U.S. Supreme Court in February, 1936. TVA was successful in confining consideration to the very narrow issue of whether the surplus power generated at Wilson Dam could be sold, on which the court divided 8 to 1 for the government. The court made clear the limited scope of the decision and its reservations concerning other phases of the TVA program:

> We limit our decision to the case before us, as we have defined it. . . . The Government is disposing of the energy itself which simply is the mechanical energy, incidental to falling water at the dam, converted into the electric energy which is susceptible of transmission. . . . And the Government rightly conceded at the bar, in substance, that it was without constitutional authority to acquire or dispose of such energy except as it comes into being in the operation of works constructed in the exercise of some power delegated to the United States. . . . We express no opinion . . . as to the status of any other dam or power development in the Tennessee Valley . . . or as to the validity of the Tennessee Valley Act or of the claims made in the pronouncements and program of the Authority apart from the questions we have discussed. . . .

Justice McReynolds, the lone dissenter, took a very different view, reminiscent of the "narrow construction" philosophy: "If under the thin mask of disposing of property the United States can enter the business of generating, transmitting and selling power as, when and wherever some board may specify, with the definite design to accomplish ends wholly beyond the sphere marked out for them by the Constitution, an easy way has been found for breaking down the limitations heretofore supposed to guarantee protection against aggression."

A few months later, a group of eighteen power companies operating in and near the TVA area joined to challenge directly the constitutionality of the TVA Act. After a year and a half of legal maneuvering, the case was tried before a special three-judge district court in Chattanooga. The court found for TVA on all counts.[11] A former general counsel of the Authority observed

---

[10] 297 U. S. 288, 56 S.C. 466, 80 L. Ed. 688 (1936).
[11] *Tennessee Electric Power Co.* v. *T.V.A.*, 21 F. Supp. 947 (1938).

that this decision has been the only one "which has squarely found the facts relating to TVA's overall power program."[12]

Nevertheless, the final decision—based on a technicality rather than on the merits—was a disappointment for those who prefer a bold advance to a sidestep. On appeal, the Supreme Court in January, 1939, by a 5 to 2 decision,[13] held that the companies lacked standing to bring the suit because none of their legal rights had been violated. Arguments that their charters and franchises included property rights protected by the Constitution were rejected on the grounds that these neither granted monopolies nor made competition illegal. This decision, putting a policy question outside judicial reach, made it possible for TVA to consolidate its power system throughout the Tennessee Valley.

THE SYSTEM THAT TVA BUILT

The first significant acquisition during the early years was from the Mississippi Power Company in 1934. TVA and the cities impatiently marked time while the judicial machinery slowly resolved the disputes with the private power companies. Finally, having had their unsatisfying days in court, the companies capitulated. TVA and Knoxville, for $7.9 million, jointly took over the Tennessee Public Service Company and its 34,000 customers in September, 1938. Three months later the Kentucky-Tennessee Light and Power Company transferred to TVA and cities in the area properties serving some 10,000 customers in northwestern Tennessee. Purchase of the West Tennessee Power and Light Company in January, 1939, brought in another 10,000.

Wendell Willkie, acting for the Commonwealth and Southern Corporation, in April, 1939, agreed to sell the subsidiary Tennessee Electric Power Company for $78.6 million. Andrew J.

---

[12] Joseph C. Swidler, "Legal Foundations," in Roscoe C. Martin (ed.), *TVA: The First Twenty Years* (University: University of Alabama Press; Knoxville: The University of Tennessee Press; 1956), p. 33. Swidler began work with TVA in 1933 as power attorney and served as general counsel from 1945 to 1957.

[13] 306 U. S. 118, 59 S.C. 366, 83 L. Ed. 543 (1939).

May of Kentucky, chairman of the House Military Affairs Committee, almost blocked a congressional appropriation to finance this purchase because he saw TVA as a threat to his state's coal industry. (TVA, by a neat historical irony, is now the nation's largest coal buyer!) A rider on another bill saved the day, the deal was consummated in August, 1939, and TVA power was extended to some 142,000 customers in Nashville, Chattanooga, and other cities.

In 1934 the people of Memphis, by 32,735 to 1,868, voted for a municipally owned power system by construction or purchase. Three years of negotiations ensued, during which time the city built a partial duplicating system that served over 6,000 customers. Finally, in June, 1939, the Memphis Power and Light Company transferred its electric and gas properties to TVA and Memphis for the sum of $17,360,000.

Other small purchases from several utilities were made in 1939 and 1940. Properties of the Kentucky-Tennessee Light and Power Company in five cities and nine counties of western Kentucky were acquired in June, 1942. The last big acquisition came in March, 1945, when TVA and the cities of northeastern Tennessee joined in buying the East Tennessee Light and Power Company for approximately $8,750,000.

Thus was built the TVA power system. Nearly the entire state of Tennessee now uses TVA power distributed by municipal, county, and cooperative organizations. The area in the state served by privately owned companies, which probably does not exceed 100 square miles, consists of the city of Kingsport and immediate surroundings, and a tiny sliver with twenty-nine customers in the vicinity of Bryson Mountain. One small city —Bells (pop. 1,232)—is served by a private company under a contract to deliver TVA power at TVA-prescribed rates; another company that served Franklin under such a contract for more than thirty years was acquired by the city of Franklin in 1969.

Tennessee is by far the largest user of TVA power. In 1968, sales to distributors and customers in Tennessee were 64 per cent of total TVA sales, excluding sales made directly to federal agencies. Alabama was in second place with 18 per cent. The five states of Georgia, Kentucky, Mississippi, North Carolina, and Virginia accounted for the remaining 18 per cent.

THE DOMINANCE OF THE POWER PROGRAM

Power development was the most controversial aspect of the prolonged debate on what to do with the Muscle Shoals properties. To appease those who were opposed to public ownership and to meet the certainty of a test on constitutionality, the TVA Act declared the power program to be subordinate to all other programs. A 1935 amendment directed TVA to operate "any dam or reservoir in its possession and control to regulate the stream flow primarily for the purposes of promoting navigation and controlling floods." Only "so far as may be consistent with such purposes" was TVA authorized "to provide and operate facilities for the generation of electric energy at any such dam . . . in order to avoid the waste of water power."[14] The only mention of a steam plant in the TVA Act was in a provision authorizing issuance of bonds up to $50 million to construct "any future dam, steam plant, or other facility" and Congress repealed this authorization in 1939. The clear implication of the act was that only hydroelectric power would be generated, and this was recognized in TVA's first annual report: "The more general purposes of the Authority are . . . generation of electric power incidental to and consistent with flood control and navigation, the disposition of the surplus power thus produced. . . ."[15]

As the economy of the Valley developed, this limited concept gradually gave way to the principle that TVA was obligated to supply all of the power needed in its service area (its contracts make it the sole supplier for all municipal and cooperative systems). Increasingly this meant steam generation. In 1933–1934 hydroelectric generation accounted for 99.88 per cent of total TVA power output; in 1966–1967 hydropower produced only 20 per cent of the total—75 per cent was steam generated and 5 per cent came from other systems. Private companies took advantage of the favorable climate of the Eisenhower administration and made a determined effort to limit the Authority's power, as exemplified by the "Dixon-Yates" deal,[16] and the effort

[14] U. S., *Statutes at Large*, XLIX, Part 1, 1076.
[15] *TVA Annual Report, 1934, op. cit.*, p. 1.
[16] For a blow-by-blow account see Aaron Wildavsky, *Dixon-Yates: A Study in Power Politics* (New Haven: Yale University Press, 1962).

certainly posed a temporary threat. TVA survived, however, and apparently its future as the source of any and all power in the Valley is fairly well assured. Nuclear-fired units, being evaluated on a basis of relative costs, are now in the offing. Three such units, aggregating a capacity of almost 3.5 million kilowatts, are scheduled for operation in 1971 and 1972 at Browns Ferry in northern Alabama. A second nuclear plant on a site near Chattanooga is now in the planning stages.

The increasing significance of electricity in a modern industrialized state (consider the consequences of the gigantic New York power failure in November, 1965) and the competitive handicaps of waterway transportation have led inexorably to an ascendancy of the power program in TVA's scale of priorities. Although official statements continue to accord higher priority to broader goals of regional resource development, social objectives, and the like, realistically the tail now wags the dog. Most of the power decisions are made by the administrators of the power program; although formal action by the TVA board of directors is sometimes required, rarely has the board modified the recommendations on power policy that come to it from the power staff.

A longtime supporter of TVA has observed that "a secondary activity, the production and sale of surplus power, has come to overshadow other program goals, some say to the considerable disadvantage of the whole."[17] In a similar vein, a former TVA staff member has noted that "for a variety of reasons, development [after World War II] took on a narrower focus, emphasizing particularly the problems of electric power."[18] A journalist quoted President John F. Kennedy as criticizing the Authority because it should be "in the business of resource development, and I want to feel that you will be giving thought to the problems which go beyond the production and sale of power."[19]

Whether the power program is or should be the most important or the most significant of TVA's multiple purposes might

[17] Roscoe C. Martin, "Retrospect and Prospect," in Martin (ed.), *TVA: The First Twenty Years, op. cit.*, p. 267.
[18] Norman Wengert, "The Politics of Water Resource Development as Exemplified by TVA," in John R. Moore (ed.), *The Economic Impact of TVA* (Knoxville: The University of Tennessee Press, 1967), p. 73.
[19] John Ed Pearce, "The Creeping Conservatism of TVA," *The Reporter*, XXVI, No. 1 (Jan. 4, 1962), 34.

18 *Sparks at the Grassroots*

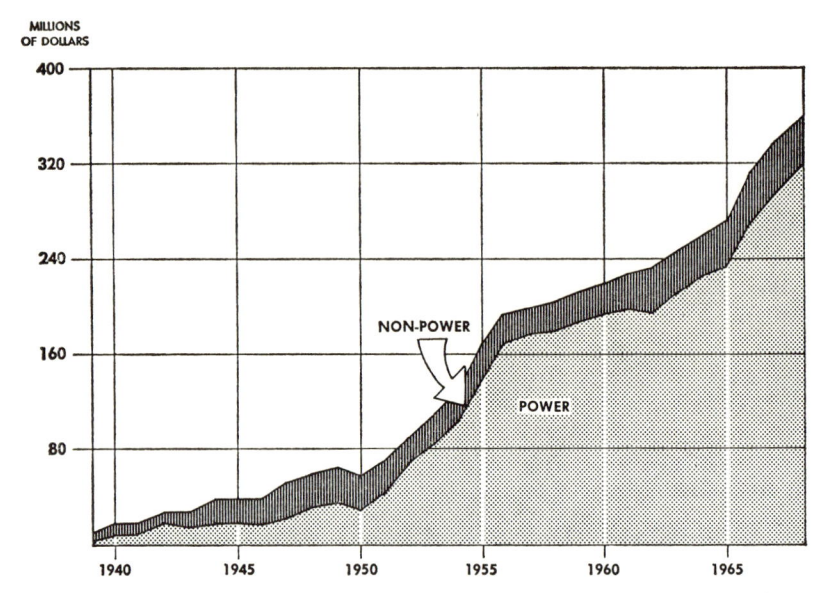

Figure 1. Total power operating expenses and gross expenses of nonpower programs of TVA, fiscal years 1939–1968.

Source: Annual TVA *Financial Statements,* 1939–1968.

be debated, but there can be no disputing the fact that it is now the largest program, in terms of both expenditure and manpower effort. Figure 1 compares total power operating expenses (including depreciation, which results in spreading construction costs over a long period of time) with the gross expenses of all other programs for fiscal years 1939 to 1968. Figure 2 shows the relative percentages of administrative and general expenses allocated by TVA to power and nonpower programs, based on TVA's own carefully devised criteria and procedures for allocating such expenses according to manpower effort devoted to the various programs. (Allocations are also made for a third category—construction—that has been omitted from this comparison.)

Percentages of TVA power sales according to major categories under which TVA reports such statistics, for the fiscal years 1950 to 1968, are presented in Appendix 1. These statistics indicate that domestic and rural consumers—the class accorded top priority in the TVA Act—in this period did not use a large propor-

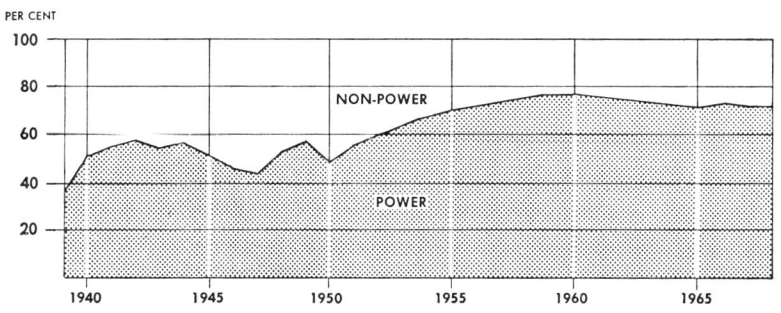

Figure 2. Relative percentage allocations of TVA administrative and general expenses to power and nonpower programs, fiscal years 1939–1968.

Source: Annual TVA *Financial Statements*, 1939–1968.

tion of TVA's total output, fluctuating from 22.9 in 1951 to a low of 13.6 in 1956, and to a high of 27.0 in 1968. Use by federal agencies and commercial industrial consumers is more important. The federal agencies' share jumped from 14.6 per cent in 1950 to 58 per cent in 1956, but declined to 22.9 per cent in 1968 (as a result of cutbacks by the Atomic Energy Commission in production of atomic materials and growth of demand by other consumer classes). Sales to commercial and industrial customers, including both direct sales by TVA and distributors' sales, have varied from 55.1 per cent in 1950 to a low of 27.1 per cent in 1956 and back up to 46.8 per cent in 1968.

THE QUESTION OF STATE CONTROL

The extension of TVA power service into the Valley states was accompanied by occasional brushes with state regulatory agencies empowered to regulate the rates and services of utilities. The first of these encounters occurred in Alabama and involved a claim of state power over federal activity. The Alabama Public Service Commission on July 14, 1934, declared that under "the well-settled law of the country . . . when municipalities and states engage in a business like that of a private individual . . . [they] render themselves subject to the laws of the land applying to . . . an individual." Applying this law the commission decided that the "Federal government in its proprietary business . . . [would be subject] to the police powers of the state."[20] The TVA board of directors, citing constitutional grounds and foreseeing an intolerable condition if TVA were accountable to "two sources of authority," refused to acknowledge the commission's jurisdiction. The matter was resolved the following year when the Alabama legislature exempted certain federal agencies, instrumentalities, and corporations (in such a way as to exempt TVA) from the commission's jurisdiction.

A short time later a similar encounter occurred in Tennessee. When a contract between TVA and the Commonwealth and Southern Corporation, estimated to save consumers some $400,000 annually, came before the Tennessee Railroad and Public Utilities Commission in 1934, approval was withheld for the rate reduction with a declaration that the commission could not be "deprived and denuded of its powers and duties . . . by the contracts of parties establishing rates to be maintained."[21] TVA responded as in Alabama, that it "could not be subjected to two sources of authority and would not permit its rates to be controlled by state regulatory commissions."[22] A prominent state senator threatened to abolish the commission, but less drastic action solved the problem. The Tennessee legislature, on the governor's recommendation because "the TVA wishes it," in 1935 exempted from the commission's jurisdiction "any corporation owned by or any agency or instrumentality of the United States," municipal corporations, and political subdivisions of the state.[23]

Years later a bitter battle between public and private power interests was fought in Kentucky, where a judicial ruling had prevented the city of Middlesboro from contracting with TVA. The court in a sharp assertion of state independence saw the contract as permitting "TVA to say how, when and where the City shall carry on its business of distributing electricity . . . free from the state's regulation or control. . . . Any and everything that the city may wish to do in relation to the manage-

[20] Re Alabama Power Co., *Public Utilities Reports* (New Series), IV, 225 (1934), quoted in Alexander T. Edelmann, "The T.V.A. and Inter-Governmental Relations," *American Political Science Review*, XXXVII, No. 3 (June, 1943), 465.
[21] *Ibid.*, p. 467.
[22] *Knoxville News-Sentinel*, Oct. 10, 1934.
[23] *Public Acts of Tennessee, 1935*, ch. 42.

ment is subordinated to the will of the federal agency...." The court refused to approve this "voluntary abdication of power ... [and] the assumption or acceptance by the City of complete subjectivity to the domination and control of the federal government . . . without legislative sanction thereof. . . ."[24] Legislative sanction, in a 1942 act,[25] passed by a narrow margin with strong support from the governor, ended the short-lived defiance by the Kentucky court.

The scene was peaceful in Mississippi, where the Mississippi Power Company had voluntarily sold properties to TVA in 1934. One case involving an effort by a small town to obtain TVA power found its way to the Mississippi Supreme Court, which washed its hands of the whole affair with a dictum expressing some doubts: "Although the duplication of service may, to many, appear foolish, the wisdom of such a venture cannot be judicially inquired into. In such circumstances, the burden must rest upon the conscience of the citizenship. Private enterprise has been a boon to this country, and many people believe that its life ought not to be snuffed out by the competition of the government through subsidized agencies."[26]

TVA INFLUENCE ON TENNESSEE LEGISLATION

In Tennessee, where TVA was most active, the Authority received top-level executive and legislative support from the beginning. The 1933 session of the Tennessee General Assembly adopted a resolution authorizing the governor "to appoint a Committee of six outstanding citizens . . . to be known as the Tennessee Valley Commission" and directed the commission "to co-operate with the Federal Government and all other agencies in the development and improvement of Muscle Shoals and the Tennessee Valley . . . and to report to the Governor and

[24] *City of Middlesboro v. Kentucky Utilities Co.*, 284 Ky. 833, 146 S.W. 2d 48 (1940).

[25] *Acts of the Kentucky General Assembly, 1942*, ch. 18, codified as secs. 96.550–96.900 of the *Kentucky Revised Statutes* (Cleveland: Banks-Baldwin Company, 1963). Unlike the other Valley states, where multiple laws exist, Kentucky has only this one act and it governs the operations of all of the thirteen TVA municipal distributors in the state.

[26] *Mississippi Power and Light Co. v. Town of Coldwater*, 234 Miss. 615, 106 So. 2d 375 (1958).

Legislature all necessary Legislation needed to protect the interest of the people of this state."[27] Almost one year later, on April 1, 1934, the governor announced his appointments to this commission.[28] Its members, working with the TVA staff and others about the state, especially legislators from the Chattanooga area, very soon initiated action to develop a legislative program. Early in the 1935 session the commission brought a dozen bills to the state capitol. The governor, with the support of the Shelby County legislative delegation, announced that all twelve bills must be passed and that any amendments would be opposed "on the grounds that the bills are now written as the Tennessee Valley Authority wants them passed."[29]

The *Knoxville News-Sentinel*, in a summary of the work of the legislature, reported that it had passed "11 measures, sponsored by the Tennessee Valley Authority, clearing the way for political sub-divisions to acquire their own electric distribution plants for TVA power, and authorizing creation of planning commissions and zoning districts." The high priority given to TVA's desires is indicated by the newspaper's report that the same session gave "no attention" to a "group of bills which the Public Works Administration insisted be enacted to clear the way for Tennessee to participate in the national public works program . . . despite a special message from the governor, who said it 'would be a calamity if we failed to meet the conditions required by the national administrator.'"[30]

TVA's influence at that time is also indicated by newspaper accounts of private legislation[31] for the city of Nashville: "The City Council Legislative Committee agreed with TVA officials yesterday that the Mayor and the Board of Public Works should be denied veto power over actual operations of Nashville's proposed Power Board. . . . The committee

---

[27] House Joint Resolution No. 38, *Public Acts of Tennessee, 1933*, pp. 516–17, approved April 22, 1933.

[28] *Knoxville News-Sentinel*, April 3, 1934, editorially implied that pressure had been necessary: "Congressman Ed Crump recently wired Governor McAlister . . . declaring that 'the people want' TVA power. That, apparently, has had results. Governor McAlister has just appointed a Tennessee Valley Commission."

[29] *Memphis Press-Scimitar*, Jan. 25, 1935.

[30] *Knoxville News-Sentinel*, April 22, 1935.

[31] *Private Acts of Tennessee, 1939*, ch. 262.

The Foundations of the TVA Power Program 23

agreed to a suggestion of J. A. Krug, TVA power planning engineer, and J. C. Swidler, TVA counsel, that no geographical limitations be imposed on the Power Board."[32] Later, Senator Newman announced that "final passage will be held up" so he could explain "some differences of opinion between TVA officials and the committee" and obtain Swidler's approval of the final draft of the bill.[33] This hurdle was soon cleared:

> Approval by the Tennessee Valley Authority of Nashville's power board bill was verified late Saturday by State Senator James A. Newman, who revealed that he will ask final passage of the bill by the General Assembly Monday night.
>
> Senator Newman said that a letter was received by Mayor Thomas L. Cummings Saturday containing complete approval of the bill by James Lawrence Fly, chief counsel for TVA.[34]

The principal enabling act in Tennessee, one of the eleven measures mentioned above, is the Municipal Electric Plant Law of 1935.[35] Thirty-six city systems are organized under this law (including some systems that used other legislative acts for issuance of bonds and later elected to organize under this law). It authorizes any municipality or county (three county-owned systems are also under this act) "to acquire, improve, operate and maintain" an electric plant for retail distribution of electricity. Operations outside the corporate or county limits are permitted, except that the consent of any other municipality to be served is required. Power is delegated "to make all . . . contracts and execute all . . . instruments as in the discretion of the municipality may be necessary, proper or advisable in or for the furtherance of the acquisition, improvement, operation and maintenance of any electric plant and the furnishing of electric service."

If bonds are issued under authority of this act, a board of public utilities must be appointed unless the municipality has a population of less than 2,000 or employs a city manager;

---

[32] *Nashville Banner*, Feb. 3, 1939.
[33] *Ibid.*
[34] *Nashville Tennessean*, Feb. 12, 1939.
[35] *Public Acts of Tennessee, 1935*, ch. 32, codified as secs. 6-1501–6-1534, *Tennessee Code Annotated* (Indianapolis: The Bobbs-Merrill Co., 1955), hereinafter cited as *Tennessee Code*.

other cities not using this act for bond authority may also appoint such a board and operate under its provisions. The board is empowered to determine programs, improvements, rates, and financial practices, to adopt "necessary or appropriate . . . rules and regulations . . . to govern the furnishing of electric service," and to disburse moneys in the electric plant fund. Bonds may be issued with approval by a majority vote of the electorate; the municipal governing body has the option of pledging the municipality's full faith and credit or securing them by electric revenues only. Permissible uses of revenue are specified, in much the same language as the TVA power contracts. A subsequent act[36] passed at the same session, to reinforce and clarify the contracting powers of municipalities, authorized "such covenants, terms and conditions as the governing body thereof may deem appropriate."

At a subsequent extraordinary session in the same year, the Revenue Bond Law[37] was enacted; it appears to be the sole legislative authority for only one city system (Lexington). It follows closely the provisions of the foregoing act, except that a board of public utilities is absent and no vote is required to issue bonds. An added provision probably reflects TVA concern over absence of a power board: "no municipality shall operate such public works for gain or profit or primarily as a source of revenue to the municipality, but shall operate such public works for the use and benefit of the consumers served. . . ."

Twenty-two city systems are operated under private acts. These contain provisions of great diversity, ranging from simple authorizations such as "to provide the City with water and light by waterworks and light plants" (Lebanon) and "operate works and plants for furnishing water and light to the town and the inhabitants thereof" (Cookeville), to complete acts for Memphis, Nashville, Knoxville, Chattanooga, and several smaller cities.

CHALLENGE IN THE COURTS: ROUND TWO

Several attacks were mounted by private companies against

[36] *Public Acts of Tennessee, 1935*, ch. 37, codified as secs. 6-1535–6-1537, *Tennessee Code*.
[37] *Public Acts of Tennessee, 1935 Ex. Sess.*, ch. 33, codified as secs. 6-1301–6-1318, *Tennessee Code*.

Tennessee cities in the early days of TVA, but the courts ruled for the cities on all counts. Charter authority to engage in the business of electricity distribution was sustained in *Tennessee Public Service Co. v. City of Knoxville*.[38]

A charge of unconstitutional delegation of legislative power was beaten back in *Memphis Power and Light Co. v. City of Memphis*.[39] The company argued that the city's contract conferred on TVA the governmental power of rate-making in contravention of the state constitutional provision that "the Legislative authority of this State shall be vested in a General Assembly." Noting that this provision "says nothing about rate making as to utilities," the Tennessee Supreme Court rejected the delegation theory on the grounds that the power had been delegated to the city, not to TVA, and was actually exercised by the city through its contract with TVA that included resale rates. In the court's view such a contract did not empower TVA to increase or reduce rates but merely gave it a "supervisory privilege" to approve any increase which "must be exercised reasonably and not arbitrarily, and, being a servant of the general public, it is presumed that in exercising this right it will conform to the spirit of the contract." The distinction was made that the city in distributing electric power was exercising a proprietary, not a governmental power. However, in extending its remarks the court declared that "the regulation of rates, however accomplished, is subject to the continuing police power of the state." The court seemed to be saying that it was not going to be a party to the complete abdication of state power. In view of TVA's original position that it would not submit to state control of its rates, it is difficult to conceive of how such power could be exercised.

In the case of *Tennessee Electric Power Co. v. City of Chattanooga*,[40] the company alleged that a private act[41] had unconstitutionally delegated to an appointive body, the Electric Power Board, the sole determination of whether bonds would be issued for purchase or construction of a distribution system and whether a tax would be levied for their payment. In

[38] 170 Tenn. 40, 91 S. W. 2d 566 (1936).
[39] 172 Tenn. 346, 112 S. W. 2d 817 (1937).
[40] 172 Tenn. 505, 114 S. W. 2d 441 (1937).
[41] *Private Acts of Tennessee, 1935*, ch. 455.

support of its contention, the company pointed to a provision that "it shall be the duty of the Mayor and Board of Commissioners of the City to provide by resolution or ordinance for the issuance of said bonds as directed by said Electric Power Board." The court saw this as being a power of implementation and held that the provisions of the act authorizing and empowering "the City of Chattanooga in its corporate capacity" to purchase or construct an electric system and to issue and sell its bonds meant that these powers were "conferred exclusively upon the City of Chattanooga and not upon the Power Board." After the city "in its corporate capacity" had made the basic decision the Electric Power Board could require the issuance of bonds to meet its requirements up to the maximum of $8 million. Although the act delegated to the power board the sole discretion to determine whether the bonds would be retired from electric revenues, and a negative decision would have required a tax levy to retire the bonds, the court did not see this as a delegation of the taxing power to the power board: "Nowhere in the act is authority conferred upon the Power Board to levy a tax.... The fact that the city is under the necessity of borrowing the money, needed by the board, by a sale of the city's bonds, which must be repaid out of tax levy, cannot, we think, be held a tax levied by the board."

Answering the contention that the power board was unconstitutionally authorized to fix rates, the court said that the legislature possessed such power and could delegate this power to a municipality or to a subsidiary board of a municipality. "The Power Board ... is but the creature of the Legislature and may be abolished by it at any time." The objection that this authority had been given to an appointive body instead of the elected legislative body of the city was summarily rejected.

In a federal district court the private companies, in the case of *Tennessee Electric Power Co.* v. *T.V.A.*,[42] charged that the congressional act constituted "an unlawful interference with the police power of the states because they regulate the rates of utilities which themselves are subject to state regulation," that TVA's rates "will inevitably force complainants to lower their

[42] 21 F. Supp. 947 (1938).

rates" (an accurate forecast), and that "TVA in its operations is not subject to the police power of the state." The court gave short shrift to these arguments, saying that the acts had been "authorized by the states themselves" and that there had been "no abdication of any state right." However, the primary basis of rejection was that no state had intervened to raise such questions before the court.

GOVERNOR BROWNING'S PROPOSAL
FOR STATE OPERATION

Governor Gordon Browning, on the same day (January 22, 1938) that victory in the case of *Tennessee Electric Power Co. v. T.V.A.* was announced, suggested that the state might expedite TVA power distribution by buying the private systems and setting up a state power administration. He proposed that the state be divided into power districts, to be operated under the Tennessee Rural Electrification Authority.[43]

The governor's proposal generated a small tempest. Senator McKellar immediately expressed opposition to state management of power distribution, and E. H. Crump of Memphis released a statement that Governor Browning "is with the power trust" and "at heart is not in sympathy with TVA and never will be."[44] Browning protested that his only objective was "to give the people of Tennessee TVA power without the necessity of waiting out endless litigation," and that he was simply trying "to do on a big scale just what Memphis, Jackson, Knoxville and other regions have tried to do for months, and that is to purchase existing facilities for the use and distribution of TVA power instead of duplicating them."[45] The *Knoxville News-Sentinel* (January 23, 1938) editorially undertook to speak for the people: "We must insist that any participation by the State of

[43] Creation of this agency was directed by *Public Acts of Tennessee, 1935 Ex. Sess.*, ch. 3, which, according to the *Knoxville News-Sentinel*, July 26, 1935 (date of signing by the governor), "was desired by the Tennessee Valley Authority." The governor on Aug. 5, 1935, appointed a three-member board as directed by the act, but the agency was never activated.

[44] *Knoxville News-Sentinel*, Jan. 23 & 24, 1938.

[45] *Ibid.*, Jan. 23, 26, 1938.

Tennessee in public power be subject to the approval and control of this non-political TVA. . . . It is ironical that the people should have more confidence in a Federal agency appointed by the President than in a state government which they have elected directly by their votes. But such is the fact."

Some thirty mayors, attending a meeting called by the Tennessee Municipal League, unanimously adopted a resolution which included the following:

> We are unalterably opposed to the proposal made by the governor of Tennessee. . . . We look with disfavor upon any plan for the purchase of utility properties . . . by any of the officials, departments, boards, commissions, or their agencies of the Government of the State of Tennessee.
>
> [We favor] local self-government and local management of electric distribution facilities [and] to that end . . . [propose division of the state into approximately 25 areas which would] elect boards or commissions charged with the duty of acquiring by purchase or construction electric distribution facilities for the distribution of TVA power . . . vested with authority to manage, control and supervise such electric distribution facilities . . . free from any regulation, control or interference of the state of Tennessee or any of its agencies.[46]

Mayor W. D. Hudson of Clarksville, speaking for the mayors, stated, "We're not trying to take anything over the heads of TVA. We conferred with TVA officials before we met, and we did not consult with any politicians."[47]

TVA Director David Lilienthal, when interviewed concerning Browning's proposal, said that the governor had not been in consultation with TVA and that it "is not the plan favored by TVA . . . nor does it hold promise of that 'decentralization and democratization' of power distribution which the TVA hopes to bring about."[48] On the same day Governor Browning met with President Roosevelt in Washington for a discussion of the proposal; at a press conference the next day the President indicated that no encouragement had been given to the governor. This was not a surprising outcome, in view of the widespread

[46] *Ibid.*, Jan. 26, 1938.
[47] *Ibid.*, Jan. 27, 1938.
[48] *Ibid.*

lack of support in his home state. The proposal soon faded into the limbo of forgotten things.

VALLEY STATES RELINQUISH POWER

Although the states theoretically can prescribe the terms and conditions of power contracts between TVA and municipalities, Kentucky is the only state that has exercised such power with any independence (but even there in only minor respects in relation to TVA's major policy objectives). A law researcher concluded that the "decisions are in accord that the police power of a state can not be abdicated or bargained away, . . . nor can it be limited by contract. . . . The power is not subject to national supervision. . . . Regulation of utility rates in intrastate commerce is under the jurisdiction of the state pursuant to this power."[49] This was acknowledged by TVA in its brief in the Ashwander case and was restated in the court's opinion: "There is no purpose in the Act to regulate matters reserved to the States by the Ninth and Tenth Amendments. The contracts with the municipalities are subservient to the law of Alabama no less than if the municipalities had made contracts with a private wholesaler. The State of Alabama has exercised its regulatory powers in the instant case by authorizing the municipalities to enter into contracts with the Authority under certain stated conditions."[50]

In a 1968 opinion the Tennessee Court of Appeals struck down a TVA power contract provision preventing refunds to members of a cooperative because such refunds are specifically authorized by state law, and it said: "It is a well settled principle of law that an agreement or contract which violates a provision of a constitutional statute is illegal. . . . We do not intend to leave the impression that the entire contract between defendant and TVA is void. . . . it is only that part of the contract which is in direct conflict with T.C.A. 65-2516 that is not binding or enforceable upon the parties."[51]

---

[49] Helen M. Martell, "Legal Aspects of the Tennessee Valley Authority," *George Washington Law Review*, VII, No. 8 (June, 1939), 1005-6.

[50] *Ashwander* v. *T.V.A.*, 297 U. S. 288, 313 (1936).

[51] *Shadow* v. *Volunteer Electric Cooperative*, unreported opinion filed June 20, 1968.

TVA has played a dominant role in shaping state policies of power distribution. The situation could hardly have led to any other outcome. The economic and political climate of the New Deal favored dominance by the federal government in nearly all areas of activity. A new government agency with promises of wider and better service at lower rates was taking over from elements of the discredited power trust, and TVA interpreted its congressional mandate to require the attachment of certain conditions to its sale. The Authority's multiple-purpose program of regional improvement in the Valley—then regarded as one of the country's most economically depressed areas—offered great hopes to the people and favorably influenced their acceptance of the TVA power program. It was natural that state officials would be sensitive and responsive to the widespread public support of the agency. In this new field of activity for state governments, state officials also lacked the expertise so readily available from the staff of TVA.

The net result has been that the Valley states have confined their roles to the enactment of enabling legislation permitting municipalities (and cooperatives) to contract with TVA. The provisions of such acts are similar, reflecting the influence of TVA. Governor Frank Clement of Tennessee testified that "the only function of the state was enactment of legislation pronouncing a public power policy and provision of necessary machinery. There has been no need to create state departments of electricity to intervene between the TVA and our localities."[52]

The policy of Tennessee, as expressed by the legislature and interpreted by the courts, has made each municipality virtually a free agent in dealing with TVA—which also means that it must shift for itself. Acting alone, the municipality is weak in relation to the monolithic power of TVA, is very much at the mercy of TVA, and very little real negotiating occurs during the contracting process. The wisdom of this voluntary abdication of power on the part of the state may be questioned. As will be seen later, the state in some instances should have been more concerned

---

[52] Presented by the governor before the National Commission on Intergovernmental Relations, at New Orleans, La., Dec. 2, 1953 (copy of MS in files of the Tennessee Municipal League).

about the interests of its creatures and less subservient to the desires of TVA. An independent stance by the state, soundly based on its regulatory powers, might be a healthy antidote to the prevailing notion that TVA is always right.

2 PARTNERSHIP: A QUESTION OF BALANCE

TVA TALKS OF PARTNERSHIP with its distributors, but careful examination reveals that they are closely supervised and circumscribed and that their roles are considerably less than that of full partners. Spokesmen for the Authority have eulogized local governments as the grassroots of democracy, but in practice they regard municipal officials as politicians from whom power system personnel should be insulated to avoid the contamination of politics. In this chapter we will examine this aspect of TVA policy and related details of its power contracts with municipalities.

THE BASIC POLICY: LOCAL AUTONOMY THROUGH LOCAL DISTRIBUTION

TVA could have created an organization to carry electricity all the way to consumers, following the practice of utility companies displaced by the Authority. According to Lilienthal, this approach was urged upon TVA by its engineers "in the interest of economy." Viewing this approach as an undesirable step toward overcentralization, he said that TVA instead undertook "to find ways, practical ways, through which the expanding powers of our central government can be administered without weakening the strength of our local governmental units."[1]

As TVA approached this problem, Lilienthal recalled that earlier he had written: "the obvious lack of public confidence in the utility industry was due in large measure to . . . overpowering size and remoteness of control . . . [and] people almost by instinct want such essential services as electricity as

[1] Remarks at the annual meeting of distributors of TVA power, Chattanooga, Feb. 16, 1943 (MS in TVA Technical Library, Knoxville).

close to them as possible."[2] In his opinion, if TVA exercised such "enormous centralized power and responsibility":

> The people of the hundreds of communities and cities would not in any way participate in the operation of the distribution systems that serve them in their home communities. They would not have a part to play in management nor in the selection of their representatives, nor would they have a responsibility for good or for bad management or for financial results. And they would not feel, as they do today—and I say this with great satisfaction—that the TVA is theirs, that TVA's problems are theirs.[3]

TVA's solution to the problem, motivated largely by the need for local support for the TVA program,[4] was a partnership with local agencies to distribute power to the consumers, formalized in power contracts. It was a sound approach, as evidenced by the many times the people of the Valley have aided the Authority in its battles with the private power lobby in Congress and elsewhere. After a few years, Lilienthal elaborated on the partnership theme:

> Your communities and the other agencies and institutions, local and state, have learned through the years that TVA is not interested in superseding or weakening but rather in strengthening the important and necessary functions of its community partners. TVA is opposed to overcentralization and remote control in the administration of federal functions. TVA does not want to dominate or dictate the governmental and economic affairs of this region. This is a partnership between TVA and the people and their state and local agencies. The TVA is as much interested in the strengthening and invigoration of communities and local and state agencies, as the local communities have shown themselves to be interested in the strengthening of the TVA.[5]

---

[2] David Lilienthal, "The TVA: An Experiment in the 'Grass Roots' Administration of Federal Functions," address before the annual convention of the Southern Political Science Association, Knoxville, Nov. 10, 1939 (MS in TVA Technical Library, Knoxville).

[3] Remarks, Feb. 16, 1943, *op. cit.*

[4] This hypothesis is developed by Philip Selznick in *TVA and the Grass Roots* (Berkeley: University of California Press, 1949).

[5] "The TVA: A Step Toward Decentralization," an address at the New School for Social Research, New York, April 3, 1940 (MS in TVA Technical Library, Knoxville).

TVA was cool to Governor Browning's proposal to create a state-administered distribution system because, according to Lilienthal, the Authority wanted systems "operated by the communities they serve whose citizens would have direct democratic control of their administration."[6] Another, more practical, consideration has probably figured heavily in TVA's policy. The risks for TVA are substantially less in dealing with individual cities and cooperatives, binding each to the provisions of a power contract, than in negotiating with a state. The former, one by one, present no serious problems in contract negotiations; if they want the power they must take it on TVA's terms. But the latter might be inclined to follow somewhat of a "states' rights" line that could be troublesome. An earlier study of this subject concluded that "TVA attempted to build a limited area of state collaboration and consent without jeopardizing its fundamental control over program content."[7]

In 1947 an official TVA statement declared that "a jointly-planned program [and] . . . its administration and partnership with state and local agencies places the program in the hands of agencies aware of the people's needs and close enough to them to be subject to local control by the people."[8] On the occasion of TVA's twentieth anniversary, Chairman of the Board Gordon Clapp stressed the autonomy of the local power systems and indicated a degree of deference to local governmental institutions:

> The most interesting thing about this arrangement, and the most significant for TVA's method of operation, is that the Authority has no coercive power whatever with regard to the long-established governments of the region. In fact, TVA has chosen almost uniformly to work through existing governments instead of through its own organization in discharging its manifold responsibilities. This policy has brought it into

---

[6] *Knoxville News-Sentinel*, Jan. 27, 1938.

[7] Elliott Roberts, *One River—Seven States*, The University of Tennessee *Record*, Extension Series, Vol. XXXI, No. 1 (Knoxville: The Bureau of Public Administration, June, 1955), p. 92. Roberts documents at some length the means by which TVA excluded the states from meaningful participation in its various programs.

[8] *Tennessee Valley Resources: Their Development and Use* (Knoxville: Tennessee Valley Authority, 1947), p. 8.

close relations with governments over which it has no control, and thus has placed a high premium on the ability to negotiate agreement and to enlist voluntary cooperation. TVA spokesmen may entreat, cajole, and argue, but they may not threaten and they may not order, for the very good reason that in the end they do not have the power of sanction. It follows that a good share of government in the Tennessee Valley is carried on through what may be called a system of co-operative administration.[9]

Reality has fallen far short of these idealistic statements by TVA's leading spokesmen. As will be developed in some detail on the following pages, TVA's contractual arrangements, even though appearing to preserve local autonomy, have in fact resulted in extensive control by TVA of the distributors' policies and operations. The question of whether the ideals have been overstated or whether practice should conform more closely to ideals is probably unanswerable.

TVA ORGANIZATION AND DISTRICT OFFICES

The TVA Act delegates to the board of directors full discretion to determine organizational structure, staffing, and personnel policies "without regard to the provisions of Civil Service laws."[10] Initially, administrative responsibilities were divided among the three directors; the power program was placed under Lilienthal's supervision. After this division of administrative responsibility proved to be unworkable, the board in 1937 created the office of general manager. An Office of Power, established by the board in 1941, is responsible for power program administration. Under this arrangement the board establishes policies and programs, fixes the basic organization, reviews progress and results, and approves annual programs,

---

[9] "The Meaning of TVA," in Roscoe C. Martin (ed.), *TVA: The First Twenty Years* (University: University of Alabama Press; Knoxville: The University of Tennessee Press; 1956), p. 9.

[10] TVA Act, secs. 2(g), 3. The agency has developed a personnel system which, in the opinion of many observers, is excellent. See Robert S. Avery, *Experiment in Management: Personnel Decentralization in the Tennessee Valley Authority* (Knoxville: The University of Tennessee Press, 1954).

projects, budgets, contracts, and individual actions of major importance.[11]

The Office of Power, as now constituted, has five major divisions and five district offices. The Division of Power Marketing, particularly its Distributor Marketing Branch, supervises the power distributors; responsibilities of this branch include the following:

> In accordance with the TVA Act and established policies and working through its district offices, the Distributor Marketing Branch initiates, develops, negotiates, and administers contracts, amendments, and agreements with municipalities, counties, and distributors of power having to do with the sale, delivery, and use of power. . . .
>
> The branch performs studies, utility practice research, and field investigations to prepare individual distributor analyses and reports on resale rates, financial forecasts, and management procedures. It recommends policies on such matters as rate application, retail power marketing practices, joint-use buildings, and the handling of funds. . . .
>
> It prepares special studies from distributor cost data on trends of total and unit distribution plant cost, taxes, tax equivalent payments, and adequacy of rate structures. . . .[12]

The *TVA Manual* states that the district offices "are the principal points of contact in the Office of Power with the distributors of TVA power, state and local agencies and officials, and the public." Duties of district managers and their assistants include administering and interpreting power contract provisions, advising TVA distributors concerning their contractual obligations, and giving advice "on such matters as management problems, rate application, financing, relations with governing bodies of municipalities, problems of customer relations, etc."

The actual involvement of TVA district office staffs in management operations of municipal systems varies widely. The larger

---

[11] John Oliver, "Administrative Foundations," in Martin (ed.), *TVA: The First Twenty Years, op. cit.*, pp. 46–47.

[12] *Administrative Release Manual* (Knoxville: Division of Personnel, Tennessee Valley Authority, loose-leaf compilation variously dated), I POWER, Power Marketing, p. 9 (April 6, 1961). Hereinafter referred to as *TVA Manual*.

systems, able to employ well-trained and specialized personnel, seldom call for assistance and receive little attention from TVA. Smaller distributors often rely heavily on TVA for guidance and are subject to fairly close supervision. Power system managers also differ in their qualities of self-reliance, and some cities object more than others to the strictures of power contracts. TVA has also found that some systems should be checked more carefully than others.

TVA district staff personnel are heavily involved in the operations of distributors. "Negotiation of contracts and agreements" and "encouragement of and participation in service area agreements between distributors" headed a long list of thirty specific activities mentioned by a TVA district manager.[13] The following sampling of these activities is revealing. He said they sell rate reductions and answer numerous questions on rate applications. Discouragement of various types of donations is another duty. In financial administration, assistance includes preparation of distributors' operating budgets, working with them on arrangements to issue bonds, endeavoring to assure proper accounting practices, and negotiating allocation of expenses of jointly used personnel and buildings among different departments of a city. To assist on personnel matters, they provide salary data and recommended salary adjustments for distributor personnel, encourage the employment of power-use representatives and properly trained personnel, and provide training for personnel in a variety of activities. They are called upon to "attend all types of meetings, particularly distributor board meetings," and to "develop programs for managers' meetings and other associated organizations." Other activities he listed included the preparation of recommendations for heating, lighting, air conditioning, water systems, feed handling, Electrofarm, Gold Medallion Homes, and PHA projects, the development of demonstration material and training aids for home agents, home economics teachers, and power distributor personnel, and assistance to power distributors in planning and conducting promotion campaigns, advertising, and public relations programs.

[13] Jack W. Eakin, central district manager, paper presented at an assemblage of TVA personnel in the Office of Power, Chattanooga, Oct. 16, 1964 (MS furnished by TVA director of power marketing).

LOCAL POWER BOARDS AND LOCAL DEMOCRACY

A policy statement adopted by the board of directors in 1933 revealed an important preference of the Authority: "sound business management of the municipally-owned utility [should be established] by providing an administrative agency apart from the city council or town board, and by selection of a competent superintendent."[14] From this and subsequent statements, it is obvious that the local agencies, which TVA desires as partners in the power program, are not municipal governments but special power agencies largely autonomous and more amenable to TVA control than politically chosen bodies might be. According to TVA spokesmen, a municipal government and a power board should work at "arm's length" to keep power distribution "out of politics." (Contrast this with Chairman Clapp's statement quoted earlier, that TVA encourages "close relations with governments.") In Lilienthal's opinion, power administration in the hands of elected officials would result in "political management," which would lead to increased costs, increased electric rates, and a reversal of the trend toward commercial development of the region. He envisioned "grievous injury" if the "effort to infiltrate politics" were successful, warning of such consequences as political awards of contracts, systems improvements or expansion dependent on political campaigns, failure to collect bills from those on the "inside track" politically, and political employment.[15] He later reported that "the reaction [to his antipolitical stand] in the Valley was excellent," including unanimous adoption of a resolution at the annual convention of the Tennessee Municipal League "putting them on record against politics in these power systems."[16]

Negative reactions among municipal officials soon developed, however. Out of a conference in 1940 came this report:

[14] "A Plan of Action for Carrying out the Power Program" (Exhibit 8-22-33b in the files of TVA).
[15] "Politics and the Management of the Public's Business," address before a meeting of the Knoxville Kiwanis Club, July 9, 1942 (MS in TVA Technical Library, Knoxville).
[16] *The Journals of David E. Lilienthal: Vol. I, The TVA Years 1939–1945* (New York: Harper and Row, 1946), p. 517.

Mayor Walker of Athens deplored the fact that after municipalities purchased the distribution systems, they were turned over to Power Boards who were afraid to speak to city officials for fear of political contamination.

"They are responsible to no-one," the Mayor declared, "while I must run every two years for re-election."

Mayor Walker's point was instantly seized upon by other mayors and city managers present, who pointed out the lack of cooperation between Power Boards and city administrations.

. . . .

It was the opinion of several speakers that this phase of the TVA contract would have to be revised, and that Power Boards would have to "come down to earth" and realize that cooperation with existing city governments would best serve all.[17]

In opposition to the TVA approach, Herbert J. Bingham, executive secretary of the Tennessee Municipal League, in 1953 pointed out that TVA fostered a "splintering of municipal functions and the removal of responsibility from elected representatives of the people." Chairman Clapp conceded that this is an undesirable trend, but he seemed to reject the argument because "too close contact between the two parties might have adverse effects on electric consumers."[18]

The effusive praise by TVA officials of democratic government, such as has been noted, is inconsistent with their condemnation of political processes that are inseparable from democratic government. Speaking before a power distributors group, Lilienthal in 1943 said that TVA had carried out its program "without destroying, indeed, with a strengthening of local and state governments, with an increase in the participation of the citizens, the twentieth century equivalent of the eighteenth century Town Meeting."[19] A suggestion today that TVA's power operations have increased citizens' participation or have en-

---

[17] *Knoxville Labor News*, Nov. 28, 1940, reporting on the Southern Institute of Local Government at the University of Tennessee, Knoxville.

[18] My notes on a conference of TVA personnel and representatives of the Tennessee Municipal League, at TVA offices in Knoxville, Jan. 29, 1953, which I attended.

[19] David Lilienthal, remarks at the annual meeting of distributors of TVA power, Chattanooga, Feb. 16, 1943 (MS in TVA Technical Library, Knoxville).

couraged anything resembling a town meeting would evoke laughter anywhere in the Valley.

Why TVA Likes Power Boards

Power boards, of course, have certain advantages. Paul S. Button, TVA's director of power marketing, cites several reasons for TVA's advocacy of this form of organization. He sees it as a means of minimizing the possibility of using the power system as a tax-collecting agency. Planning and operations are superior to what a municipal department would accomplish. He feels that the electric utility deserves this kind of recognition and representation in a municipal government structure. Members of a city council can avoid political involvement in matters concerning the power system, on the grounds that all such matters are under the power board's jurisdiction. The staggered terms of power board members, appointed instead of being elected, make for less turnover and better continuity of policy. He alleges that interest rates are lower on revenue bonds as direct results of this policy. Power board members are more likely to appreciate the highly technical and exacting nature of electric utility work, and the resulting increase in job security minimizes the costs and inefficiencies caused by high labor turnover. Finally, he said that a power board will more readily accept "the principles we insist upon."[20] This approach may be justified in the name of efficiency, but it seems to be incompatible with vesting control in the people themselves or strengthening municipal government.

A typical power board has little contact with the city governing body. Its policies and operations are closely supervised by TVA, and citizens' participation is nonexistent. In the fields of planning, recreation, industrial promotion, community improvement, and tributary development, TVA has worked in close cooperation with local government officials. However, in power distribution, where the potential for close cooperation is the greatest, TVA has exerted little effort to implement the democratic ideals enunciated by its leaders. Perhaps the use of the power board creates a situation that virtually precludes a realization of these ideals. If so, then TVA's protestation of demo-

[20] Interview on June 25, 1964.

cratic ideals is little more than a farce. TVA would have to live with these ideals more if power distribution were carried out, as other functions are, under the general control of municipal governing bodies.

A practical consideration, undoubtedly given great weight by TVA, was mentioned by a mayor when he referred to TVA personnel: "they exert too much influence on systems to establish independent power boards and then use the board to operate the system entirely as they direct. They could not do this operating directly with the elected officials." As compared with an appointive power board, most elected officials are more likely to have stronger feelings of local autonomy, to feel stronger ties to local interests and pressure groups, and some might even be tempted to divert electric revenues to other uses. Moreover, if TVA were to exert its contractual and supervisory powers upon elected officials, it would incur greater risks of friction and alienation of local support.

TVA Success in Tennessee

The establishment of power boards has provoked controversy in some instances. Provisions for the popular election of power board members in an early draft of a Nashville bill were eliminated as a result of TVA objections. According to Senator James A. Newman, TVA recommended instead that the "exclusive nomination of new members [be] made responsibility of the board subject to confirmation by the mayor and City Council."[21] An effort made in Chattanooga, in 1949, to place the mayor and one city commissioner on the five-member power board brought forth a declaration from the board that this would lead to "political entanglements" and "ultimately destroy the successful operation of the system."[22] After a three-hour meeting with the area's legislators, even a reduced proposal of "at least one

---

[21] *Nashville Tennessean*, Feb. 8, 1939. The bill was enacted as ch. 262, *Private Acts of Tennessee, 1939*, and provided for nominations by the board of public works (composed of mayor and two administrative officials), with confirmation by the city council, for twelve-year terms (initially four, eight, and twelve years). This was changed to appointment by the mayor only for five-year terms, by ch. 246, *Private Acts of Tennessee, 1947*.

[22] *Chattanooga Times*, Jan. 20, 1949.

representative" of the city commission on the power board was abandoned.[23]

In the early stages of Knoxville's planning, the city's two newspapers opposed a power board as inconsistent with the council-manager form of government; the proposed salary of $600 per year for each board member was also viewed as a political plum. The city's law director was quoted as saying that the proposed board of five members, to be appointed by the city manager, "follows proposals of the TVA,"[24] but city council, by a vote of 8 to 2, rejected it.

Three years later, after conclusion of the long fight to acquire the privately owned system in Knoxville, the establishment of a power board again became an issue. In the meantime the city had abandoned the council-manager form of government, which for many removed the reasons for adhering to a departmental setup. The mayor indicated his preference for a five-member, nonsalaried board with staggered terms. The entire city council was reported to be in favor of "keeping politics out of the system."[25] Both newspapers were also converts to the new cause. The principal front-page story of the *Knoxville News-Sentinel*, October 27, 1938, began: "Legislative machinery to guarantee that the city's electric and water utilities will be protected against politics and politicians was put in motion today by Mayor Walter Mynatt." The story reported that the plan had been "unanimously and enthusiastically endorsed by the business men's group [thirty prominent business leaders] . . . meeting in [the mayor's] office this morning," and that it would provide for a five-member board nominated by the mayor and confirmed by the city council for staggered ten-year terms. Finance Director Allen Frierson was quoted as saying that the purpose was "to take the water and power departments clear away from City Hall and place them in the hands of qualified business men."

Revisions were made on recommendation of a city charter committee, including nomination of new members by remaining members of the board with the concurrence of the

---

[23] *Ibid.*, Jan. 30, 1949.
[24] *Knoxville News-Sentinel*, March 15, 1935.
[25] *Knoxville Journal*, Aug. 26, 1938.

mayor, subject to confirmation by the city council.[26] The vice-mayor said revisions were made to keep the proposed board as "free from the influence of politics as possible."[27] The Central Labor Union, represented on the charter committee, urged labor to be "very skeptical of the Power Board proposal—which takes out of the hands of the people the management of their own property" and observed that if politics should become involved, the people would be "responsible under a democratic form of government." However, a simple test was suggested to settle the matter: "Does the TVA want a power board to administer TVA power in Knoxville? If the TVA wants it, we're for it; if the TVA doesn't want it, we're again' it. . . . We believe TVA can supervise all that is necessary. We'd rather trust TVA than some of these so-called 'non-political' theorists."[28]

Power boards have been established with little controversy in most other cities in response to TVA recommendations. In a few instances, the power board has been adopted after long promotional efforts by TVA personnel and the local power manager. One mayor reported that the power manager supported by TVA personnel complained so much about inattention by the governing body to problems of the power system that a power board was finally created. Another city changed to a power board as a result of the manager's lobbying with members of the state legislature.

TVA has done well in promoting power boards in Tennessee. Of the 59 city systems, 50 are so organized (including some "utility boards," which also administer other utilities such as water, gas, and sewer systems), and 9 have the departmental form (in 2 of these council committees act informally as power boards). Five of the "departmental" cities owned their electric systems prior to the advent of TVA, and one is the relatively new city of Oak Ridge (1959), where the people strongly support integrated government under the council-manager form.

The preferences of municipal and power system officials seem to be influenced by the form of organization in their respective

[26] The *Knoxville Journal*, Jan. 15, 1939, partially dissented by calling for shorter terms and election by the city council as a means of assuring control by the people.
[27] *Knoxville News-Sentinel*, Jan. 15, 1939.
[28] *Knoxville Labor News*, Nov. 3, 1938.

cities. On questionnaire returns from 32 mayors and other general government officials in the 9 departmental cities, 62 per cent favored this form, 28 per cent favored the power board form, and 9 per cent expressed no preference. Of 109 such officials in cities with power boards, 75 per cent favored the board form, 18 per cent the departmental form, and 7 per cent were neutral. Power board members and managers, as would be expected, heavily favored the board form—97 per cent of 137 respondents; 2 favored the departmental form, and 2 indicated no preference.

The reasons most often advanced by municipal officials for the board preference were to keep politics out, to avoid overburdening the governing body which must deal with all municipal matters, and to permit pay increases for utility employees without the necessity of across-the-board increases for other city employees. Some thought that higher pay was justified by the technical nature of utility work and the need to compete with other systems for competent personnel. The cause of good municipal government would be advanced if municipal officials would realize that such treatment for all employees would improve their levels of performance. TVA claims that its high standards have spill-over effects on municipal governments, but we see here the antithesis: the good things are available only in the power system by insulating it from the remainder of the city government.

AUTONOMY OF POWER BOARDS

A power board usually has full control of the electric system. Participation by the municipal government is generally limited to the selection of board members, taking title to property, and approving power contracts and bond issues. The Tennessee Municipal Electric Plant Law makes a broad grant of authority to power boards:

> Subject to the provisions of applicable bonds or contracts the supervisory body shall determine programs and make all plans for the acquisition of the electric plant, shall make all determinations as to improvements, rates, and financial practices, may establish such rules and regulations as it may deem necessary or appropriate to govern the furnishing of electric

service, and may disburse all moneys available in the electric plant fund hereinafter established for the acquisition, improvement, operation, and maintenance of the electric plant and the furnishing of electric service.[29]

Private acts contain provisions such as the following:

> [The board shall have] full control and complete jurisdiction over the management and operation of the System and may make all contracts and do any and all acts and things that are necessary, convenient or desirable in order to operate ... the System.[30]

> Electric Power Board ... shall have exclusive management and control of said electric power plant and/or distribution system.[31]

> [The electric system] shall be operated by the Board of Public Utilities independently and free from supervision or control of any kind by the Board of Commissioners.[32]

Power boards exercise a fair amount of control over their own membership in some municipalities, more through informal influences than by formal procedures. Vacancies on the power boards of Chattanooga and Knoxville are filled from nominations by the remaining board members (in Knoxville the mayor must concur). Two other Tennessee cities, LaFollette and Shelbyville, tried such an arrangement, but subsequent charter amendments gave the governing bodies full authority to fill vacancies.[33]

Control by Municipal Governing Body

Memphis seems to be the only city in Tennessee that has retained substantial control over its utility board, reflecting the strong government and independent spirit of the city that existed under E. H. ("Boss") Crump during TVA's first twenty

---

[29] Municipal Electric Plant Law of 1935, *Tennessee Code*, secs. 6-1514, 6-1515.
[30] *Private Acts of Tennessee, 1955*, ch. 176 (Maryville).
[31] *Private Acts of Tennessee, 1939*, ch. 262 (Nashville).
[32] *Private Acts of Tennessee, 1943*, ch. 325 (LaFollette).
[33] LaFollette: *Private Acts of Tennessee, 1943*, ch. 325, amended by *Private Acts of Tennessee, 1953*, ch. 479. Shelbyville: *Private Acts of Tennessee, 1941*, ch. 293, amended by *Private Acts of Tennessee, 1957*, ch. 202.

years. The charter provides for five members to be appointed by the city board of commissioners (replaced by a thirteen-member city council under a charter amendment effective January 1, 1968) for three-year terms. They may be removed "at the will and pleasure of the board of commissioners [city council] ... without the necessity of a hearing, or notice, [which] ... shall be final." Appointments to positions with an annual salary of over $4,000, power purchase contracts with a term of over five years, any purchase contract of over $5,000, and any changes in retail rates are subject to approval by the council.[34]

Some city officials feel that it should be possible to abolish a power board as well as to create one. They say that creation of a power board by a governing body should not necessarily be binding for all time to come and that the same body should have the power to reverse the action. This issue came to a head in one city in 1954. A disagreement arose between the mayor and board of aldermen over nominations for membership on the utilities board. After more than a year of public feuding, the board of aldermen, over the mayor's veto, adopted an ordinance abolishing the utility board and placing the electric system under the board of aldermen. Two months later, another ordinance created a new power board to operate the system. One of the aldermen explained these actions as a maneuver to change the hand-picked membership of the power board which was too subservient to the power manager. The state attorney general, at the request of the mayor, gave an opinion that the enabling act contained no provision for abolition of the power board and therefore the action was illegal. The same view was expressed in a letter from TVA's general counsel, who also pointed out that the terms of bonds issued in 1939 committed the city to the board organization as a binding contractual obligation. His letter also stated that such a board "is a creature of the State Legislature and can be abolished only by it."[35]

The foregoing case illustrates the principal argument against

[34] The applicable private acts are (years and chapters): *1939*, ch. 381; *1941*, ch. 327; *1947*, ch. 723; *1951*, ch. 388.

[35] Even though the board had been created by local action under a permissive enabling act, the legal view is that it became a creature of the state legislature, and as the enabling act contained no provision for abolishing the board it could not be done without additional legislation by the state legislature.

easy abolition of a power board. With such power, the governing body could take action at any time, regardless of motives. Still, a case might be made for giving such authority to the governing body, on the basis of its political responsibility to the people. However, the main reason for a board—its relative independence from political considerations—would be threatened if its continued existence were placed in such jeopardy. Others may argue, though, that this is simply a means of assuring some degree of responsiveness and accountability to the governing body, elected by the people to be responsible for the whole municipal government. Mississippi handled the problem by permitting a referendum by the electorate on the question of abolishing a power board.[36] Under Tennessee law a change might be made through a private legislative act amending a city charter and local ratification by two-thirds of the governing body or by a majority vote in a referendum, but this could be construed as an unauthorized conflict with the general law.[37] This procedure would not be available to the nine Tennessee "home rule" cities which have municipal power systems, as the state constitution requires the legislature to deal with such cities only by laws which are "general in terms and effect."

Consternation Over Effects of Metropolitan Government

As is characteristic of organized groups, TVA and municipal power boards have developed a vested interest in existing organizational arrangements and stoutly oppose change. A case in point is the in-fighting that occurred in 1957 when the Tennessee legislature was considering a bill to empower each of the four largest counties and their central cities, by consolidating the county and city governments, to form a "metropolitan government."[38] The bill provided for a ten-member charter

[36] *Mississippi Laws, 1962*, ch. 549, codified as sec. 3519-04 of the *Mississippi Code*.

[37] An extension of the theory in *Johnson City* v. *Allison*, 50 Tenn. App. 532, 362 S. W. 2d 813 (1962), which upheld a private act that added three nonresident members to a power board created under the general law, would sustain a private act abolishing a power board.

[38] Shelby County and Memphis; Davidson County and Nashville; Knox County and Knoxville; Hamilton County and Chattanooga. The act was made available for all counties by an amendment in 1963, but it has been adopted only by Davidson County. It is codified in *Tennessee Code*, secs. 6-3701–6-3724.

commission selected by one of two methods: five members selected by the governing body of the county and five members named by the governing body of the principal city, or the ten candidates receiving the highest number of votes in a county-wide election. The commission was made responsible for preparing a charter for submission to the voters, which would become effective if approved by dual majorities in the principal city and in the remainder of the county. Such procedure is common for charter adoptions and amendments by home-rule action, and it would seem to be thoroughly compatible with TVA's oft-stated principles of local determination and control by the people. Yet it evoked the Authority's vigorous opposition.

The chairman of the fringe-area committee of the Tennessee Municipal League, Frank Gray, Jr., asked for TVA's opinion because "great confusion has arisen in the minds of legislators, the general public, and others due to forecasts by certain power system spokesmen of the dire consequences and the unwholesome conditions in operation of the electric distribution system if the attached bill is enacted."[39] The letter pointed out that a charter commission could continue the electric system as a part of the metropolitan government without any change in the system's management, administration, personnel, operation, and disposition of revenues, or the provisions of any law or bond ordinance. The letter also presented nine questions bearing on the issue of whether the bill in any way threatened municipal power systems.

The TVA chairman's letter of reply commenced with a discussion of the evil effects of diverting electric revenues and asserted that there was "nothing in the bill which would continue [existing safeguards] . . . contained in the currently applicable special laws." The letter pointed out that implementation of any provision that would violate "current TVA power contracts" would be invalid, but the bill as drafted gave no assurance of any protection "after the expiration of the current contracts." It suggested that a charter commission might even propose a charter that would "prohibit the signing of a new power contract which provided against intermingling of electric

[39] Letter from Frank Gray, Jr., chairman, fringe-area committee of the Tennessee Municipal League, to Aubrey J. Wagner, general manager of TVA, Jan. 12, 1957 (in the files of the league).

system revenues with other metropolitan government revenues."

The TVA letter declared that the "basic issue involved in [four of] these questions seems to be whether the legal status of the electric systems would be more secure under the proposed bill than they are under existing legislation"; it continued:

> The answer would seem to depend largely, not upon the bill itself, but upon the actions taken under the bill. Any charter proposed under the bill could cover the electric system without specifically referring to it. As we read the bill, upon approval of such a charter in the necessary referenda, the power board would be abolished. Whether the private act governing the operation of the electric system would remain in effect in other respects is open to serious question. In such a case, nothing in the charter or the referenda proceedings would necessarily put the voters on notice of the proposed change in the management or operation of the electric system, unless the power board or some other interested organization took it upon itself to inform the voters of this effect of the charter....
>
> ... the charter would provide expressly for continuation of the existing power board and the provisions of the private act under which it operates. Upon approval of such a charter the existing electric system might be less vulnerable to changes in legal status than at present. On the other hand, the charter could merely authorize the metropolitan governing body to abolish or create boards as it saw fit for the furnishing of municipal utility services. It is obvious that in that event the existing power board and any successor board would be less secure than they have been at any time in the past when they could not be abolished or interfered with short of an act of the legislature.
>
> In conclusion, if our interpretation of the proposed bill is correct, nothing in the bill necessarily affords greater security and stability than the electric systems now have. They could be made subject to changes in management and operation at the will of the metropolitan government without approval of the electorate.[40]

The intention manifested in the original bill was to grant to a charter commission and the electorate full discretion with

[40] Letter from A. J. Wagner to Frank Gray, Jr., Feb. 5, 1957 (in the files of the Tennessee Municipal League).

respect to all parts of the city and county governments, excepting only a few constitutional offices. However, TVA and municipal power system personnel were unwilling to run any risks of such tampering with governmental organization and successfully insisted that the municipal power systems be accorded a special privileged and protected status (the only agencies accorded such treatment). Under the act, any proposed charter must include "such terms and provisions as are contained in any private act or municipal charter with respect to any municipally owned utility supported by its own revenues and operated, administered and managed pursuant to said private act or municipal charter...."[41]

The home-rule advocates won a partial victory, in a proviso that was added to this section: "such terms and provisions of the charter may subsequently be amended pursuant to subsection (t) hereof"; subsection (t) requires an amendment procedure that must include a countywide majority of the voters voting thereon. The effect was to prohibit any change respecting the power system in an initial charter proposed under this act but to authorize subsequent changes by amendment.

THE VIEW FROM THE MUNICIPAL SIDE

TVA unquestionably has a delicate problem of public relations when it undertakes to establish uniform policies as to rates, financial and accounting practices, and operating procedures for a utility system divided among 160 distributors, including 105 cities. It would of course not be humanly possible for any administration to keep everyone happy at all times under these circumstances. A TVA district manager described the problem this way:

> One phase of the districts' job is like trying to walk a tight rope. We must see that the power distributors live up to their contracts and at the same time gain respect and understanding of the TVA program to the degree that they will fight for TVA on a national level. This means that the districts must explain the TVA idea year after year in the face of the highly

[41] *Public Acts of Tennessee, 1957*, ch. 120, sec. 10(v), codified as sec. 6-3711 (v) of the *Tennessee Code*.

financed and organized opposition. The power distributors not only provide the practical means of local participation in the power program but they also provide the public relations support which TVA must have.[42]

Roughly a third of general government officials and power system officials voluntarily made favorable remarks on our questionnaires. Fifteen per cent of those in the former group and 6 per cent in the latter group offered critical remarks. A large proportion in both groups, 52 and 59 per cent respectively, made no remarks.[43] A former mayor wrote a short critical treatise which merits repeating here in full:

> It is my basic political belief that an official elected by the people and answerable to them must also have the power to determine the course of the public function. This is not true under a strong power board operation backed up by a determined agency. In order to justify its operation as a public agency TVA must admit certain facts but in its relationship with municipalities, TVA has usurped practically all of the managerial responsibilities which, in my opinion, belong rightfully with elected officials. TVA stands on its tax free status as a public entity but tries to place local operation strictly outside the public control.
> The question of "being outside politics" is completely distasteful to me. Ours is traditionally and historically a nation whose precepts are based on the control and operation of government by duly elected officials who must depend on proper stewardship for re-election. It is this constant cry of "take it out of politics" that has brought about the present day attitude in the minds of many of the image of an office holder or politician being dishonest and immoral and therefore untrustworthy. I am, and have been for years, opposed to taking this responsibility from elected officials.
> Although I think the relationship between our city and the TVA has been fine and pleasant I feel that they exert too much influence on systems to establish independent power boards and then use the board to operate the system entirely as they

---

[42] Jack W. Eakin, Oct. 16, 1964, *op. cit.*

[43] The bias of the statistics is favorable to TVA. Supplementary personal interviews indicated that respondents were more prone to talk critically than they were to write critically.

direct. They could not do this operating directly with the elected officials. The fact that because of the affluency of most power systems allowing higher pay they should have preferential treatment as a "sacred cow" is obviously wrong.

Other comments of general government officials pointed to TVA's dictatorial methods: "TVA never plans with you. They dictate to you. All dealings are unilateral." "TVA has power to be dictatorial and frequently is." One reported that TVA had been "more or less dictatorial, threatening to take any reserve in the case of no contract." Other comments from such officials included: "TVA has too much control; local government too little." "Provisions of the power contract hold the power system's feet to the fire rather closely, yet leave TVA wide latitude as to what it can require of the power system." A power system manager similarly noted that the arrangement was "too inflexible with regard to the system's powers and too flexible with regard to TVA's powers." Power board members thought there should be "room for negotiation and less rigidity in TVA's interpretations" and that "local government should have more to say about operation." Board members also commented on dictatorial tendencies: "TVA is inclined to be dictatorial in some cases of local management." "Benevolent dictatorship!" One declared that "domination of local governmental units by TVA should be eliminated."

Favorable comments ranged from matter-of-fact commendations to effusive eulogies. The lengthy remarks of three power system managers (one in a city without a power board, and the other two in cities that operated for many years without power boards) reveal the strong bond that has developed between TVA and managers:

> Relationship is excellent. If any TVA personnel ever attempts to influence or advise us regarding matters over which they are not given jurisdiction by the power contract, we simply disregard the advice, unless we wish to follow it. We value very highly the services they offer regarding industrial engineering, advertising, contracts with customers, etc. I sincerely believe our customers are much better off because of TVA's enforcement of provisions in the power contract, than they would be if our city government had sole jurisdiction over our power system.

The second manager looked upon TVA as his protector:

> TVA has a good organization with well qualified employees. These employees are dedicated, in most cases, to the Public Power Idea. Much support is given to management of local power systems and without such support many distribution systems would be used as revenue sources for City or County Government. The TML [Tennessee Municipal League] should not advocate the "City Government Operation" of power systems since most small cities would impose on the power systems for many favors. There is a need for educating city leaders that power systems are a "part of city government services" (in our case) and that the better the service, the better the Government and that the citizens are better off financially and better satisfied.

The third manager expressed very strong views—he would even take a private company over the municipal government:

> The TVA has always been fair and honest in their dealings with us and this city government. They have only insisted that the provisions of the Power Contract be carried out, which is drawn up to comply with a congressional act to provide the most electricity at the lowest possible rate to all classes of consumers and is the only protection that the electric consumers in the State of Tennessee have to protect them against high and exorbitant electric rates. Generally speaking, municipal governments want to control the operations of their electric utilities, so they can use them as a revenue raising operation and there is a natural conflict between TVA and the municipalities because of this. The third party, the customer, is demanding more and better service at all times, which requires a constant plough-back of earnings to keep up with the fast rate of growth. The interest of all concerned will be served best by a complete and separate operation under an electric power board working with TVA. It would be better to go back to private ownership and operation than to have the municipalities operate the electric systems for revenue and political gain.

However, critical remarks from several managers indicate that all are not so enamored with TVA; one said, "TVA is always right and everyone else is always wrong—no one in TVA will listen to us since Vogel [H. D. Vogel, board chairman, 1954–1962] left."

The TVA manager of power has lauded the "spirit of cooperation" between TVA and its distributors, who "work out their mutual problems so that the best and lowest cost arrangements are developed as if there were only one owner instead of two."[44] However, he was speaking to representatives of power systems, and his statement should be evaluated in the context of typical dealings by TVA with power system officials—not with officials of municipal governments. Municipal officials are generally involved only when they must approve a contract, when they have a grievance or problem and seek a conference with TVA, or when the Authority finds that their participation is necessary to work out a problem.

Reactions of municipal and power system officials to TVA's influence and their feelings of pressure from TVA are summarized in Tables 1 and 2. Table 1 indicates significantly higher influence on power system officials than on general city government officials. Thirty-seven per cent of general city government officials and 18 per cent of power system officials reported "no

TABLE 1

ESTIMATION BY TWO GROUPS OF MUNICIPAL OFFICIALS
OF DEGREE OF TVA'S INFLUENCE*

Questionnaire response	General city gov't officials No.	Per cent	Power system officials No.	Per cent
Sometimes a negative reaction	14	10	5	4
No influence	53	37	25	18
Slight influence	15	10	21	15
Influence about 50 per cent	40	28	67	49
Dominant influence	9	6	13	9
No reply	13	9	7	5
Totals	144	100	138	100

* Question: "Which of the following comes nearest to describing any influence of TVA information and/or policy statements on the performance of your duties?"

[44] G. O. Wessenauer, address before an annual meeting of the Distribution Practices Section, Tennessee Valley Public Power Association, at Nashville, Oct. 30, 1962 (MS in TVA Technical Library, Knoxville).

influence"; 28 per cent of the former group and 49 per cent of the latter group stated that TVA's influence had been "about 50 per cent." The high score for TVA on feelings of pressure—62.5 per cent of general city government officials and 68.2 per cent of power system officials reporting "no pressure"—no doubt reflects in part a reluctance of many officials to say anything critical of TVA. Many probably failed to return questionnaires for the same reason; one power board member who failed to do so said, "We are not a customer of TVA—we are just their lackey." Even so, 25 per cent of all respondents reported some pressure and 7 per cent thought it had been more than "mild pressure."

TVA'S INFLUENCE ON LOCAL GOVERNMENT

Does TVA policy, especially its advocacy of power board ad-

TABLE 2

ESTIMATION BY TWO GROUPS OF MUNICIPAL OFFICIALS OF DEGREE OF PRESSURE EXERTED BY TVA*

Questionnaire response	General city gov't officials No.	Per cent	Power system officials No.	Per cent
No pressure	90	62.5	94	68.2
Mild pressure:				
Seldom	11	7.6	21	15.3
Occasionally	9	6.2	9	6.5
Frequently	1	.7	1	.7
Strong pressure:				
Seldom	3	2.1	3	2.1
Occasionally	4	2.8	2	1.4
Frequently	2	1.4		
Unnecessarily strong pressure:				
Seldom	1	.7		
Occasionally	3	2.1		
Frequently	2	1.4		
No reply	18	12.5	8	5.8
Totals	144	100.0	138	100.0

* Question: "In situations involving conflict between local interests and TVA interests, in your own dealings with TVA personnel do you feel they have exerted—"

ministration, conflict with principles of local autonomy and democratic government at the municipal level? Is local government, as a democratic institution responsible to the people, strengthened by a policy which writes off the politicians and their administration of public affairs as hopelessly political? Is TVA's policy a short-run approach aimed at power systems only? Should TVA use its great prestige to influence the course of municipal government generally, in the long run to upgrade the caliber of all governmental services—not just electric power service?

On a number of occasions TVA has expressed a broad interest in local governments, even a desire to participate in reforms aimed at greater efficiency and more democratic responsibility. A member of the TVA staff in its early years observed "that enlightened management of electric utility operation may be expected to touch and influence the direction of other local governmental affairs is also a hope implicit in TVA since its objectives transcend power service and reach into the broad sphere of the general welfare."[45] Lilienthal has also spoken on this point:

> The dividends of such decentralization are already appearing, not merely in high returns in cash to these community systems—returns in excess of 15 and even 20 per cent on investment are being reported—but dividends of other kinds, socially even more significant. I invite your study of the effect of these added responsibilities of operating an essential public service upon the level and tone of city management generally in communities where TVA power is being distributed; the effect upon the evils of patronage in city services, of slip-shod accounting, and of lack of citizen interest in municipal affairs.[46]

A TVA publication released in 1960 contains a similar statement: "It appears that the high quality of operation required by TVA in reference to the municipal power systems has had a subtle influence in up-grading administrative and personnel practices, accounting controls, fiscal management, and other performance

---

[45] Ormond C. Corry (Research Associate Professor, the University of Tennessee), "TVA Contractual Regulation of Electric Distribution Systems" (unpublished MS, 1942).

[46] Lilienthal, address on Nov. 10, 1939, *op. cit.*

standards of all local utility operations. Moreover, this influence seems to have carried over to an extent in regard to general activities of municipal government in some communities —although objective evidence on this point is not readily available."[47]

Apparently, the rationale of such assertions is that an example of nonpolitical administration will be set which will be emulated by other branches of a municipal government—about the only theory by which the separate board setup could be reconciled with the concept of strengthening local government. Presumably the power board "nonpoliticians" will set an example that will cause other city officials to act less like politicians. Though probably not a part of TVA's rationale, another possibility is that municipal governments will be induced to transfer functions to power boards or to other boards. A reliable source has reported that the officials of one city suggested that all municipal services might be transferred to its power board and that TVA power personnel were flattered by the proposal (it was not adopted). Utility boards in a few cities are responsible for sewers. A couple of small cities have been giving serious consideration to a transfer of public works activities to such boards. Is such encouragement to city officials to reduce their accountability to the electorate an undesirable side effect of power board administration?

A small Tennessee city provides a case in point. The electric system had been poorly managed as a department of the city government, and delinquent electric bills totaled about $10,000, some of them as old as three years. The city, however, resisted TVA's efforts to have the system placed under a power board and instead employed a competent city manager. It could not have done so if the electric system had been separated from the general city government, because the scope of remaining operations would not have warranted a full-time city manager nor justified a salary attractive to a competent person. The new manager soon put the affairs of the electric system in good shape, with TVA's assistance, which he sought, and he also introduced the beneficial effects of good manage-

[47] Government Relations & Economics Staff, *Tennessee Valley Authority Program: The Role of the States and Their Political Subdivisions* (Knoxville: Tennessee Valley Authority, 1960), p. 19.

ment for other operations of the city government. Included in his improvements was a new building for all departments, constructed with electric system funds, which most likely would not have been possible under a power board setup.[48]

Another small Tennessee city furnishes an opposite example. Influenced by the efficient operation of the electric system under a power board, the governing body decided to transfer to it the water and sewer operations. Later, members of the governing body became interested in the council-manager form of government, but full implementation of the plan is unlikely because the scale of remaining operations is too small to justify employment of a full-time, professional manager.

Unquestionably, most observers would agree that municipal power systems, judged on efficiency alone, are superior to other branches of municipal government, and most would also say that in large measure this stems from TVA's close oversight and technical assistance. Some would also concede that concepts and practices of efficient management have permeated other municipal functions to some extent, but, in the words of TVA, "objective evidence on this point is not readily available." The opinions of general city government officials on this point are tabulated in Table 3. The high degree of affirmative opinion they expressed is subject to qualification. The extent to which the respondents correctly identified the influences that brought about improvements can be questioned. Also, the question may have been misinterpreted by some; several respondents checked "improvements" and then added a comment that these had occurred only in the electric system. Only 18 per cent of officials in cities without power boards checked "no improvements," as compared with 24 per cent in cities with power boards, which is slight evidence that the influence of TVA on municipal government may be greater where no power board exists.

The point needs to be made also that influences other than TVA-oriented power systems have been active in upgrading

[48] The city pays no rent for that part of the building used for nonelectric operations, on a basis that such a rental would be almost exactly the same as a tax equivalent computed by applying tax rates to the book value of the building, which was waived by the city as a consideration for nonpayment of rent.

municipal government in Tennessee. Agitation for personnel reforms that began with the Pendleton Act in 1883, establishing a federal civil service, has swept across the country, affecting all levels of government. The Tennessee Municipal League, under enlightened and progressive leadership, has stressed professionalization of municipal personnel and improvement of municipal government. For more than twenty years the Tennessee Municipal Finance Officers Association has promoted modern accounting procedures and improved financial practices. For the past decade or so, public works officers, city managers, and inspection officials, through their professional organizations, have been similarly active in their respective fields. Since 1949 the experienced and competent staff of the Municipal Technical Advisory Service at The University of

TABLE 3

QUESTIONNAIRE RESPONSE OF GENERAL CITY GOVERNMENT OFFICIALS: THE EFFECTS OF TVA ELECTRIC SYSTEMS ON GENERAL CITY GOVERNMENTS*

Respondents	No reply	No improvements	Better-qualified employees	Better training for employees	Less politics in personnel policies	Better working quarters	Use of modernized equipment	Better accounting practices
Mayors	1	14	28	24	32	34	37	35
Other members of governing bodies	1	8	19	20	18	24	20	18
Other city officials		9	7	4	6	10	8	7
Repr. of gov. bodies on power boards	1	4	8	6	7	8	9	9
Totals	3	35	62	54	63	76	74	69
Per cent of total number (144) of respondents	2%	24%	43%	38%	44%	53%	51%	48%

*Questionnaire item: "TVA claims that it promotes 'good management' practices by power systems. Please indicate your opinion below as to whether the power system in your city has tended to bring about improvements in the general city government."

Tennessee has provided technical assistance to municipal officials.[49] For an even longer period the Tennessee State Planning Commission has provided technical assistance to local planning agencies through several regional offices staffed by qualified planners.

POWER CONTRACTS

TVA has achieved a major feat of public administration by welding together 160 distribution systems (105 city systems, 50 cooperatives, 3 county systems, and 2 private companies) in such a manner that they are operated essentially as a unified system, in terms of both technical operational details and policies. Unification has been accomplished through the device of the power contract between TVA and each of its distributors. A utility observer very early noted that "the power contract . . . has become the instrument or vehicle for codifying whatever degree of central supervision is exercised and coordinating the operations of multiple independent distribution units."[50]

TVA might argue that municipal resentment against its domination and restrictions should be directed to Congress, on the grounds that it is carrying out congressional policy. In the Authority's first year, the board of directors declared that the act of Congress made it "clearly manifest . . . that the Board . . . should not only have the power but should be under the duty, to specify in the contracts . . . the terms and conditions upon which it [surplus electric power] is to be purchased, [and] . . . only upon terms and conditions that would assure its utilization in the public interest."[51] A veteran of the electric utility industry also concluded that the situation logically called for tight controls by TVA: "There is no question that

---

[49] Personnel of TVA's Government Research Division participated in making plans for the Municipal Technical Advisory Service, created in 1949, and one of them (Gerald W. Shaw) left this division to become MTAS' first executive director.

[50] E. W. Morehouse, "The New Administrative Problems of Municipal Electric Plants and Rural Cooperatives," *Proceedings: Southern Institute on Local Government*, The University of Tennessee Record, Extension Series, Vol. XVII, No. 1 (May, 1941), p. 19.

[51] *TVA Annual Report for the Fiscal Year Ended June 30, 1934* (Washington, D. C.: U. S. Government Printing Office, 1935), p. 22.

Congress set out in the laws establishing the TVA, and to a lesser extent the REA, the policies of promoting public ownership, stimulating increased use of electricity, and directing primary consideration of consumers. These provisions of law, without stating them in detail, plus the financial and practical reasons underlying them will usually be cited, among many reasons which might be advanced, for the measures of control over local operations thus far adopted."[52]

But the entire burden for policy-making cannot be placed on Congress. There is a large area of discretion for interpretation of the public interest by TVA officials within the framework of congressional legislation. Furthermore, TVA personnel have played a large part in writing the laws. Many battles have been fought in Congress over bills relating to TVA, and sometimes the Authority has been the loser; in the main, however, the prestige and expertise of its personnel have commanded enough respect to cause their views to be significantly reflected in the final acts. Two TVA staff members concluded that the act of Congress "perhaps by design . . . left many questions of policy unanswered, [and] gave many opportunities for varying interpretations of its scope. . . ."[53]

Preferences to Public Distributors

Congress clearly indicated that public agencies are to get first call on TVA power. Section 10 of the TVA Act directs the Authority to "give preference to States, counties, municipalities, and cooperative organizations of citizens or farmers, not organized or doing business for profit, but primarily for the purpose of supplying electricity to its own citizens or members." A similar provision appeared in all of the bills sponsored by Senator Norris. In a report recommending rejection of Henry Ford's bid for the Muscle Shoals properties, he and four other senators recommended instead adoption of S. 3420, his first bill, and expressed their belief "that power developed on navigable streams, power that originates from property owned by the people of the country, ought to receive as wide a distribu-

---

[52] Morehouse, "New Administrative Problems," *op. cit.*, p. 18.
[53] Lawrence L. Durisch and Robert E. Lowry, "The Scope and Content of Administrative Decision—The TVA Illustration," in *Public Administration Review*, XIII, No. 4 (Autumn, 1953), 219.

tion as possible; it ought to be furnished to municipalities at as near cost as possible; it ought to be divided in such a way that all of the people, both rich and poor, will receive a proportionate benefit of the cheapening of electric energy."[54]

TVA has reversed itself on the question of whether or not municipal and cooperative distributors should have preference over the needs of federal agencies. During the near brownout enforced by the Eisenhower administration, when the power supply situation in the Valley showed signs of becoming critical, the question was raised by a number of municipal leaders. The point was also debated in the course of congressional hearings on proposed TVA appropriations for 1957. Congressman Glenn R. Davis of Wisconsin, referring to "the rather frequent statement you hear that if we do not increase the capacity of the TVA . . . we are simply going to prevent the Atomic Energy Commission from getting the power that it needs," went on to say that "if the Atomic Energy Commission is an arm of the Federal Government and has a priority over some of the other present users, then that statement falls completely."[55] At that time the AEC was taking about one-half of TVA's total output. TVA's general counsel responded as follows:

> The TVA Act was drafted before the Federal Government was a very large consumer of electric power itself and there was no anticipation in the legislation of the kind of demands for power by the Federal Government which has developed. The TVA Act, like the other preference statutes, makes no provision for a priority for Federal agencies. This is true not only of our own act but it is true of the preference provision in the Flood Control Act of 1944 under which the Interior Department disposes of the power output of the dams constructed by the Army engineers and it is true also of the Bonneville law and the Boulder Canyon law and so forth.
>
> The TVA Act is a regional development act and the act makes clear the intention of Congress that the power generated by TVA was intended as one of the means of accomplishing the objectives of improving the economy of the

[54] U.S., Congress, Senate, Committee on Agriculture and Forestry, *Muscle Shoals*, 67th Cong., 2d Sess., 1922, S. Rept. 831, Part 1, p. 32.

[55] U.S., Congress, House, Subcommittee of the Committee on Appropriations, *Hearings, Public Works Appropriations for 1957*, 84th Cong., 2d Sess., 1956, pp. 278–79.

Tennessee Valley. So that all of the preferences run in a direction of regional development.

This much was included in the original act on the problem of Federal loads: There is a provision in Section 20 that if Federal needs necessitated, in case of war or national emergency declared by Congress, the projects of the authority would be appropriated by the Government for national defense needs upon payment of compensation to any customer of TVA whose power contract was affected by that action of the United States. That takes care of any emergency situation, but the act does not provide that the units which have been installed and committed to the power needs of the area may be diverted at will to the service of a new Federal use which might appear upon the scene.[56]

TVA's early contracts obligated it without qualification to supply power up to a fixed maximum and to increase the maximum to higher quantities upon the giving of notice by the distributor (the greater the increase, the longer time notice required—up to two years).[57] However, a new policy of giving the federal government higher priority was soon adopted. The Trenton contract of 1937 added the qualifying language, "provided that the requirements of AUTHORITY and/or United States reasonably enable it to do so," and the Ripley contract of 1938 added: "to the extent that Authority, in its judgment, has power available after all requirements of Authority and/or the United States and prior contractual commitments have been met." A similar provision was included in all distributor power contracts until the early fifties, in language similar to that of the 1952 version of the standard power contract obligating TVA to furnish additional power "only to the extent that Authority, in its judgment, has power available after all requirements of Authority, the United States of America, and prior contractual commitments have been met, and subject to acts of God and other contingencies beyond Authority's control."

Relative priorities of local distributors, federal agencies, and industries were discussed in a conference in 1953 which was

---

[56] *Ibid.*, p. 279.
[57] Such contracts were made with Pulaski (1934), Bolivar (1935), Somerville (1935), and Chattanooga (1937).

64 *Sparks at the Grassroots*

attended by high TVA officials and representatives of the Tennessee Municipal League. Most of the discussion centered on the problems of meeting expanding industrial needs; as to federal agencies, TVA Board Chairman Gordon Clapp stated simply that they "get priority on the power supply if needed, because the national defense requires it."[58]

Prior to renewing the contract of its first municipal distributor (Tupelo, Mississippi) on February 6, 1954, TVA gave a comprehensive review to its standard power contract. This renewal contract omitted any qualifying language respecting higher priority of federal needs. The requirement of specific advance notice to increase maximum power supply was also dropped. The amended provision, still in use in 1968, follows:

> Municipality shall keep TVA currently informed of any important developments affecting its probable future loads or service arrangements. TVA shall take account of all available information in making its forecasts of the loads of Municipality and of TVA's other customers. TVA shall make every reasonable effort to increase the generating capacity of its system and to provide the transmission facilities required to deliver the output thereof so as to be in a position to supply additional power therefrom when and to the extent needed to meet the increases in their loads.
>
> . . . .
>
> TVA may, as a condition precedent to TVA's obligation to make power available, require Municipality to provide such assurances of revenue to TVA as in TVA's judgment may be necessary to justify the reservation, alteration, or installation by TVA of additional generation, transmission, or transformation facilities for the purpose of supplying power to Municipality.[59]

It is thus apparent that TVA prior to 1954 accorded to the federal government a priority beyond that contemplated in the statute. This now may be a matter of only historical interest, in view of the omission of such priority from TVA's power contracts. The self-financing basis of the power program, initiated in 1959, also should provide sufficient assurances of adequate power for all claimants.

[58] My notes on conference, Jan. 29, 1953, *op. cit.*
[59] Renewal contract with Knoxville, July 1, 1968.

TVA as Sole Supplier

A key feature of TVA's plan is that it must be the sole source of electric power for any of its distributors. A standard provision in early contracts was that "Municipality agrees to purchase from Authority, and Authority agrees to supply, the entire electricity requirements of Municipality." The 1952 edition of the standard power contract covered the point more elaborately:

> Authority shall, from the date of initial delivery and for the term of this contract, supply for Municipality's use and for resale all of Municipality's power requirements up to a maximum demand specified in section 3 hereof. . . . Municipality shall in no event obtain, by generation, purchase, or otherwise, power from any source, other than Authority's electric system, without the consent of Authority, unless Authority has refused to supply Municipality such additional quantities of power as may have been applied for as provided herein, and then only to the extent of its requirements in excess of the power available from Authority.

Since 1955 the concept of TVA as sole supplier has been expressed in a prefatory clause: "Whereas Municipality . . . is presently purchasing and desires to continue to purchase its entire power requirements from TVA." The policy has also been restated in the body of the contracts, in language similar to the following: "TVA shall produce and deliver to Municipality at the delivery point or points specified in or hereafter established under section 3 hereof and Municipality shall take and distribute the electric power required for service to Municipality's customers."[60]

The TVA Act contains no provision specifically authorizing or directing that the Authority shall be the sole source of power supply for its distributors. The legislative basis for this policy is found in Section 10 of the TVA Act, which authorizes the board "to include in any contract for the sale of power such terms and conditions . . . as in its judgment may be necessary or desirable for carrying out the purposes of this Act. . . ."

Spokesmen of private utility interests have been critical of

[60] *Ibid.*

this aspect of TVA policy, saying that it makes "captive cities" of TVA's municipal distributors. However, only one instance is known where it has posed any problem for a municipality. When Memphis was made the target of private utility penetration under the Dixon-Yates deal fostered by the Eisenhower administration, at a time (1956–1957) when TVA was really concerned about meeting future load requirements, the city did not have the option of supplementing TVA power from its own generating facilities. Memphis had to choose between continued sole dependence on TVA (through which the private power would be channeled) or constructing generating facilities adequate to supply all of its requirements. It chose the latter course and did not renew its contract with TVA, which expired in 1958. The decision by the city to build a steam plant instead was a *quid pro quo* for cancellation of the Dixon-Yates contract, which was announced by President Eisenhower at a White House conference in the presence of the mayor, the chairman of the TVA board of directors, and other high governmental officials. TVA viewed loss of the city as a small sacrifice in comparison to the infiltration of private power through the Dixon-Yates contract and later, similar undertakings then being planned. Another benefit to TVA was that it greatly eased the strain on the Authority's power resources.

Term of Contracts

The TVA Act authorizes the board of directors "to enter into contracts for such sale [to a preference customer] for a term not exceeding twenty years." If a distributor builds and maintains its own transmission line to a TVA generating station or transmission line, a term up to thirty years is authorized.[61] In the early years a few cities that were near TVA hydroelectric plants, including Chattanooga, constructed their own transmission lines to take advantage of a 10 per cent discount on the wholesale price for "nontransmitted power."[62]

[61] The Senate-passed bill authorized up to thirty- and forty-year contract terms, but the conference committee recommended twenty- and thirty-year terms included in the House-passed bill.
[62] The first section constructed by Chattanooga was a transmission line to Chickamauga Dam. The city's contract of June 17, 1937, was for thirty years, which was extended by a 1940 amendment to thirty years from the date of initial delivery of power (Jan. 23, 1939), but at the same time the

Original contracts, except with the few cities that built or acquired their own transmission lines, uniformly have been for twenty-year periods. Practice for amendatory contracts has varied; some have been for the balance of a contract term; others have been for new twenty-year terms. Such variations, and the entry of cities into the TVA system over an extended period of time, have staggered contract terms. By thus spreading the work, TVA personnel can give more attention to negotiation of particular contracts. This situation also tends to discourage concerted action by municipalities, as municipal officials typically are not concerned until the time approaches for renewal of their own city's contract.

Prior to the 1954 Tupelo, Mississippi, revision, contracts contained no provision for termination. The Tupelo revision and subsequent contracts added a clause permitting either party to terminate a contract "on not less than four years' prior written notice," to be "effective not earlier than 10 years" from the effective date of the contract.

Other Contract Provisions

Provisions respecting rates, disposition of funds, payments in lieu of taxes, street lighting, and service to large industries are considered in subsequent chapters. At this point brief mention of other provisions of the power contracts will give some idea of their general scope.

In addition to obligations of the parties respecting power supply, other technical matters are covered: exact delivery points, wholesale power voltage, distribution system voltage, responsibility of each party for protecting the other's equip-

---

10 per cent discount was limited to 60,000 kw. Florence and Tuscumbia, Ala., in the vicinity of Muscle Shoals, were given thirty-year contracts with the 10 per cent discount on all power; both of these contracts expired in 1967. Two other Alabama cities—Sheffield and Muscle Shoals—were treated similarly, but their twenty-year contracts expired years ago. Bessemer and Tarrant City, Ala., jointly constructed a transmission line to Guntersville Dam, a distance of more than 100 miles, which subsequently became overloaded and was taken over by TVA; both cities received 25-year contracts which have expired. All of these contracts were entered into before TVA, about 1939, declared there could be no "nontransmitted power" in a grid system that makes it impossible to identify the source of electric power energy, and therefore discounts would be discontinued. (Telephone interview with Elbert Pearson, TVA Office of Power, April 26, 1965).

ment, temporary use of distributor's lines for transmission by TVA, equipment to be furnished by each party, method of determining peak demand, testing of metering equipment, submission and payment of wholesale power bills, adjustment of the wholesale cost of power in the event of higher production costs, interference with availability or use of power, voltage and load fluctuations, and balancing of loads. Because of their technical nature such matters seldom give rise to differences of opinion or problems of contract interpretation.

Another part of each power contract is a "Schedule of Rules and Regulations" to govern distributors' operations. Some early contracts gave TVA blanket authorization to make changes, as illustrated by the 1934 Knoxville contract under which the city agreed "to be bound during the term hereof, by any future additions or amendments of such Schedule of Rules and Regulations prescribed after conference with representatives of Contractor, the same as though such additions or amendments were incorporated herein." The *Knoxville News-Sentinel* observed that such provisions were "not as flexible" as those contained in other contracts and noted that a contract with Memphis (November, 1935) permitted changes "from time to time . . . by agreement of Board (city) and Authority."[63] The 1952 standard power contract contained an even more liberal provision: "Municipality hereby adopts said Schedule of Rules and Regulations. The provisions of said schedule may be amended, supplemented, or repealed by Municipality at any time upon ten (10) days' written notice to Authority setting forth the nature of and reason for the proposed change. No change shall be made in said schedule, however, which is inconsistent with or in violation of any of the other provisions of this contract." The 1954 Tupelo revision and subsequent contracts contain substantially the same provision, except that the time period for the notice is changed to thirty days.

The scope of rules and regulations may be indicated by reciting the section headings: application for service, deposit, point of delivery, customer's wiring-standards, inspections, underground service lines, customer's responsibility for distributor's property, right of access, billing, discontinuance of ser-

[63] *Knoxville News-Sentinel,* Jan. 19, 1936.

vice by distributor, reconnection charge, termination of contract by customer, service charges for temporary service, interruption of service, voltage fluctuations caused by customer, additional load, standby and resale service (resale is prohibited), notice of trouble, nonstandard service, meter tests, relocation of outdoor lighting facilities, billing adjusted to standard periods, revisions, and conflict (if any with rate schedule, latter prevails).

Contracting Agents for Municipalities

TVA officials have indicated the lack of uniformity among municipal officials with whom contracts have been negotiated:

> Mr. Clapp [board chairman] stated that TVA negotiates contracts with local agencies designated as being responsible for the electric systems, and that TVA cannot be placed in a position of trying to iron out differences between local electric boards and city councils. . . . Mr. Watson [director of power utilization] said that most of the early contracts were made with city councils, but that more recently many electric system boards had been given such authority and that therefore contracts had been negotiated with them. In response to a question, Mr. Swidler [general counsel] said that authority had been delegated to electric system boards by special legislative acts and by ordinances, and that no standard practice prevails.[64]

Table 4 is a tabulation of the officials acting on behalf of Tennessee municipalities to execute original, renewal, and amendatory power contracts. If these figures are adjusted to reflect execution of forty-four original contracts by mayors before power boards were created (when the option of power board chairmen did not exist), 49 per cent of the total for which this option existed were executed by chairmen of power boards. One is inclined to suspect that the relative ease of negotiating contracts with power boards, whose members are oriented more toward TVA's policies, might have been a factor in the selection of these agencies to act for cities. However, the pattern of recent years seems to have been to secure the mayor's approval (who presumably must have the governing body's

---

[64] My notes on conference, Jan. 29, 1953, *op. cit.*

authorization to sign) for renewal and amendatory contracts of any policy substance; only one (Nashville, May 4, 1939) executed in this manner bears a date prior to July 1, 1956. Although some contracts have continued to be signed on behalf of cities by power board chairmen only, generally these seem to be concerned with technical matters—an additional delivery point, increasing the power supply, installation of power-conserving equipment, and the like.

Some cities are governed by private acts that delegate contracting powers to power boards, but most of Tennessee's municipal distributors are organized under the general law. This law clearly designates the governing body to represent a municipality in contracting with TVA: "Any municipal corporation . . . is authorized, in any contract or arrangement with the Tennessee Valley Authority . . . to stipulate and agree to such covenants, terms and conditions as the governing body thereof may deem appropriate, including but without limitation, covenants, terms and conditions in respect to the resale rates, financial and accounting methods, services, operation and main-

TABLE 4

TENNESSEE MUNICIPAL OFFICIALS EXECUTING
TVA POWER CONTRACTS, 1933–1964

Officials executing contracts for municipalities	No. of contracts	Per cent of total
Cities with no power boards		
Mayors	23	100
Cities with power boards	162	100
Mayors	54*	33
Power board chairmen	58	36
Power board chairmen, approved by mayors	26	16
Power board chairmen and mayors	11	7
Power system managers	6	4
Majority of both governing body and power board	7	4

* Includes two by the city manager of Knoxville.

tenance practices and the manner of disposing of the revenues, of any such system. . . ."[65]

Negotiation of Contracts

The TVA district manager's comment that his job is "like trying to walk a tight rope" is a fair description of the dilemma facing TVA officials when they present draft contracts to municipal officials or power board members: they must give an impression of negotiation, yet they must avoid breaching the terms of the standard power contract if TVA is to maintain a position of dealing on equal terms with all of its distributors. TVA has perhaps been more successful in attaining the latter objective than it has been in creating an atmosphere of negotiation—which implies some give-and-take, of which there has been very little. TVA personnel are patient and thorough in their explanation of contractual provisions, and they may even create an impression that some matters will be governed by the wishes of local officials—but in the end one realizes that a contract has been offered and the only real choice is to take it or leave it. As one mayor commented on his questionnaire, "TVA is rather inflexible in its attitudes toward consumer utilities."

TVA in 1967 served notice on Chattanooga that its power contract expiring in January, 1969, would not be renewed unless the legislature repealed a private act[66] which gave the city a slightly better tax-equivalent base than the standard book-value base. A bill introduced in the 1967 session for this purpose was generally acceptable, except that one representative (James Caldwell) objected to a provision barring the city from levying a sales tax on electricity sales. He explained that he was not advocating such a tax but he thought that the city's hands should not be tied for the future. High officials of TVA conferred with him, but he was unshaken by their threats of no power contract and a consequent increase of some 20 per cent in the city's power costs. Caldwell created a furor when he proposed that the legislature adopt a resolution calling for a congressional investigation of this matter. Supporters of TVA

[65] *Tennessee Code*, sec. 6-1535.
[66] *Private Acts of Tennessee, 1945*, ch. 53.

in the House secured fifty-five signatures on HJR 94 which, after several "whereas" clauses, resolved "that this legislative body not go on record as condemning or criticizing TVA." This resolution never came to a vote, primarily because the resolution of criticism was never introduced.

In the 1968 session Caldwell maintained his stance that the restriction was unreasonable, but all other members of the Hamilton County delegation fell in line and the bill was adopted.[67] TVA could easily have conceded on this point, as the general law of the state prohibits a local sales tax levy on electricity sales. It is puzzling, with such a law of statewide application, that TVA would go to such lengths to insist on the same provision in a private act. Apparently TVA is unwilling to rely on the general law and wants a second line of defense in contract prohibitions on each distributor.

One of the few cases when TVA was not the winner can be reported, however. Commenting on the new draft contract presented to Tupelo, Mississippi, the *Tupelo Journal* observed that "the new TVA contract indicates greater suspicion regarding the ability of local officials to run local affairs than did the agency's first contract signed by Tupelo twenty years ago.... Tupelo's mayor and board of aldermen cannot afford to yield ground."[68] Shortly thereafter, the same source reported that over three hours of negotiations had failed to break the deadlock over two issues: a provision permitting TVA to assess a penalty if the city should serve a large industry without TVA approval, and a provision barring use of revenues for new construction such as new substations, warehousing, or line improvements. "Mr. Jim Watson said the provisions had been inserted to provide TVA with adequate protection against some TVA distributors that had been abusing the terms of the old TVA contracts."[69] Just one week before the contract was to expire, it was announced that TVA had made an agreement possible by dropping these two proposals.[70]

Some municipal leaders have felt that municipal interests have not been adequately presented or defended in this

[67] *Private Acts of Tennessee, 1968*, ch. 310.
[68] Jan. 18, 1954.
[69] *Ibid.*, Jan. 21, 1954.
[70] *Ibid.*, Jan. 29, 1954.

process, which involves the monolithic power of TVA pitted against the relative weakness of a single municipality. Although the Tennessee Valley Public Power Association, representing local *power systems*, has conducted vigorous negotiations with TVA and at times has even managed to wring some concessions out of TVA, this organization has not adequately represented the interests of *municipal governments*. One city official suggested on his questionnaire return that the "owners should suggest or draft a typical contract." A similar suggestion was made at a conference of TVA and municipal officials in 1953. In that conference TVA spokesmen indicated that a revision of the standard power contract was underway, and the executive secretary of the Tennessee Municipal League, Herbert J. Bingham, requested that a "League Committee be permitted to comment on the provisions of the standard power contract as it underwent the process of revision." The TVA board chairman, Gordon Clapp, replied, "That will be arranged."[71] For reasons that have never been explained, the chairman's commitment was never carried out.

[71] My notes on conference, Jan. 29, 1953, *op. cit.*

3 POWER RATES: AN OVERHEATED ISSUE

LILIENTHAL EARLY GAVE expression to TVA's dominant theme:

> The consumer is often referred to, and usually accurately, as "the forgotten man." Workers are organized. Farmers are organized. Finance is organized. Rarely the consumer. In fact it isn't often that anyone has a responsibility to the consumer; it isn't often that the consumer is the No. 1 man.
>
> That is not so in the case of TVA electricity. Congress has provided by law that you and I in disposing of TVA electricity *owe our first duty to the consumer* and particularly, says the law, to the domestic and rural consumer.[1]

In this chapter, we shall look at considerations that have influenced TVA's rate policies. The Authority sees low rates as the principal justification of its power program, and some observers think that too much weight is given to this objective. TVA power contracts require distributors to agree to lower rates, and sparks have flown at times when such agreement was not readily forthcoming.

LOWEST POSSIBLE RATES: MANDATE OR POLICY?

"Lowest possible rates" could be identified as TVA's motto. These words, lifted from the TVA Act, are declared to be primary in every power contract and are used frequently by TVA spokesmen. For example, the chairman of the board in the opening remarks of a speech quoted the TVA Act as directing that TVA projects "shall be considered primarily for the benefit of the people of the section as a whole and particularly the

---

[1] David Lilienthal, address before a meeting of the Eastern Division Power Distributors' Association, Chattanooga, Aug. 10, 1945 (MS in TVA Technical Library, Knoxville).

domestic and rural consumers to whom the power can economically be made available . . . at the lowest possible rates and in such manner as to encourage increased . . . use of electricity [ellipses as in his manuscript]."[2]

Such statements and the paraphrasings in power contracts aren't quite the same as the full provision in the congressional act:

> It is hereby declared to be the policy of the Government so far as practical to distribute and sell the surplus power generated at Muscle Shoals equitably among the States, counties, and municipalities within transmission distance. This policy is further declared to be that the projects herein provided for shall be considered primarily as for the benefit of the people of the section as a whole and particularly the domestic and rural consumers to whom the power can economically be made available, and accordingly that sale to and use by industry shall be a secondary purpose, to be utilized principally to secure a sufficiently high load factor and revenue returns which will permit domestic and rural use at the lowest possible rates and in such manner as to encourage increased domestic and rural use of electricity.[3]

The congressionally declared objective of handling "sale to and use by industry" in such a way as to "permit domestic and rural use at the lowest possible rates" has been modified by TVA

---

[2] A. J. Wagner, "Objective: Low-Cost Power," address before a meeting of the Accounting Section of the Tennessee Valley Public Power Association, Knoxville, Nov. 13, 1961 (MS in TVA Technical Library, Knoxville). Wagner was then a TVA director; in 1962 he was made chairman of the board.

[3] TVA Act, sec. 11. Only the first sentence was included in the bill as it passed the Senate under the sponsorship of Senator George Norris, TVA's godfather. The second sentence was one of a few provisions in the House-passed bill accepted by the conference committee; the Senate version prevailed on most matters of consequence; one House member remarked that the so-called conference bill looked like the Senate bill. The second sentence was copied almost verbatim from the 1931 act which created the Power Authority of the State of New York, the only differences being the opening words through "provided for," substitution of "section" for "state," and "which will permit" was "to permit" in the New York act. The New York law is still in effect; see *New York Public Authorities Law* (Rochester: The Lawyers Co-operative Publishing Co., 1962), sec. 1005. This is worthy of note because Franklin D. Roosevelt, as governor of New York at the time this law was enacted, expressed a preference for distribution through existing companies if they would do so at reasonable rates.

to the unqualified objective of "lowest possible rates" governing every phase of the power program. The Authority's spokesmen endeavor to establish this as a policy determined by Congress, but in fact it is more of a TVA product than a congressional mandate.

An early policy statement, prepared by Lilienthal and approved by the TVA board, closely followed the statute: "The municipality, in fixing its rates, will observe the principle that the sale to and use by industry shall be secondary purpose, to be utilized principally to secure a sufficiently high load factor and revenue return which will permit domestic and rural use at the lowest possible rates and in such manner as to encourage increased domestic and rural use of electricity."[4] The foregoing language was included in the 1934 contracts with Pulaski and Dayton, but such a provision is missing from subsequent contracts. The 1954 Tupelo revision and subsequent contracts have declared the primacy of "lowest possible rates" as follows:

> WHEREAS, the TVA Act provides that the sale of such power shall be primarily for the benefit of the people of the section as a whole and particularly the domestic and rural consumers, to whom it is desired to make power available at the lowest possible rates and in such manner as to encourage increased domestic and rural use of electricity;
>
> . . . .
>
> 1. *Purpose of Contract.* It is hereby recognized and declared that, pursuant to the obligations imposed by the TVA Act, Municipality's operation of a municipal electric distribution system and TVA's wholesale service thereto are primarily for the benefit of the consumers of electricity through the development of the fullest and widest use of electricity at the lowest possible cost.

An observer may agree that low rates are desirable yet question whether this objective sometimes receives too much emphasis to the detriment of other considerations, such as the

---

[4] Memorandum on "Basic Provisions for Contracts between the Authority and Municipalities for Power," approved by the TVA board of directors on Oct. 16, 1933, and rescinded on March 14, 1936 (in the files of TVA).

payment of adequate tax equivalents, the use of revenues for capital expansion, and TVA's oft-stated deference to local desires in the management of distribution systems.

The theory that higher use leads to lower costs, originated by TVA in the power field, has proven to be sound, probably even beyond the Authority's expectations. In 1932 the average yearly residential consumption in Knoxville was 579 kilowatt-hours, at an average rate of 6.68 cents per kilowatt-hour; in 1937, the last year of private operation, consumption had risen slightly to 967 kilowatt-hours and the average rate had fallen to 3.72 cents per kilowatt-hour.[5] In the 1967–1968 fiscal year, average residential use in the Valley was 12,668 kilowatt-hours, at an average rate of 0.93 cent per kilowatt-hour, which compared with a nationwide average of 5,788 kilowatt-hours at an average rate of 2.14 cents per kilowatt-hour.[6]

Commercial and industrial rates cannot be so simply compared because of the complexity of rate schedules, but illustrative comparisons can be made from data in the "Typical Electric Bills" series published by the Federal Power Commission. Table 5 compares 1940 and 1968 commercial and industrial billings in Chattanooga with national averages and billings in nine cities served by privately owned companies. (Chattanooga was using TVA's second and fourth retail rate schedules—many municipal systems apply lower rate schedules.) The 1940 commercial bill in Charlotte was the only one in this comparison that was lower than Chattanooga's. For the three typical billings in the table, 1940 national averages were, respectively, 90, 53, and 56 per cent higher than Chattanooga's bills and in 1968 were 128, 67, and 77 per cent higher. Commercial billings in 1968 in the other cities ranged from 66 to 187 per cent higher than Chattanooga's bills, and 1968 industrial bills were 9 to 99 per cent higher. The spread in these comparisons may be reduced as a result of TVA's two wholesale rate increases effective in 1969 (see below).

---

[5] Joseph C. Swidler, address at a meeting of the National Lawyers Guild, New York, May 31, 1940 (MS in TVA Technical Library, Knoxville).

[6] *TVA Power Annual Report 1968* (Knoxville: Tennessee Valley Authority, 1968), pp. 4, 5.

TABLE 5

MONTHLY COMMERCIAL AND INDUSTRIAL ELECTRIC BILLS
National Averages, Chattanooga, and Nine Selected Cities, 1940 and 1968

City	Commercial 6,000 kwh. used 30 kw. demand 1940	1968	Industrial 30,000 kwh. used 150 kw. demand 1940	1968	Industrial 200,000 kwh. used 1,000 kw. demand 1940	1968
Monthly bills in dollars						
Chattanooga, Tenn.	90	70	370	379	1,810	1,932
Birmingham, Ala.	130	138	413	413	2,550	2,550
Charlotte, N. C.	86	116	395	414	2,277	2,381
Cincinnati, Ohio	153	165	593	613	2,994	3,189
Jackson, Miss.	177*	146	570*	586	2,956*	2,934
Louisville, Ky.	150	135	516	538	2,599	2,935
Macon, Ga.	159	163	496	558	2,553	2,783
St. Petersburg, Fla.	195*	201	713*	677	3,141*	3,854
Syracuse, N. Y.	142	157	502	502	2,342	2,673
Terre Haute, Ind.	151	125	604	601	3,184	3,652
National average	171	160	565	634	2,828	3,428
indices, Chattanooga = 100						
Chattanooga, Tenn.	100	100	100	100	100	100
Birmingham, Ala.	144	197	112	109	141	132
Charlotte, N. C.	96	166	107	109	126	123
Cincinnati, Ohio	170	236	160	162	165	165
Jackson, Miss.	197*	209	154*	155	163*	152
Louisville, Ky.	167	193	139	142	144	152
Macon, Ga.	177	233	134	147	141	144
St. Petersburg, Fla.	217*	287	193*	179	174*	199
Syracuse, N. Y.	158	224	136	132	129	138
Terre Haute, Ind.	168	179	163	159	176	189
National average	190	228	153	167	156	177

* 1941
Source: Federal Power Commission, *Typical Electric Bills* (annual series). Rates are those in effect on January 1 of the years indicated.

WHOLESALE RATES

Except for minor variations in adjustment clauses and small increases for large industrial customers, TVA's wholesale rates remained essentially unchanged from 1933 to 1967. Citing the increased costs of coal-produced power as compared with hydrogeneration, the Authority increased the large-industry rate in 1952 to produce additional revenue estimated at $750,000 to $1 million annually. The TVA manager of power predicted that this would affect fewer than 500 customers,[7] but it was reported later that more than this number had been affected in only two cities: 387 in Nashville[8] and about 300 in Knoxville.[9] A report from Knoxville indicates that TVA's attempt to explain the necessity of this increase was not completely successful: " 'I don't like it a bit,' snapped Vice Chairman William C. Ross. Other members [of the Knoxville Utilities Board] voiced their agreement with Ross.... Bartlett [system manager] said ... 'TVA has us over a barrel, but the agency has not instituted much of the increases it could legally put into effect.' Richard P. Immel, board member, declared, 'We are passing this under duress.' "[10]

An increase on January 1, 1957, based on an escalator clause tied to the price of coal, affected only directly served large industries ("no more than a 'handful' in the entire seven-state area") and added less than 1 per cent to their bills.[11]

The first general increase in TVA's wholesale rate schedule was effective in August, 1967. Distributors' costs were increased by an average of about 7 per cent (some as high as 15 per cent) and of directly served large industries with high load factors by an average of about 4 per cent, to produce an estimated $27 million annually in additional revenue. TVA cited increased costs of interest, labor, and fuel as the cause of this increase.

On October 16, 1968, TVA announced a second general increase in its wholesale rates for all classes of customers. The Authority said this increase was brought about by increased costs of materials, interest, labor, and fuel, and "TVA's determination to maintain increasingly higher standards of air and water quality."[12] After negotiating with its distributors on the structure of retail rate schedules, TVA put a new wholesale rate schedule into effect in March, 1969, for most distributors and

[7] *Chattanooga Times,* Nov. 8, 1951.
[8] *Nashville Tennessean,* April 17, 1952.
[9] *Knoxville News-Sentinel,* July 6, 1952.
[10] *Ibid.,* May 16, 1952.
[11] *Ibid.,* Dec. 8, 1956.
[12] *Knoxville Journal,* Oct. 17, 1968.

TABLE 6

TVA WHOLESALE POWER RATES

	1933–1967	1967	1969[a]
Monthly demand charge per kw.	$.90	$1.00	$1.05
Monthly energy charges per kwh.		in mills	
First 100,000 kwh.	3.5[b]	3.6	4.1
Next 200,000 kwh.	3.0	3.1	3.6
Next 700,000 kwh.	2.5	2.6	3.1
Excess over 1,000,000 kwh.	2.0[c]	2.1	2.6

[a] The complete 1969 schedule is reproduced in Appendix 3.
[b] Originally 4.0; reduced to 3.5 in 1952.
[c] From 1952 to 1956 was 1.95 mills; in 1956 re-established at 2.0 mills with a reduction of .05 mill for any distributor with no customer having a demand over 5,000 kw.

directly served industries. Table 6 compares the major features of TVA's wholesale rates since 1933.

The operation of a contract escalator clause, reflecting rising interest and fuel costs, brought another general increase in August, 1969. TVA estimated that these three rate adjustments—the one in 1967 and two in 1969—on the average amounted to 29 per cent of the wholesale costs of Tennessee municipal power systems in the year ending October 31, 1968. The range for individual systems ran from 27 per cent for Harriman and Memphis to 39 per cent for Sparta. Since these percentages are based on data for a year that reflected the 1967 rate increase, percentages expressed on the basis of costs prior to this increase would be even higher.

Interest costs, initiated in 1961 under the "TVA self-financing act,"[13] undoubtedly have figured heavily in the 1967 and 1969 rate increases. In the seven fiscal years ending June 30, 1967, payments of interest totaled $290.6 million[14]—14 per cent of TVA's power operating revenues. These payments have been based on the outstanding balance of appropriations for the power system, which stood at about $1.2 billion in 1961 (the balance had been reduced some by repayments of principal initiated in 1948). Although the obvious intent was to charge

[13] Public Law 86-137, as amended by Public Law 86-157; U.S.C., sec. 831n-4.
[14] *TVA Power Annual Report 1967* (Knoxville: Tennessee Valley Authority, 1967), p. 28.

interest on the capital thus provided to the Authority (the statute prescribes a rate equal to "the computed average interest rate payable by the Treasury upon its total marketable public obligations as of the beginning of said fiscal year"), TVA prefers to use the term "dividend payments" and succeeded in having "return on the appropriation investment" written into the act. Actually, these payments represent a reimbursement of interest costs to borrow the funds provided to TVA, recaptured in this manner from the consumers of TVA power.

Load Density Credit and Other Adjustments

TVA's rate and distribution policies involve a substantial subsidy by urbanized customers to lower rates in rural areas. TVA in its 1967 wholesale rate schedule introduced a new feature (continued in the 1969 schedule) that increases this subsidy: a decrease in a distributor's monthly bill of .05 mill per kilowatt-hour for each 25 kilowatts or major fraction thereof by which the load density in the distributor's service area is less than 100 kilowatts per square mile.

Estimates by TVA indicate that the beneficiaries of the load density credit are forty-three cooperatives (all but seven) and nine municipal systems with large rural service areas (six in Tennessee). The total annual reduction for these fifty-two systems is estimated to be $900,000 (91 per cent of this for cooperatives), which TVA of course must recoup from its other customers. This no doubt represents a pragmatic approach by TVA to the revenue-costs problems of the least urbanized systems, and evaluation largely depends upon the premises postulated for policy-making. One question that might be raised is whether this type of system-wide priority, which benefits all customers alike, including those in the commercial and industrial classifications, is contrary to the statutory policy of benefiting "particularly the domestic and rural customers."

TVA's 1967 wholesale rate schedule included several new adjustment clauses in addition to the energy rate increases shown in Table 6.

The previous fuel clause reflected only coal costs: for each .1 cent or major fraction thereof below 17 cents per million Btu of all coal received by TVA at its steam plants, deduction of an amount equal to .01 mill per kilowatt-hour of the average monthly amount of energy resold to large lighting and power customers under the final block of the retail energy rates, calculated for six-month periods ending in December and June; addition on the same basis if the coal costs went above 19 cents per million Btu. The 1967 change called for decreases or increases in the monthly wholesale bill equal to .1 mill per kilowatt-hour for each .1 mill or major fraction thereof by which TVA's fossil and nuclear fuel expense falls below or exceeds 1.45 mills per kilowatt-hour during the last fiscal year ending with June, to be effective for twelve months commencing with the first meter reading after August 1. The 1969 rate schedule provides for the same adjustments, except at the rate of .01 mill per kilowatt-hour for each .01 mill of change in fuel expense.

The 1967 rate schedule also introduced for the first time an adjustment clause to reflect interest costs. Each monthly bill is to be decreased or increased by 5 cents per kilowatt of billing demand for each 5 cents or major fraction thereof by which TVA's cost of money falls below or exceeds 40 cents per kilowatt of the sum of the monthly billing demands of power sold by TVA in the most recent fiscal year ending with June, to be effective for twelve months commencing with the first meter reading after August 1. Under the 1969 rate schedule, the same adjustment is to be made at the rate of 1 cent per kilowatt of billing demand for each 1 cent of change in the cost of money.

Facilities Rental

An innovation in the 1967 wholesale rate schedule (and retained in the 1969 schedule), a "facilities rental charge," was the culmination of earlier moves by TVA to transfer transformation costs to distributors. For many years TVA built and maintained substations to supply power at whatever voltages were desired by the distributors, but measures (possibly induced by the tight budgets of the Eisenhower administration) were initiated in the fifties to shift these costs to the distributors. Replacing a contractual obligation to coordinate developmental plans, TVA in 1956 instituted a contractual provision that new development would be financed by TVA or a distributor on the basis of "the most economical combination of transmission and distribution service facilities . . . in the same manner as if all such facilities belonged to one owner." The result, as seen by distributors, was to burden them with TVA's costs:

> TVA accomplishes this by proposing various entangling arrangements whereby the distributor will perform construction of substations and transmission lines that should normally be the responsibility of TVA. TVA's costs of delivery points are so high that distributor is always at a disadvantage and is asked to go ahead under the "single owner" concept, because distributors let construction contracts and TVA uses its own forces. Examples of comparative costs: 69 kv transmission line, by TVA $22,500/mi., by a distributor $12,500 to $15,000/mi.; 7,500 kva substation, by TVA $225,000, by a distributor $175,000.[15]

The "facilities rental charge" provides another way for TVA to accomplish this objective. It is more favorable to the Authority because the charge applies to existing facilities rather than construction of new facilities. Any distributor that receives power from TVA at a voltage below 161 kilovolts must pay a monthly facilities rental charge equal to 15 cents per kilowatt for the first 10,000 kilowatts of the highest billing demand established at each delivery point during the latest twelve-consecutive-month period (the 1969 schedule increased this part of the charge to 20 cents per kilowatt if delivery is at less than 46 kilovolts) and 5 cents per kilowatt for the portion of such demand in excess of 10,000 kilowatts. Memphis is the only system not now subject to this charge. Thus TVA imposes on distributors alleged higher costs of delivery at less than 161 kilovolts.

The charge even applies where it would be economically unfeasible for TVA to construct a 161-kilovolt transmission line or for the distributor to install the necessary transformation facilities. Only the very large systems are likely to find that it is economical to make the change, and in these cases the charge might be justified as an incentive to a distributor to upgrade its system. In regard to most distributors, however, the charge

[15] Summary of discussions at a meeting of the Tennessee Valley Public Power Association in Huntsville, Ala., Sept. 7, 1962 (in the files of the association).

seems to be simply another way for TVA to increase its wholesale revenues. TVA estimated that the charge produced $10.8 million in the first year—about 40 per cent of the total realized from the 1967 rate changes. One advantage from the Authority's point of view is that such revenue is separately reported by TVA and distributors and thereby excluded from cost of power statistics. An adverse effect on the states is that such revenue is not subject to TVA's 5 per cent payments in lieu of taxes.

The Minimum Bill

Contrasting sharply with TVA's "single owner" concept for construction of new facilities is its insistence that each distribution system be treated as an isolated system for purposes of calculating a minimum bill. Until 1956 the minimum of 60 per cent of the highest demand in the preceding eleven months worked no hardships on any system, but a much higher minimum was instituted in that year: an amount, exclusive of any adjustments, *equal to* the highest demand charge in the preceding twelve months. With the rapid increase in electric house heating, only one cold snap was needed to establish a high demand that would hold until the next winter. As seen by one system manager, it was unfair for TVA to impose such a penalty and at the same time urge the distributor to undertake promotional efforts to sell electric house heating. He calculated that his system actually would be better off without such loads in suburban residential areas.

Two small municipal systems in Tennessee have been severely penalized by this provision. In the four fiscal years ending June 30, 1967, the additional amount for one ranged from $24,406 to $33,654 per year—3.0 to 4.9 per cent of its total annual wholesale bill; for the other the amounts ranged from $13,229 to $44,025—2.7 to 9.0 per cent of the annual wholesale bill. TVA imposed this higher minimum by contract amendments with all distributors. Two questionnaire respondents from one of these systems stated that the amendment "was unintentionally misrepresented," but another respondent from the same system stated simply that it "was misrepresented." Adversely affected distributors view the provision as a penalty for peak loads and not a minimum bill. Although only these two systems have felt the impact, concern was expressed by managers of two other systems over the potential effects of the penalty.

TVA apparently looks on the minimum bill as a means of putting pressure on distributors to sell more power in order to raise their load factors. One system that attempted to secure a change in policy was given the answer: "Get out and sell more air conditioning." Even the power board's bargaining proposition that rates would be reduced if TVA would eliminate the penalty failed to get any results.

This policy of TVA is subject to attack on several grounds. It is inconsistent with numerous statements made by the Authority's spokesmen about the unity of the combined TVA-distributors system, as well as the "single owner" concept. TVA applies uniform wholesale rates for all distributors, though some are located so close to generating plants that virtually no transmission costs are involved in delivering power to them. All distributors must adhere to standard retail rate schedules so that those using a particular schedule will not compete with one another. TVA insists on serving large industries directly so that the profit therefrom will be spread throughout the system; otherwise, one distributor, lucky enough to get a big industry, could capture the whole profit for the benefit of its customers only. About the only effective way to avoid the penalty is an increase in industrial loads, because air conditioning sales in summer bring proportional increases in winter heating loads. Furthermore, the policy may conflict with the principle of lowest possible rates for the domestic and rural customers of small distributors.

Another argument against the penalty is that TVA has entered into an interchange agreement with the Southwest Power Pool, the purpose of which is to balance summer and winter loads—the southwest area needing more power in summer, and the TVA area requiring more in winter. With such balancing on a system-wide basis, the viewpoint of the small distributor is that it should be considered a part of the TVA system and not an isolated system standing on its individual consumption record for peak-billing purposes.

A change initiated in the 1967 wholesale rate schedule and retained in the 1969 schedule may give some relief. Instead of the minimum being the highest demand charge within the preceding twelve months, it is fixed at 85 per cent of the highest demand charge during the previous thirty-six months. The manager of one system was not optimistic—he said one very cold day every three years could result in substantial penalty payments for summer months.

TVA CONTROL OF RETAIL RATES

Control of retail rates logically flows from TVA's premises: a congressional mandate to favor domestic and rural consumers, and TVA's own policy of lowest possible rates. Giving a municipality complete freedom to fix rates and use revenues would make possible the levy of taxes camouflaged as utility charges, which could defeat the low-rate policy. The original TVA Act did not clearly give such control to the Authority, but an amendment in 1935, passed at the request of the TVA board, authorized "resale rate schedules" in power contracts with distributors.[16]

One of the principal points in the Plan of Action adopted by the board of directors on August 22, 1933, was that TVA should require "fair and non-discriminatory rates at retail, to insure that the general principles of a more extensive use of power and other objectives of the Authority may be achieved." The Authority's third annual report declared that "TVA's sole permanent interest in retail distribution lies in its role as a party to a bulk power contract in which low rates are agreed upon."[17] The Tennessee Supreme Court also took note of this policy: "One of the objects of TVA is to supply the inhabitants within its territory with cheap electric current. It does not operate for profit. The contract which it has entered into with the city is predicated upon reasonable rates, and there can be little doubt but that in order to effectuate the purpose to protect the public against unjust charges, it reserved the right to approve any increase in rates."[18]

---

[16] Probably as the result of a disagreement with Florence, Ala., which was extensively aired in the press. The city wanted higher domestic rates and lower industrial rates, and the mayor (also an attorney) claimed that TVA lacked legal authority to control resale rates. *Knoxville News-Sentinel*, Feb. 12, 1934.

[17] *TVA Annual Report for the Fiscal Year Ended June 30, 1936* (Washington, D. C.: U. S. Government Printing Office, 1936), p. 31.

[18] *Memphis Power & Light Co.* v. *City of Memphis*, 172 Tenn. 346, 360, 112 S. W. 2d 817 (1937).

Retail Rate Schedules

By 1961 TVA had developed four retail rate schedules. For a number of years it provided only one, which, with minor modification, was continued as the highest or "basic level" of these four schedules. It soon became apparent that the rates of the original schedule were too high for some distributors, but the shortages of World War II and the resulting need to conserve electric power rather than to encourage increased consumption delayed the introduction of lower schedules. Two lower schedules were introduced in 1944 and 1945. The fourth schedule, designated the Norris Centennial rate, was announced at a White House ceremony on July 11, 1961, to commemorate the 100th anniversary of the birth of TVA's godfather, Senator George W. Norris of Nebraska. Compared with the basic level schedule, these were, respectively, approximately 6 per cent, 15 per cent, and 20 per cent lower.[19] The Norris Centennial rate lowered rates for all customers except those in the outdoor lighting class, made up mostly of local governments.

Concurrently with the increase in wholesale rates in 1967, TVA established nine retail rate schedules. Five new schedules were added, one higher, one lower, and one between each of the four existing schedules, which were modified only slightly to compensate for the added wholesale cost to the distributor. Based on studies by its power staff, TVA prescribed one of these schedules for each distributor. Some distributors objected on the grounds that the prescribed rates were too low, but in nearly every case TVA was adamant and would not authorize a higher level. Generally the response by the Authority was that the matter would be reconsidered on application of a distributor if future operations would seem to indicate a need for higher rates. One Tennessee municipal system that objected to the squeeze on its profit margin was advised by a TVA district manager that the solution might be a lowering of tax-equivalent payments to the city. In a number of cases recent upward adjustments in such tax equivalents, within the limits of TVA's power contracts, caused difficulties for TVA personnel as they

---

[19] Estimates by TVA Office of Power, through Gilbert Stewart, Jr., TVA Office of Information, March 15, 1967.

strove to negotiate new retail rates low enough to meet their concepts of lowest possible rates.

TVA's contracts with distributors require the application of specified retail rate schedules, subject to subsequent modifications or changes by mutual agreement. The contracts specify that "all municipal and governmental customers and departments" shall be charged under such schedules—no other class of customers is specified. This apparently reflects TVA's concern over possible diversion of electric revenues through free service or lowered charges to such customers. All contracts have prohibited discrimination among customers in the same class by incorporating almost verbatim the following provision in Section 12 of the TVA Act: "All contracts entered into between the Corporation and any municipality or other political subdivision or cooperative organization shall provide that the electric power shall be sold and distributed to the ultimate consumer without discrimination as between consumers of the same class...."

The Application of Rate Schedules

TVA follows through very closely, sending its accountants into the field to check the resale schedules applied for new consumers taken on by distributors, as well as reviewing any significant changes by existing customers. A former TVA board chairman has justified this degree of control as being necessary to prevent the development of "competitive relationships among the distributors [that] would make it difficult over a period of years for most of them to avoid abandoning the rate standard, much as they might regret having to do so." Without such restraint he could see municipalities "almost inevitably ... driven to compete with each other for industrial customers through excessive and discriminatory concessions either to industries as a class or to specific industrial customers, while maintaining their earnings level through high charges to other customers."[20]

Most local rate problems involve commercial and industrial consumers. A TVA district manager reported that sometimes a

[20] Gordon R. Clapp, in an address before a meeting of the Tennessee Valley Public Power Association, Nashville, March 29, 1954 (MS in TVA Technical Library, Knoxville).

local manager will promise a prospective industry "the world with a fence around it" before TVA district personnel are informed. They must then enter the picture and negotiate an agreement in accordance with the power contract that will not discriminate against existing industrial consumers. He also reported that local power system officials are sometimes eager to pass the buck upstairs, e.g., when a minister tries to get a residential classification for his church on the grounds that it is neither "commercial" nor "industrial," or a school superintendent protests the higher rate classification of his school.[21]

Not surprisingly, municipal officials are sometimes unhappy with the results of TVA's review. A power board member reported that TVA was "somewhat adamant re: interpretations and applications." Trouble can even develop with respect to residential customers, as in one case where a municipal system wanted to collect a higher deposit for temporary service to a trailer home, to be refunded if service continued for five years. TVA insisted, however, on the same treatment as accorded to any other residence. One system reported that competition could bring some relaxation—that "TVA never lets us break the power contract unless someone is 'going gas' [about to use natural gas instead of electricity]." A power manager who evinced strong support for TVA made this questionnaire comment: "All contracts are written by TVA personnel who assume they know all the details in a distributor's area. This makes it difficult for distributors to serve certain type loads and makes said distributor subject to their opinions."

Amortization Charges and Surcharges

Another phase of rate-making subject to control by TVA under the power contracts is the imposition of "amortization charges" and "surcharges." The former were authorized or required, dependent upon TVA's analysis of the financial prospects of a system, for the purpose of amortizing the principal of bonded debt and were to be discontinued when the debt was retired (some have been terminated earlier by agreement). A few contracts required discontinuation for customers after

[21] Jack W. Eakin, in an address to an assemblage of selected personnel of the Office of Power, Chattanooga, Oct. 16, 1964 (MS furnished by director of power marketing).

periods of service to the customers ranging from seven to twelve years. The rate was 1 cent per kilowatt-hour per month, from a minimum of 25 cents to a maximum of $1.00.[22] Such charges have been levied by eighteen Tennessee cities at various times, but all had been eliminated by 1967.

Surcharges have generally been authorized for commercial and industrial customers only, and usually for a maximum of 10 per cent applied to basic bills. Forty-seven city-owned systems in Tennessee have utilized this extra source of revenue for limited periods. In 1966 surcharges were being collected only in the rural part of the Fayetteville system, and no municipal system was authorized to levy such charges under the new retail schedules adopted in 1967. The theory of surcharges was that they provided an extra margin of fiscal solvency during a developmental period while a distributor was building up its load and gaining experience.

Memphis was a notable exception; it levied a surcharge of 15 per cent on commercial and industrial bills from the time that it acquired the privately owned system (June 27, 1939) until it left the TVA system in 1958, and on residential bills until April, 1943.[23] A prolonged and determined attack by the local press and pressure by TVA could do no better than secure termination of the residential surcharge. Memphis justified its policy on the grounds that such revenues were needed for expansions and improvements. Year after year record profits were reported, and substantial amounts of bonds were called prior to maturity. Said the *Commercial Appeal* (April 8, 1943): "The present industrial and commercial consumers . . . are paying a 15 per cent surcharge in order that ratepayers of 1967, 1968 and 1969 will be relieved of the burden of paying off bonds maturing in those years." A city policy of using utilities as profit-

[22] The 1960 Sparta contract and an amendment in 1962 for Fayetteville fixed the maximum at 50¢ per month.

[23] An article by Cecil Holland in the *Chattanooga News*, Nov. 9, 1935, based on an interview with Maj. Thomas H. Allen, chairman of the Memphis utility board, reported: "Memphis does not contemplate surcharges even to the 10 per cent limit in the original TVA contract, and this provision was written into the new instrument merely as a precaution." The *Commercial Appeal* (July 5, 1942) called the city "an island of high rates in the Tennessee Valley Authority area because of the 15 per cent surcharge on electric bills" and estimated that this was denying to consumers "a $750,000 savings on their electric bills."

making enterprises was also a contributing factor; for this reason Boss Crump had refused to approve the purchase of the electric system unless the gas system was also sold to the city. In 1944 he even proposed that the utilities carry all city taxes.[24] One of the conditions specified by TVA for re-entry of Memphis into the TVA system in 1965 was that no such surcharges could be imposed.

Nashville insisted upon a like authorization when negotiating its contract in 1939. Lilienthal said TVA would agree "with the understanding that, if this were done, 'the authority would be free to state its view to the public on this matter.'" He further advised the power board chairman of "our view that surcharging domestic customers is not sound electric rate policy, and that we are convinced it will work against rather than for the soundest financial results."[25] The press launched an attack on the Nashville surcharge, and within less than two months the TVA Power Consumers' League had obtained 10,000 signatures on a protest petition. Soon it was announced that the residential surcharge would be removed, effective November 1, 1939.[26] Its application to commercial and industrial bills was discontinued in 1945.

RETAIL RATE REDUCTIONS

A questionnaire comment by one mayor is a valid generalization of TVA policy: "TVA is continually requesting rate reductions." Since the rates must be formally established by the distributors, this is the only means by which TVA can achieve its objectives. If a system's earnings seem to be excessive to TVA, as compared with regulatory standards used in the electric utility field, recommendations for a rate reduction are made. This is one of the principal areas of controversy between TVA and its distributors, and varying degrees of pressure and resistance have been involved. Recent indications point to a hardening of TVA policy in this respect—that rates *will* be reduced no matter what the resistance may be.

The contractual basis for forcing rate reductions is some-

[24] *Chattanooga Times*, Jan. 12, 1944.
[25] *Nashville Tennessean*, Aug. 9, 1939.
[26] *Ibid.*, Oct. 21, 1939.

what tenuous; no specific standard, such as a maximum rate of return on the investment, is prescribed.[27] Contracts of the first twenty years or so, including the 1952 edition of the standard power contract, implied that rate reductions would be made whenever possible. Beginning with the 1954 Tupelo, Mississippi, revision, under certain conditions the power contracts have required agreement on rate reduction: "If the rates and charges in effect at any time provide revenues that are more than sufficient for such purposes, as more particularly described in section 6 hereof [which prescribes permissible uses of revenues], the parties shall agree upon a reduction in said rates and charges, and Municipality shall promptly put such reduced rates and charges into effect." Section 6, referred to above, includes the following provision respecting the use of surplus revenues: "resale rates and charges shall be reduced from time to time to the lowest practicable levels considering such factors as future circumstances affecting the probable level of earnings, the need or desirability of financing a reasonable share of new construction from such surplus revenues, and fluctuations in debt service requirements."

Why Cities Balk

Sometimes cities resist rate reductions because they feel the need to increase a power system's tax-equivalent payments to the owner-city, but most frequently they want to build up reserves for system improvements to avoid borrowing money. A prevalent view among municipal power board members was expressed by a questionnaire respondent: "TVA suggested lowering rates and issuing additional bonds for construction. Board felt present bonds should be paid off before reducing rates and issuing more bonds." Power boards sometimes stand their ground when their conservative financial philosophy collides with what they call the "deficit financing" policies of TVA.

---

[27] An exception was noted in the 1937 contract with Trenton: "MUNICIPALITY need not reduce its rates nor reduce or eliminate surcharges unless net earnings, defined as the amount remaining after deducting from the total income of the electric system all operating expenses as defined in subsection (d) (1) of this section, exceed Sixteen Thousand Dollars ($16,000) annually, and then only to the extent of such excess."

The opposing point of view is well expressed by a spokesman from outside the Valley:

As to the first suggestion—a utility plant free of debt—with this I have no patience at all.

The achievement of this objective means to me simply that one generation of ratepayers has been forced to pay the total of all costs truly attributable to the service rendered, and, by way of surcharge, has been forced to purchase a utility plant for the service of the next generation.

To me it seems clear that rates should be sufficient to cover a depreciation annuity equal to the diminution in value of the plant used in the service for which the rate is charged but, at the same time, it seems equally clear that the impulse to charge rates sufficient to provide for depreciation, plus amortization of debt, plus any additional sum necessary to finance current net additions and betterments is dead wrong.[28]

Chattanooga supplies an example of the conservative financing policies that characterize many municipal systems. In 1963 its power system called $3,397,000 in bonds due for retirement from 1964 to 1967, which carried interest rates of 2 per cent or less, in order to make it "the first large publicly owned electrical system in the nation to be debt-free."[29] The funds used for this purpose could have been invested to return more than the interest due to be paid on the retired bonds. Following this action the system lowered rates for residential and outdoor lighting customers to save them about $1 million per year.

Nashville's short-lived 15 per cent surcharge in 1939 was declared to be "absolutely necessary" for the orderly development of the power system. Citing the provisions of the city's contract with TVA, the power board chairman said, "TVA has no right to pass on the amount of our surcharge, and we could have made it 16 or 17 per cent or more, if we had wanted to, without consult-

[28] Gilmore Tillman, "The Place of the Municipal Utility in Modern America," a paper presented before a meeting of the California Municipal Utilities Association, Long Beach, Cal., Nov. 8, 1950, reprinted in U. S., Congress, House, Committee on Ways and Means, *Hearings, Revenue Revision of 1951*, 82d Cong., 1st Sess., 1951, Part 2, pp. 1120–21.

[29] *Knoxville News-Sentinel*, May 5, 1963, quoting the chairman of the Chattanooga power board.

ing TVA." He also pointed to a "huge saving in interest" amounting to $2.5 million on its $15 million, twenty-year bond issue, as compared with Chattanooga's $13.2 million, thirty-year issue.[30] The *Nashville Tennessean* editorially commented that there was "no real reason" for such acceleration "but the procedure is quite orthodox, and comforts ultra-conservatives."[31] Twelve years later the Nashville power board chairman had swung around to the TVA position:

> Nashville power consumers have paid for $16,000,000 in system expansions in the past 12 years, W. C. Baird, power board chairman, said yesterday.
>
> Baird, who urgently recommended a residential rate cut to the power board yesterday, said "these expansions and improvements are of a long term nature and, from now on, should be financed out of new capital.
>
> "This capital can be obtained from the sale of bonds at 2 per cent, which at the present rate of earnings for the system, will pay a return of about nine per cent," Baird continued.
>
> "I think we have depended too long on the consumer to pay the major share of costs for permanent improvements that will be here for the next generation."[32]

His recommendation was not accepted and Nashville in 1969 was still on the same schedule of rates.

In mid-1945, six Tennessee municipal systems were free of debt. On June 30, 1968, the number was twenty-six;[33] fifteen had long-term debts less than 20 per cent of net plant value, and only seven had debts in excess of 50 per cent of net plant value (Memphis, at 132 per cent, headed the list, followed by Sparta, at 81 per cent).

This is an interesting conflict between a policy that ap-

---

[30] *Nashville Tennessean*, Aug. 9, 1939. The two issues were sold about a week apart; Nashville's interest rate was 2.3 per cent, and Chattanooga's rate was 2.7 per cent.

[31] Jan. 12, 1940.

[32] *Nashville Tennessean*, June 9, 1951.

[33] 1945: Clarksville, Harriman, Milan, Newbern, Somerville, and Trenton. 1968: Bristol, Brownsville, Chattanooga, Clarksville, Cleveland, Clinton, Columbia, Elizabethton, Erwin, Harriman, Humboldt, Jackson, Jellico, Johnson City, Maryville, McMinnville, Milan, Mt. Pleasant, Newbern, Newport, Oak Ridge, Ripley, Rockwood, Sevierville, Shelbyville, and Winchester; Somerville and Trenton, on the 1945 list, had debts of $35,000 and $10,000, respectively.

proaches the private companies' practice of perpetual debt, encouraged by TVA because it lowers power rates (at least in the short run), and local conservatism that opposes deficit financing and favors a pay-as-you-go policy to save interest costs, even if it is at the expense of the present generation. This represents a turnabout for TVA; in the early years the Authority was also in favor of retiring debt:

> All of us agreed that we wanted to get rid of the debt as quickly as possible. We were familiar with the fact that the privately-owned utilities had been piling up tremendous indebtedness, and that instead of providing for the regular and constant wiping out of that debt, the utilities were refunding their bonds when they would mature. . . . And so a definite addition to the rate of 1¢ per KWH for the first 100 KWH was agreed upon . . . [to] be used to pay off the debt as quickly as possible.[34]

How and Why TVA Prevails

Generally TVA has been more successful with the smaller systems—a tenable hypothesis might be that the Authority's influence is in inverse proportion to the size of a local power system. Prior to 1967 Chattanooga was the only one of the four large cities that had lowered rates below the basic level. Memphis in 1967 went one step lower, and in 1969 another step lower, on the nine-step stairway of rate schedules, but TVA has given unusual attention to Memphis as a "special situation." However, occasionally, a smaller system has been stubborn about rate reductions. In one case a power system serving a city of about 10,000 population and a small rural area made its first rate reduction in 1958 after declining to act on TVA recommendations made in 1950, 1952, 1954, 1955, and 1956. TVA's 1950 report to this system included the following:

> For the 12 months ending June 30, 1950, . . . the System earned approximately $217,900, representing an 18.9% return on the investment. . . .

---

[34] David E. Lilienthal, address at a meeting of the American Farm Bureau Federation, Nashville, Dec. 12, 1934, reporting on TVA's first contract with the Alcorn County Cooperative in Mississippi (MS in TVA Technical Library, Knoxville).

The basic TVA power policy and the agreement between TVA and the City of . . . as set forth in the power contract, are dedicated to the non-profit operation of the electric properties for the benefit of the electric consumers in order to assure the widest possible use of the electricity at the lowest possible cost to the consumer. Only in this way can the benefits of the federally owned and operated system of TVA be passed on to the consumers in a manner which will result in the maximum development of the area and maximum benefit to the country as a whole. Under the program each distributor should examine its operation from time to time and make such adjustments in its rate policies as will best promote this joint program.

Last year [the system] earned a return on its investment of 18.9%. The private utility companies of the country whose rates are controlled by public service commissions are generally permitted by such commissions to earn something in the neighborhood of 6% return of capital employed.[35]

TVA has found that sometimes agreement cannot be required and that during the term of a contract the approach must be, in Clapp's words (see p. 35), to "entreat, cajole and argue." However, when a contract is about to expire, stronger measures can be taken; the Authority can "threaten" and even issue what some would regard as an "order."

Events at Bristol were exceptional, but they illustrate what can happen within the TVA system. Councilman O. T. Powell, of Bristol, Virginia, in 1957 reported that Wilson House, district manager of the eastern district, had told him that TVA had attempted "for some time" to secure a rate reduction in both Bristols; in 1963, Powell, then mayor, "said TVA officials had indicated to him they would demand a rate reduction be enforced before a new contract is signed . . . in 1965."[36]

In May, 1964, the three-member Bristol city commission refused to approve the action of the city's power board to lower rates on the grounds that "the city needs the surplus monies for other purposes." The mayor asserted that expanded services at

[35] *Elizabethton Star*, Jan. 25, 1951. The system did remove, in 1951, a 10 per cent surcharge on industrial bills. In 1963 the second intermediate level was put into effect, and on June 30, 1965, under some compulsion from TVA, the system adopted the lowest level (Norris Centennial) rate schedule.
[36] *Bristol Herald-Courier*, Sept. 11, 1957; Nov. 27, 1963.

the same rates in effect was a reduction of rates in a time of inflation and rising price levels, and that TVA could not "demand" a reduction under the power contract unless the power system had a surplus.[37] About a month later C. A. Reidinger, TVA's chief power attorney, appeared before the city commission and informed them that "rates will have to be reduced . . . before it grants Bristol a new contract to supply the city's power." He also advised them that this matter was not within the jurisdiction of the city commission and that the power board had the authority to reduce rates under Tennessee law (a doubtful point—see footnote).[38] This threat was sufficient to persuade the city commission to reverse its previous stand and approve the rate reduction.

In another case a contract was not renewed for almost two months after its expiration; according to an official of the city, "TVA said our return on investment was too large and forced a rate reduction that the city council was not in favor of." The means of forcing the reduction was a threat of a higher wholesale rate (about 25 per cent) which TVA customarily charges to customers for short-term power. TVA personnel on other occasions have used this threat in contract renewal "negotiations" with stubborn distributors.

Some of these latter-day actions are contrary to earlier policy guidelines of TVA, exemplified by this statement by former Board Chairman Gordon R. Clapp:

> The distribution of electricity . . . is a direct concern of the consumers. In the Tennessee Valley this part of the job is in the hands of the locally owned and operated systems.

[37] *Ibid.*, May 6, 1964.
[38] *Ibid.*, June 12, 1964. Exception may be taken to Reidinger's advice that the power board could cut rates on its own. Although ch. 32 of *Tennessee Public Acts, 1935,* gives the "supervisory body" power to "make all determinations as to improvements, rates and financial practices," a later act passed for clarifying purposes (*Tennessee Public Acts, 1935,* ch. 37), empowers a municipality to enter into contracts with TVA and "to stipulate and agree to such covenants, terms and conditions as the governing body thereof may deem appropriate, including but without limitation, covenants, terms and conditions in respect to the resale rates, financial and accounting methods. . . ." A more tenable argument is that the later act is the source of specific contracting authority and that since rate reductions are accomplished through the means of amendatory or renewal contracts the terms and conditions thereof are subject to approval by the municipal governing body as required by this act.

Their officials set the policies and make the decisions within the framework of their agreement with the TVA. *Shall surplus revenues be used to pay off indebtedness, for expansion of the system, or a reduction in rates?* [emphasis added] Down which highway will the next new rural lines go? What steps shall be taken to build load, or acquaint new rural consumers with the multiple uses of electricity on the farm? These are questions that are decided, not by some remote "higher-up" in a Federal office or a private utility headquarters, but by local power boards and system managers who are in daily contact with the people they serve and for whom they work.[39]

TABLE 7

NUMBER OF TVA MUNICIPAL DISTRIBUTORS APPLYING VARIOUS RETAIL RATE SCHEDULES, 1957, 1966, 1967, AND 1969

Rate schedules (pre-1967)	Rate schedules (1967)	1957	1966	1967	1969 Res.	1969 Gen. power
	1	—	—	2	2	2
Basic	2	39	21[c]	14	14	13
	3	—	—	10	10	13
First intermediate	4	37[a]	38[d]	31[f]	30[f]	29[f]
	5	—	—	8[g]	12[g]	11[g]
Second intermediate	6	23[b]	34[e]	28[h]	24[h]	27[h]
	7	—	—	9	11	8
Lowest (Norris Centennial)	8	NA	15	6	3	3
	9	—	—	—	2	2
Totals[i]		99	108	108	108	108

[a] Dickson, Tenn., applied basic level in rural part of its system.
[b] Florence, Ala., applied basic level in rural part.
[c] Chattanooga applied first intermediate level for residential and outdoor lighting customers.
[d] Athens, Ala., applied basic level in rural part.
[e] Fayetteville, Tenn., and Florence, Ala., applied basic level in rural parts.
[f] Athens, Ala., applies second level in rural part.
[g] Florence, Ala., applies first level in rural part.
[h] Fayetteville, Tenn., applies second level in rural part.
[i] Include three county-owned systems in Tennessee.

[39] "Electricity and the Public Interest," address at the annual meeting of the National Rural Electric Cooperative Association, Chicago, March 7, 1950 (MS in TVA Technical Library, Knoxville).

However accomplished, an impressive record of rate reductions has been established in the Valley, even with the extra load of amortizing debt as noted. TVA in 1957 reported that its distributors had made more than 250 rate reductions, including removal of surcharges and amortization charges. The number of municipal systems applying the various rate levels in 1957, 1966, 1967, and 1969 are shown in Table 7. Until 1967, no municipal or cooperative distributor had gone from a lower to a higher rate schedule; the only changes upward were minor increases by two cooperatives in their early developmental periods—one in the amortization charge and the other in the surcharge. The general shuffle in 1967 resulted in one-level increases (in the new nine-schedule range) by twenty-two municipal systems. Under the rate adjustments of 1969 twelve municipal systems went up one level (three for general power only and one for residential only), nine went down one level (two for general power only and one for residential only), and two went down two levels (one for residential only).

RATES IN RURAL AREAS

Before the Rural Electrification Administration was created in 1936, TVA was advocating the extension of electric power to rural areas. Its third distributor, to which TVA power was first delivered on June 1, 1934, was the Alcorn County Electric Power Association, centered around Corinth, Mississippi. Reporting on the development of a rate policy for that cooperative, Lilienthal said:

> We agreed that the rates in the town and the rates in the country should be the same. This is an extremely important point. The people in Corinth knew that . . . it costs something less to serve ten people living in a single block in town than it would cost to serve ten farmers over a three-mile stretch on a country road. But they also realized . . . that the townsman could not prosper if his farmer neighbor did not prosper . . . that it would lead to the purchase of radios, washing machines, refrigerators and electric ranges. . . . The townspeople had selfish reasons and they had unselfish reasons, and both of these led to the conclusion that the cost of render-

ing service in that county should be *averaged* over all the people of that county.[40]

The Plan of Action adopted by the TVA board on August 22, 1933, laid down this guideline: "where opportunity affords, cities and towns should seek a policy of serving adjoining rural areas, at rates within a certain range. No inflexible and uniform rule should be exacted, at least for the time being."

As the Authority was nearing the end of its first year, the chief electrical engineer, Llewellyn Evans, was asked, "Does the TVA contemplate making large users of power in Chattanooga help pay the cost of power used by farmers, small store owners and home owners in and around the city?" He released what the press report called "a verbal bombshell in the midst of an otherwise placid round table discussion" by responding:

"I'll answer that question directly and frankly, once and for all. It is time for the big users to realize that they can't enjoy lower power rates unless they do pay for a part of the power used in and about the city. . . . Our urban forces," said Mr. Evans, "must once and for all decide to join forces with the county in the distribution and reduction in cost of power. The cities must assume that responsibility of making our farms places where people will want to stay. . . ."[41]

TVA generally has required municipal systems to charge uniform rates in areas inside and outside city limits. Contracts made in 1934 with Knoxville, Pulaski, and Dayton bound the cities "to serve nearby rural and suburban areas whenever such service can feasibly be rendered, and to charge for such service such rates as may be agreed upon between CONTRACTOR and AUTHORITY." The 1935 Pulaski contract required uniform rates but it also authorized an amortization charge of 25 cents to $1.00 per month on rural customers only for debt retirement. Contracts with several other cities[42] provided for operation of the urban and rural portions as separate systems on a self-supporting basis; some authorized and some required imposi-

---

[40] Address before a meeting of the American Farm Bureau Federation, Nashville, Dec. 12, 1934 (MS in TVA Technical Library, Knoxville).

[41] *Chattanooga News*, April 24, 1934.

[42] Bolivar, Dayton, Dickson, Lawrenceburg, Milan, Paris, Pulaski, and Somerville.

tion of amortization charges for liquidation of the separate debts for urban and rural portions. Several of these cities, as well as LaFollette and Newport, for various periods levied the amortization charge (1 cent per kilowatt-hour, minimum of 25 cents and maximum of $1.00 per month) on rural bills only. Dickson from 1946 to 1963 was the only municipal system in Tennessee to charge higher rates in its rural system, and the distinction was eliminated in 1965. Fayetteville in 1963 applied a higher rate schedule to its rural system, which had formerly been the Lincoln County Electric Membership Cooperative;[43] under the 1967 and 1969 rate adjustments the rural rate was set four levels above the city rate. Only two other municipal systems apply a dual rate structure, both in Alabama: Athens, two levels higher in the rural part, and Florence, four levels higher.

TVA's policies for such separations of urban and rural systems have varied. In the earlier contracts[44] a separate accounting of revenue and expenses was required, and each system was required, "to the extent necessary, [to] make reasonable and equitable allocations in respect of the expenses incurred in the operation of its Rural System." The Milan contract of 1943 required operation so that the revenues and expenses "shall be separable," but it permitted charging to the rural system only "such incremental amounts as represent the difference between the operating expense of all of Municipality's electric properties, and the operating expense that would be incurred by the Urban System if the Rural System were not in existence." About eighteen months later this provision was stricken by an amendment which declared that the purpose was to treat both urban and rural systems "as one electric system." The 1948 Bolivar contract required the keeping of separate records "so that the receipts and expenditures pertaining to each can be accurately determined," and this was expanded in the 1955 Dickson contract to require "books and records so that the assets, liabilities, revenues, receipts and expenses of each system will be determined equitably and recorded accurately and separately."

TVA's authorization to the two Tennessee cities of Dickson and Fayetteville and the two Alabama cities of Athens and

---

[43] This takeover was accomplished under the terms of ch. 8, *Private Acts of Tennessee, 1963*.

[44] Bolivar, 1939; Paris, 1938 and 1940; Pulaski, 1939; Somerville, 1939.

Florence to apply higher rate schedules in rural areas is a deviation from consistency of policy. Many other municipal systems would have adopted this plan if the option had been available to them, especially in their early developmental stages. Authorizing amortization charges for retirement of debt on rural portions is another policy that should have been extended equally to all systems.

PROMOTION OF POWER SALES

TVA's success is partially attributable to the application of mass merchandising concepts and methods to the sale of power. One of the early New Deal creations, spawned in TVA, was the Electric Home and Farm Authority (EHFA), established by a Presidential Executive Order in December, 1933. Its directors were the three directors of TVA, and its mission was to promote the sale of electrical appliances. Lilienthal summed the situation up as follows: utilities could not lower rates because customers did not use enough power; the manufacturers said they could not lower prices because of light demand; consumers could not buy because both appliances and power were priced too high. The EHFA was created to break this stalemate. With a $10 million credit from the Reconstruction Finance Corporation (RFC), the EHFA made possible the purchase of appliances from cooperating dealers for 5 per cent down and the balance in one to four years. It carried on a broad promotional campaign; by mid-1934 a mailing list of 180,000 persons had been compiled, and a large-scale advertising program was undertaken. In August, 1935, it was reorganized as a corporation of the District of Columbia and given a nationwide responsibility. When finally liquidated in 1942, because of the wartime shortage of appliances, the RFC reported that the EHFA had earned a profit of $700,000 for the government.

In the early period TVA, on its own and by assisting distributors' personnel, engaged in promotional activities to increase power sales. Costs of these activities were included in the calculation of wholesale rates and were made a part of the Authority's annual budgets. The resulting increase in power usage, leading to lower unit costs, and the great benefits of electricity to consumers were seen as factors that fully justified the relatively small amounts budgeted for this purpose. As TVA pointed out, distributors "paid for the benefits they derive from the promotional expenditures of the Authority through their payments for the increasing amounts of power they have purchased."[45]

With the onset of World War II the emphasis shifted to conservation of electricity and promotional efforts were turned into other channels. TVA home economists, at meetings sponsored by distributors, demonstrated the proper use of appliances and explained how they should be maintained. With the cooperation of equipment manufacturers, the Authority sponsored instruction in appliance repair. Employees of distributors were educated in consumer service problems. Assistance was given to distributors on problems growing out of the increased wartime demands of industrial plants, and educational programs on school lighting were carried out in cooperation with local organizations.

Soon after the arrival in 1953 of Eisenhower's first appointee to the TVA board, Chairman H. D. Vogel, such services were placed on a contract-fee basis at the option of distributors. A "Window Display and Advertising Mat Service" is available at a cost of 10 cents per residential customer, with a minimum annual charge of $100 and a maximum of $600, plus $100 for each window display in excess of one. A "Commercial and Industrial Engineering Service" also provides advisory assistance with respect to power use by commercial and industrial customers and space heating and air conditioning by all classes of customers.[46] In 1965, of the fifty-nine city-owned systems in Tennessee, forty-seven were subscribing to both services, four took only the advertising service, four were using only the engineering service, and four[47] did not utilize either service.

TVA's management views sales campaigns as a matter of some urgency and makes an effort to stimulate distributors to greater activity:

---

[45] *TVA Annual Report for the Fiscal Year Ended June 30, 1938* (Washington, D. C.: U. S. Government Printing Office, 1939), p. 67.

[46] The charge for this service is 75¢ per commercial or industrial customer (excluding commercial farm customers) plus ½ of 1 per cent of the annual gross aggregate revenue or $25,000, whichever is less, from such customers with monthly demands of 50 kw. or more.

[47] Nashville, Chattanooga, Bristol, and Harriman.

We've been talking here as though none of you were doing anything about load growth, and we don't want to leave that impression. The TVA power distributors as a group have sold a lot of electricity. In the case of a dozen or so distributors, the selling job has been outstanding, but in the case of most of the rest, there remains a great deal to be desired. George Munger tells me that there are 55 distributors who have not conducted or taken part in a single appliance sales campaign in the last 4 years. The average expenditure for sales promotion by all TVA distributors last year was about $1.00 per customer. Those who had a real active program averaged about $2.50 to $3.00 per customer, but there were 43 distributors that spent less than 50¢ per customer for load development. . . . [He then outlined six steps for more activity in this area and concluded that growth] won't happen automatically. . . . we must show the people how our service can make it possible, and it will take hard work and it will give us aches and pains. But it will be worthwhile. We need that growth if we are to live as electric suppliers.[48]

STREET LIGHTING RATES

City officials are concerned about street lighting rates, which are one item of expense in municipal budgets.[49] On several occasions they have suggested that such costs should be paid from power system budgets, and proposals have been made, though not followed up, that the Tennessee Municipal League should make this one of its policy objectives. In one instance an especially aggressive mayor advised TVA in 1959 that his city wanted to make a change in a renewal contract then being negotiated on the grounds that "users of the streets, which are more than just the property owners, should pay for this valuable street lighting." His plea went unheeded by TVA.

After a TVA-municipal conference in 1953 disclosed that city officials often misunderstood TVA policy or lacked information,

---

[48] G. O. Wessenauer, manager of power, address at a meeting of the Tennessee Valley Public Power Association, Memphis, April 7, 1959 (MS in TVA Technical Library, Knoxville).

[49] For example, the *Commercial Appeal* of July 5, 1942, reported that the Memphis City Commission, "alarmed by skyrocketing street lighting bills," had ordered an investigation, and the result was a reduction of $25,000 to $30,000 per year.

TVA prepared a special report on "Street Lighting at Cost" (duplicated for limited distribution to officials of the Tennessee Municipal League). Declaring that the basic objective was the same as for other rates, to "develop the widest possible use at the lowest possible cost," it also noted that an additional objective was "providing a means by which a municipality may finance the installation of a street lighting system."

The 1953 report noted that "two basic approaches" could be used in fixing street lighting rates: all the costs that may fairly be allocated, or only out-of-pocket incremental costs of providing street lighting in addition to the other operations of the electric system. Until 1949 the only street lighting rate available was based on "the fully distributed costs of service"—the first approach. In that year TVA announced to its distributors the availability of lower street lighting rates, justifying the action on the following basis (as stated in the aforementioned report):

> Street lighting is a very special type of electric service. There are advantages to the electric system resulting from a high standard of street lighting which are not available to the distributor from other sales categories. A well lighted town is recognized as a progressive town, and a high level of street lighting furnishes both an effective advertisement and an example for good lighting in the homes and commercial establishments. This sales promotion value plus the special electric load characteristics of street lighting (usually the peak load period for street lighting is at a different time from the normal system peak loads) provides some justification for treating street lighting service differently than other types of service. . . . TVA has agreed that if the distributor desires [in most cases this means if the power board desires], the standard street lighting rates may be modified to recognize the special characteristics of this type of service by basing the charges on the cost of providing such service on an incremental basis.

Since 1949 the TVA standard street lighting rate has had three components: an energy charge, an investment charge, and a lamp and glassware replacement charge. Until 1969 the energy charge was on a block basis, similar to but slightly higher than the commercial rate; in 1969 this part of the street lighting rate was changed to a uniform 1 cent per kilowatt-hour. The investment charge covers the costs of furnishing physical facilities for street lights; TVA pointed out in the 1953 report that other customers furnish their own facilities. The third part covers the costs of replacing lamps and glassware, also an expense that other customers bear themselves.

On an incremental basis, energy costs are less than the normal commercial rate, because all such energy could be considered as being purchased at the rate for the highest block of power used. In constructing the new street lighting rate schedule, an estimate of three mills per kilowatt-hour was made for this saving, and only the excess above this amount for replacing lamps and glassware is charged to the municipality. The schedule also permits reduction of the investment charge "in some cases where the distributor has lower interest, taxes, or operation and maintenance expenses than the average system." Until 1969 the range of investment charges was fixed at 8 to 12 per cent per year, but the 1969 rate changes lowered the percentage for Maryville to 7 per cent and for Sparta to 6 per cent.

TVA's 1953 report advised a municipality interested in lowering its street lighting costs to first determine whether the power system management would approve the incremental cost basis. If so approved, the next steps outlined were a detailed survey of the existing street lighting system and the development of specific plans for improvements. Then the municipality was to "ask the distribution system management to work with TVA in the development of an incremental cost analysis to determine the investment charge." If the final plans developed in this manner were "acceptable to the municipal government and the power distributor," the last step was to negotiate an implementing amendment to the city's power contract with TVA.

The TVA report cautioned, however, that the new rate could not be used "merely to reduce the dollar cost of street lighting to a municipal government" but must be justified on a basis that "the street lighting system is to be developed into a high quality system providing superior lighting which will truly represent a sales promotion or advertising project of the electric system."

In accordance with its usual procedures, TVA communicated with power boards and power managers in developing and publicizing the new street lighting rate:

The rate modification was developed in cooperation with the Electrical Development Advisory Committee appointed by the power distributors and others interested in assisting in street lighting improvement. During 1949 this program was outlined to all power distributors and discussed in their regular managers' meetings. Many of these meetings were attended by mayors and other local officials [probably from the few cities without power boards]. TVA's electrical development personnel and our district offices have taken every opportunity since that time to bring the rate modification to the attention of any municipality expressing a desire to improve its street lighting.[50]

When it became evident that communication had not reached all municipal governments (for example, Mayor P. R. Olgiati of Chattanooga "said they had never been informed about the new schedule and would never have known about it if he had not stumbled across it by talking with the mayor of another city"[51]), an explanatory article was published in the official magazine of the Tennessee Municipal League.[52] Several municipal officials later indicated that this was their first notice of the new rate. On May 24, 1954, a city manager, exceptionally well qualified, wrote to me as follows:

> With whom do cities bargain for better street lighting rates, particularly with reference to investment cost and lamp replacement charges?
> Many months ago the *Town and City* gave notice that TVA would permit an amendment to its street lighting contract. Can you tell us who publicized this fact and where this information was made available, and if it was a released document by TVA can you obtain a copy for us?
> On this subject it is only fair to tell you that we have been negotiating on this matter for several months and think we will be able to receive favorable consideration, but as I probably intimated to you in the past it is the most difficult matter to get information on that I have run into as City Manager of.... I first learned by accident that it might be

---

[50] Letter from James E. Watson to me, June 29, 1953.
[51] From my notes on a conference of TVA personnel and representatives of the Tennessee Municipal League, at TVA offices in Knoxville, Jan. 29, 1953, which I attended.
[52] *Tennessee Town & City*, IV, No. 8 (Aug., 1953), 9.

possible to get a lower investment charge, and then some months later accidentally stumbled upon the fact that lamp replacement charges might also be excluded. Now I am wondering if there are other phases of street "lighting" about which I am in the "dark."

What happened was that some power managers, under power boards independent of their municipal governments, had failed to pass along information about the availability of lower street lighting rates. The most probable explanation of this failure is that the power systems did not view favorably such reductions in their street lighting revenues. Conversations in Knoxville, for example, indicated that for this primary reason the power system held to the highest rates in its new contract with TVA effective July 1, 1968, without consulting city officials. A reduction of the investment charge alone from 12 to 8 per cent would have lowered the city's costs about $114,000 in fiscal year 1969. As a part of the 1969 rate adjustments, Knoxville's investment charge was lowered to 11 per cent, but the full cost of lamp and glassware replacements was continued.

In this area of power rates TVA has made little effort to achieve uniformity. The Authority leaves the initiative to municipal power boards and makes no effort to reduce street lighting charges (unlike other retail rates, which TVA is constantly trying to push down). The manager of one small system stated that TVA provided a draft contract in 1969 and instructed him to fill in the investment and replacement charges determined by his power board.

Data in Appendix 2 indicate the wide variations that exist. Chattanooga and Knoxville paid lamp maintenance charges until 1963, although this provision soon became obsolete; it was not included in a new power contract after 1939. Chattanooga in 1963 received the benefit of the minimum 8 per cent investment charge and the excess glassware replacement cost formula, but in the same year an amendatory contract with Knoxville included the maximum 12 per cent investment charge and full cost of glassware replacements. Bolivar, though on the basic level of rates until 1961, in 1951 was given the most favorable terms: an investment charge of 8 per cent and only the excess cost of glassware replacements. Etowah adopted the first intermediate level in 1956 but was charged 11 per cent for investment (raised to 12 per cent in 1969) and the full cost of glassware replacements. Two cities paid the maximum costs from the time they entered the TVA system until 1969: Rockwood (1939) and Jellico (1940). Nashville, which by 1969 had not lowered its rates, in 1953 was given the lowest investment charge and excess glassware cost provision, but Pulaski, at the same rate level, has been on the 12 per cent investment charge and full glassware cost basis since 1947. Erwin and Morristown reduced retail rates to the second intermediate level in 1965 and 1966, respectively, but neither received the benefit of the excess glassware replacement factor. Six cities in 1969 were paying a 12 per cent investment charge; 16 were paying the full cost of glassware replacements; 21 were paying an investment charge of 8 per cent, and 2 were even lower: Maryville at 7 per cent, and Sparta at 6 per cent.

In this area of contractual relationships there has been some genuine negotiation. Municipal officials of several cities have stated that by taking hard bargaining positions they have persuaded TVA to reduce street lighting charges. In other cases municipal officials have been unsuccessful in dealing with their own power boards.

4. CONFLICTS OVER SERVICE AREAS

WHEN THE AREAS TO BE SERVED by local distributors were being established, service at low rates to rural customers became an important issue. Most service areas were built around cities, but some cities declined to serve adjoining rural areas and others were passed over in favor of cooperatives. Conflicts have developed between cities and cooperatives over service in suburban areas, and TVA has been caught in the middle. A struggle between TVA and its distributors over service to large industries has also produced some sparks.

TVA SELECTION OF DISTRIBUTORS

Two TVA staff members tell us that the Authority "encouraged arrangements for municipalities to take over distribution properties . . . and actively assisted in the organization of cooperatives to acquire rural distribution lines for service to rural territories."[1] The allocation of rural areas among municipalities and cooperatives, and the apportionment of the costs of acquiring the private companies among TVA's distributors, called for numerous and basic decisions within comparatively short periods of time. Troublesome questions had to be answered immediately, but more complex problems arose that have since become important and controversial.

TVA actively encouraged the cities selected to be distributors to serve their surrounding rural areas.[2] Some declined and

[1] Lawrence L. Durisch and Robert E. Lowry, "The Scope and Content of Administrative Decision—The TVA Illustration," in *Public Administration Review*, XIII, No. 4 (Autumn, 1953), 222.

[2] "We used every means at our disposal to encourage balanced areas—including the taking of tax equivalents on the rural parts." Paul S. Button, TVA director of power marketing, in an interview, June 25, 1964. He mentioned as "success stories" the Bolivar, Dickson, Greeneville, Lawrenceburg, and Pulaski systems.

cooperatives took on service in the suburban areas of such cities, a development destined to cause problems later.

Although TVA showed a general preference for cities, the Authority gave cooperatives first choice on many rural areas and small towns. A press report announcing agreements on the Tennessee Electric Power Company (TEPCO) acquisition quoted a "high TVA official" as saying: "the sale will strengthen electric co-operatives in rural Tennessee, since the arrangement will call for the co-operatives to serve most of the rural areas. 'They will have the opportunity to pick up the rich territory with the thin territories to which they have been confined,' the spokesman said. Small cross-roads villages and unincorporated towns unable to purchase distribution systems would become an integral part of the co-operative systems."[3]

By the end of 1936, seven municipal systems and six cooperatives were distributing TVA power in Tennessee. In two years—1939 and 1940—nine new cooperatives were organized in the state. In 1968 twenty-one cooperatives served about three-fourths of its land area and accounted for 18 per cent of total sales (in kilowatt-hours) by Tennessee distributors; fifty-nine systems were city-owned, three were county-owned, and two were privately owned.

By mid-1935 TVA had received applications for power from some 350 cities and towns in the Valley. Many small towns were applicants; e.g., Bluff City (1940 population 700) was authorized by the Tennessee legislature to issue $15,000 in bonds to establish a municipal power system. These were turned down by TVA because they were too small to constitute economic units; the only exceptions were those that already owned their electric systems, e.g., Newbern (1940 population 1,740) and Somerville (1940 population 1,570). A TVA official in 1940 stated: "the Authority advised against the formation of municipal and co-operative units having less than 1,000 customers. In systems of 1,500 members or more, however, there seems to be no advantage to size."[4] The criteria applied in these cases, as explained by the TVA manager of power, were

[3] *Chattanooga Times,* Feb. 5, 1939.
[4] Joseph C. Swidler, in an address before a meeting of the National Lawyers Guild, New York, May 31, 1940 (MS in TVA Technical Library, Knoxville).

that all of these organizations be set up to serve a reasonably large number of consumers and to serve a diversified business. The purchase of existing electric properties in this region was accomplished in such a way as to further this aim in that the properties were divided so as to give to each of the participating distributors an area in which economical operations could be carried on. This resulted in many cooperatives acquiring a number of urban areas and industrial customers.[5]

Other factors also favored cooperatives from TVA's point of view: fewer problems associated with politics, no pressures for diversion of electric revenues, lower tax equivalents, and power boards more amenable to TVA control.[6] Towns passed over in favor of cooperatives included (first figure is 1940 population, second figure is 1968 population): Smyrna (493–9,931), Manchester (1,715–6,038), Jefferson City (2,576–5,169), Crossville (1,511–4,668), and Rogersville (2,018–4,050).

Sparks in Five Cities

The City of Nashville objected to its assigned share of the purchase price in the 1939 acquisition of TEPCO. The city threatened to have a new appraisal made, to which TVA Chief Power Engineer J. A. Krug responded: "Regardless of what value you or any appraisal engineer places on the system, it will make no difference to us; our proposal stands."[7] After reluctantly agreeing to buy on TVA terms, thus decisively stated, the city asked that its power contract authorize a property tax equivalent based on the purchase price of almost $15 million. TVA would not approve this figure but did make an exception to permit use of the last assessment of the company's property within the city as the tax-equivalent base. In light of TVA's pressure to buy at the high purchase price, city officials could not understand its insistence, immediately after acquisition, that the electric plant was worth even less for tax purposes than the former assessed value of the private system.[8]

[5] G. O. Wessenauer, "TVA and Rural Electrification," address at the annual meeting of the Tennessee Rural Electric Cooperative Association, Nashville, Jan. 8, 1946 (MS in TVA Technical Library, Knoxville).
[6] Philip Selznick, in *TVA and the Grass Roots* (Berkeley: University of California Press, 1949), p. 239, n. 32, reported similar conclusions.
[7] *Nashville Times,* April 7, 1939.
[8] Letter from G. O. Wessenauer, TVA manager of power, to J. E. Carnes,

Crossville also objected to the conditions attendant on the purchase of TEPCO, balking at paying a price that city officials said was "$30,000 more than the system is worth." Months of negotiations with TVA for purchase of the properties in Cumberland County followed, which ended with a sale to the Volunteer Electric Membership Corporation despite the city's threat to refuse to award a franchise to this cooperative. The mayor was quoted as saying that TVA officials had advised him "that they prefer the Volunteer Co-op to own the system here."[9] The city made another effort in 1960 to secure a TVA contract but was unsuccessful despite the help of the powerful House Appropriations Committee, which issued a report calling on TVA to consider "the merits of these requests [Smithville and Sparta had also made such requests] . . . in the light of TVA's responsibility as the sole source of electric power supply in the area and in line with the expressed intent of congress."[10] (The "intent" provision in fact could not be of much help, because it directs TVA to "give preference to States, counties, municipalities, and cooperative organizations," with no indication of priorities among these claimants.)

Sparta scored a notable success in a direct confrontation with TVA. At the time of the acquisition of the private company, in 1939, the city agreed to accept service from the neighboring city of McMinnville only under a twenty-year franchise to that city which reserved to the city of Sparta the right to acquire the system upon expiration of the franchise. The city asserted this right when the franchise expired in 1959. TVA did its best to dissuade the city on grounds that the McMinnville service area should not be broken into smaller and less economical areas, and TVA records show that one member (possibly two) of the TVA board at one time favored litigation over giving in to the city. TVA's three directors, general manager, manager of power, general counsel, and other high staff members journeyed to Sparta for a meeting with city officials and about sixty business-

---

July 5, 1949. The Nashville system's reports to TVA indicate that it was not until the mid-1950's that the book value finally reached the level of the 1939 assessment plus the last assessments of properties acquired after 1939.

[9] *Knoxville News-Sentinel,* Aug. 16, 1939.
[10] *Nashville Tennessean,* May 20, 1960.

men and farmers, which was partially reported by the press:

General Vogel, Brooks Hays and A. R. Jones, the members of the Board of Directors, and G. O. Wessenauer, Manager of Power, spoke on the immediate benefits Sparta would receive if it would agree to purchase the system from McMinnville and in turn sell the same to Caney Fork Electric Co-Operative. Although the Co-Operative is now charging the highest rate any distributor can charge in the T.V.A. System, it is suggested by T.V.A. that a rate reduction could be obtained whereby the people within the Sparta city limits would be paying 20 per cent less for power than the people in the County.[11]

Sparta's city attorney declared: " 'We are determined to own our own system' and will not accept terms of sale as 'dictated by the board of directors of TVA.' "[12] Agreement by TVA to give the city a contract was announced on October 27, 1960, two months after the city had acquired the system from McMinnville for $350,000,[13] and the contract was formally approved by the TVA board of directors on December 8, 1960. The deciding factor in the city's favor was probably the view of TVA's legal staff that TVA, by participating in its formulation, had by implication approved the contract between McMinnville and Sparta and was therefore obligated to serve the latter city if it exercised its rights under the contract.

Smithville was initially rebuffed by TVA because of its small size (1960 population 2,348). The city, concurrently with Sparta's action, awarded a franchise in 1939 to the McMinnville power system reserving the right to buy. Upon expiration of this franchise in 1959 it was not renewed for three years while the city tried to get a TVA power contract for its own system. The franchise to McMinnville was extended in 1962 for five years and again in 1967 for a like period, with a reservation to buy at any time that TVA would agree to give the city a power contract. In February, 1969, TVA indicated its willingness to

[11] *Sparta Expositor*, Feb. 11, 1960. The TVA-recommended departure from a uniform rate level in a distributor's area, to give lower rates to the people in the city, is noteworthy.
[12] *Chattanooga Times*, Feb. 8, 1960.
[13] *Nashville Tennessean*, Oct. 28, 1960.

enter into such a contract, to be effective July 1, 1969, citing growth of the system from 975 customers in 1959 to 1,475 customers as the reason for its new position. The legal situation, being the same as Sparta's, favored Smithville. No doubt a strong plus value was a federal commitment of $8 million under the Model Cities program, to match $2 million from the city and its county (DeKalb), which gives promise of further growth by the city. Passing note may also be taken that Smithville is the home of Congressman Joe L. Evins, chairman of the House Subcommittee on Independent Offices Appropriations.

Smithville incurred a sacrifice to have its own power system. To hold retail rates at the same level McMinnville had been charging, the city agreed to freeze its tax equivalent at $10,000 annually—$8,000 less than it had been paid by McMinnville. When the mayor indicated that the city might prefer to operate the power system as a department under the board of aldermen, he was told by the TVA district manager that creation of a power board was necessary if the city wanted a power contract.

South Fulton was denied a contract in the late fifties. When the city decided in 1956 to break away from the Kentucky Utilities Company, TVA gave the city no encouragement for a contract and instead recommended service from the cooperative serving that area. This was not agreeable to the city, but it consented to defer the matter because of the self-financing battle then being fought in Congress, which might have been adversely affected by the taking of a private company's customers. Once this issue was settled, the city revived its effort to get TVA power but was refused a contract allegedly because of its small size (2,239), despite the fact that Allen and Hoshall, a well-respected firm of Memphis engineers (and one of the firms recommended by TVA power personnel for this purpose), had submitted a favorable economic feasibility report. The city finally abandoned its hopes for a contract with TVA and in 1959 awarded a franchise to the nearby Weakley County system, which constructed a new system to serve the city after the Kentucky Utilities Company refused to sell its properties.

The Question of Mandatory Contracts

No occasion has arisen to permit a test of the following provision in Section 12 of the TVA Act, which seems to make TVA service mandatory under the stated conditions:

> If any State, county, municipality, or other public or cooperative organization... shall construct or agree to construct and maintain a properly designed and built transmission line to the Government reservation upon which is located a Government generating plant, or to a main transmission line owned by the Government or leased by the board and under the control of the board, the board is hereby authorized *and directed* [emphasis added] to contract with such State, county, municipality, or other organization, or two or more of them, for the sale of electricity. . . .

The Rural Electrification Administration presented to TVA the question of "whether the Authority may refuse to serve a municipality which builds a transmission line to a main transmission line of the Authority when the applicant is already served by another municipality or cooperative." TVA's assistant general counsel replied: "Obviously the legislative intention of section 12 was to implement and define the general preference provisions in section 10 by eliminating administrative discretion as to the wisdom or feasibility of service where the public or cooperative agency has supplied the necessary transmission facilities." As to the specific question presented, however, he expressed an opinion that these provisions of law "do not require the Authority to sell power directly to a municipality already served by a preferred agency." He added that TVA "would not sell power directly to such a municipality, at least until a fair offer had been made by the municipality for the acquisition of the existing facilities."[14]

Under TVA's interpretation, Section 12 could never serve as a basis of action for a municipality wishing to break out of a TVA distributor's service area. It might help a community not receiving TVA power (South Fulton considered this approach), but virtually all communities eligible under the terms of the 1959 self-financing act,[15] which established territorial limits for the Authority, are now receiving TVA power. Whether TVA

[14] Letter from Joseph C. Swidler to K. Wilde Blackburn, July 24, 1939 (in the files of TVA). The letter was approved by the TVA board on July 20, 1939.
[15] U. S., *Statutes at Large*, LXXIII, 280, 338.

has correctly interpreted the statutory mandate that "the board is . . . directed to contract with such . . . municipality" is open to question.

RURAL SERVICE BY MUNICIPAL SYSTEMS

Indicative of the attitude of some municipal officials toward power service to their rural neighbors is the following press report on a meeting of Coffee County representatives with officials of some twenty cities to discuss the proposed TEPCO purchase:

> In spite of the fact that every municipality present owed its origin and continued existence to the support of the rural districts surrounding it . . . (we) were unable to get any statement or assurance from the representatives present that rural electrification would be attempted by any municipality accepting the TVA set-up. . . . by questions, (we) finally succeeded in having one representative of a municipality to say, "I do not think we would be bothered with the rural districts." . . . neither approval nor protest was uttered by any other representative.[16]

J. A. Krug, TVA's first chief power engineer, acknowledged that sometimes such criticisms were justified: "Frankness compels me to admit that this may be true in a few cases." But he also noted that "independent business men who comprise the municipal power boards have generally recognized this situation, and many have expressed to me a complete willingness to approve the construction of every rural extension which meets minimum requirements of economic feasibility." He said that TVA, having delegated the distribution function to local agencies, recognized that it should "not try to dictate rural electrification policy, . . . [but] we do everything in our power to persuade the distribution agencies to make every extension which is within the range of economic feasibility."[17]

The promotion of rural electrification by municipal systems in Tennessee has achieved limited success. Of the fifty-nine

---

[16] *Nashville Tennessean*, April 9, 1939, reporting on a meeting in Murfreesboro, called by the mayor of that city.

[17] J. A. Krug, address at the Middle Tennessee Farmers' Institute, Columbia, May 17, 1940 (MS in TVA Technical Library, Knoxville).

Tennessee municipal systems, twenty-nine serve rather large rural areas, twelve include little rural territory, and eighteen are urban systems. Generally lower rates prevail in the urban systems, a natural result of "skimming the cream" of the power business by taking only the more profitable urban consumers.

Questionnaire responses indicated a preponderance of agreement with TVA's policy of balancing service areas with urban and rural customers. Local situations apparently have some effect on such views: agreement was 84 per cent in systems with little rural territory, 73 per cent in those with substantial rural areas, and 54 per cent in the urban systems (even in these systems 16 per cent were neutral, and only 30 per cent disagreed).

People in Washington County in the late forties expressed dissatisfaction because the Johnson City power system had not served many areas of the county. The remedy sought by county politicians and community groups in the county was the addition of "men on the board who know the rural problem."[18] Power system officials replied that they were putting forth a maximum effort for rural electrification, working under a city charter handicap which required a referendum to issue revenue bonds. In 1949 the state legislature removed this disability and also adopted a private act which added three members to the city power board: two selected by the quarterly county court, and one by the governing body of Jonesboro, the only other municipality in the county.[19] Later that year the city received an REA loan of $515,000, to be used "to speed the work on more than 250 miles of electric lines . . . [to] serve some 1,351 customers."[20]

As late as 1963, it was alleged that the state's largest city was derelict in serving rural customers. According to the *Commercial Appeal*, attention was being given "to the possibility of the Memphis Light, Gas and Water Division matching the liberal power policy of the Rural Electrification Administration to the benefit of outlying Shelby County residents." The news-

[18] *Johnson City Press-Chronicle,* April 17, 1949.
[19] *Private Acts of Tennessee, 1949*, ch. 856. The act was later challenged by the city and sustained by the Tennessee Court of Appeals (certiorari denied by the Tennessee Supreme Court), in the case of *Johnson City* v. *Allison,* 50 Tenn. App. 532, 362 S. W. 2d 813 (1962).
[20] *Johnson City Press-Chronicle,* Sept. 23, 1949.

paper commented editorially: "Another matter urgent to rural Shelby County is the need for electricity in 8,000 homes that do not have it. Because of the Federal Government subsidy to the Rural Electrification Administration on the perimeter of Shelby County, many residents near the county line are most unhappy. They cannot understand why the MLGWD demands large extension fees when the REA would be glad to come across the line for virtually nothing."[21]

Ray Morton, president of the Memphis system, challenged the accuracy of the 8,000 estimate, claiming that the system's survey revealed only 650 dwelling units without electricity, of which no more than 200 were of construction substantial enough to be wired under city and county building codes. Later in the year, the Memphis system announced the addition of 56 new rural customers under a liberalized policy of extending lines free of charge 1,320 feet for each new customer.[22]

CONFLICTS BEYOND CITY LIMITS

Competition between municipal and cooperative systems to serve profitable fringe-area markets has been an increasingly difficult problem in recent years. Numerous annexations under a 1955 act[23] giving cities power to annex by ordinance, combined with rapid suburban residential and industrial growth, have aggravated the problem.

The cooperative's case was stated in 1964 in the magazine of the Tennessee Rural Electric Cooperative Association (TRECA). "Encroachment by municipal systems [in] . . . sprawling sub-divisions" around cities, the "service areas of the cooperatives," was seen as the "major problem." Municipalities were pictured as greedily eyeing such areas as sources of "additional taxes [and] . . . increased gross revenue . . . to their electric systems." A legal right to serve these areas was asserted because they "have always been [the cooperatives'] service areas," but the power of a municipality to annex "without referendum" operated to compel a cooperative "to sell its system

[21] *Commercial Appeal*, Oct. 8, 1963.
[22] *Ibid.*, Jan. 27, 1963; Dec. 8, 1963.
[23] *Public Acts of Tennessee, 1955*, ch. 113; codified as secs. 6-308–6-321 of the *Tennessee Code*.

in the annexed area and get out." Among specific problems mentioned were overstaffing, the relocation of feeder circuits from substations to rural areas, and "wrecking of the financial structure of the cooperative." Like any other organization, a cooperative could not "remain in business [and] continually lose its best customers."[24]

The municipal viewpoint is that cities are destined to grow, that their boundaries should keep pace with such growth, and that newly annexed citizens are entitled to all municipal services, including the lower rates offered by municipal electric systems. Although they recognize that difficulties are created for the cooperatives, municipal officials feel that these are unavoidable adjustments that must be made to accommodate urban growth. The cities negotiated from a superior legal position, grounded on municipal power to franchise utility services, under which cooperatives, lacking franchises to serve, could be ousted from annexed areas. Cities could also exercise the option of duplicating facilities of cooperatives to lure their customers by lower rates. Consistently, however, through all negotiations on this issue, the cities adhered to the principle of fair compensation to cooperatives for acquired properties.

Joseph C. Swidler, after having resigned from his post as general counsel for TVA, was retained by TRECA in 1958 to help with the settlement of such problems. Working with a committee representing this organization and a committee from the Tennessee Municipal League, he prepared a bill which was introduced in the 1959 session of the state legislature.[25] Provisions of the bill were made specifically not applicable "to electric service by a municipality within the corporate limits of such municipality as now or hereafter existing." The system with distribution facilities nearest to new premises outside cities would have been given prior rights, but the system could waive these rights in writing. It would have prohibited service to any premises "then being or theretofore . . . supplied by any other non-profit electric system" and would have permit-

[24] Frank McGregor, director of public relations, Cumberland Electric Membership Corporation, "What Future for Electric Cooperatives?" in *The Tennessee Magazine* (official publication of the Tennessee Rural Electric Cooperative Association), VII, No. 12 (Dec., 1964), 26–27.
[25] House Bill No. 285.

ted municipal service "to an industrial plant located on a site acquired for a substantial consideration and owned by said municipality at the time of location of such industrial plant, if the entire site is within two miles of the corporate limits of said municipality, and if said municipality provides, or has contracted to provide, sewerage and water services thereto."

The bill was approved by the league and TRECA, but it failed to gain the backing of the Tennessee Valley Public Power Association (TVPPA, an organization of municipal and cooperative power systems); the opposition of a number of municipal power systems was a factor in its subsequent defeat. It passed both houses and was sent to the governor but was recalled by the Senate; after a sharp legislative battle in that chamber the bill was beaten by a close vote. The speaker of the Senate and former mayor of Lebanon, William D. Baird, was principally responsible for this outcome.

Following a hard-fought battle in the 1961 session of the state legislature to preserve the annexation law against vigorous onslaughts from suburbanites and a number of large industries, and in the face of continued rumblings of opposition, the Tennessee Municipal League decided that a compromise to eliminate the opposition of the cooperatives might be a significant factor in saving this law. The cooperatives presented a direct challenge when TRECA adopted a resolution at its 1963 annual meeting calling on its members to contact candidates for the state legislature prior to the 1964 elections for the purpose of securing commitments to support the following bill:

> Any utility providing electric service in any area annexed as a result of incorporation, annexation, or otherwise, by any municipality subsequent to the effective date of this act, shall have the dominant and exclusive right to continue to provide electric service in said areas to consumers then being served and to new consumers in said area located nearer to its facilities than to the facilities of any other utility supplying electric service as all those facilities were located immediately prior to the effective date of said annexation or incorporation.[26]

As the cities were becoming more embroiled in this issue, with increasing uncertainty as to whether their views would

[26] Resolution No. 16, adopted Oct. 22, 1963 (in the files of the Tennessee Municipal League).

122   *Sparks at the Grassroots*

prevail, a spokesman for the Tennessee Municipal League asserted that TVA was primarily responsible for the situation:

> TVA has failed through all of the preceding 25 years or more to exercise its unquestioned authority to eliminate the dual franchise and the controversies resulting, having only assisted in developing a model service area agreement, and giving some encouragement to its voluntary acceptance by a few adjacent power systems. Thus, TVA has permitted to develop in its entire service area the very unwholesome concept and practice of the dual franchise for natural utility monopolies—somewhat unique in utility practice throughout the country. In my judgment, this was a failure on the part of TVA to accept its responsibility as the utility regulatory agency in its service area.[27]

Service Area Requirements

The extent of TVA's participation has been to encourage competing systems to enter into voluntary agreements for settling such disputes and to provide a model form of a "Service Area Agreement," under which TVA upon request designates a member of its staff to act as the third member of an arbitration committee.[28]

The Tennessee Municipal League reacted to the 1963 threat of TRECA by appointing a special committee to join with municipal power system managers in making plans to combat the bill. They met on February 20, 1964, and decided that the municipal effort should be directed toward promotion of service area agreements on a voluntary basis and, if this proved to be unsuccessful, should seek new legislation embodying the same principles. Representatives of TVA, REA, TRECA, the league,

---

[27] Interview with Herbert J. Bingham, Dec. 16, 1964. Such a view raises the question, difficult to settle, as to the extent to which TVA, as the sole supplier of electric power, succeeded to the regulatory powers normally exercised by the states. However, in defense of TVA's position of not assuming jurisdiction in such matters, it may be pointed out that the state of Tennessee exercised no such controls over municipally owned systems prior to the advent of TVA, and that the settlement of disputes between creatures of a state may more properly be a responsibility of the state.

[28] Such an agreement between the city of Murfreesboro and the Middle Tennessee Electric Membership Cooperative, Sept. 4, 1958, placed this responsibility on TVA as a party to the contract, and was given a TVA contract number of "TV-20747A" (in the files of TVA).

and TVPPA consulted together on the terms of TVA's model Service Area Agreement and by mid-1964 had agreed on a revised version incorporating the following features: a map of the respective service areas; either party prohibited from serving in the other's area without its written approval; in the event of annexation require the municipality within sixty days either to grant the cooperative a twenty-year franchise or serve notice of its intent to purchase the cooperative's properties; if the municipality exercises its option to buy, the cooperative would make a study of the value of its properties, applying a number of criteria set forth in detail; if the two cannot agree on a basis of this study, each to appoint one member and TVA a third member[29] of an arbitration committee, which would make a determination "binding on both parties" except that in no event could compensation to the cooperative be less than the book value of its properties plus its reintegration costs.

At the beginning of 1964, TVA reported that twenty municipal systems had entered into some type of agreement with adjacent systems, ranging from simple letter agreements on boundaries to formal service area agreements of the type described above. Questionnaire returns from managers of forty-five municipal systems indicated that seventeen had annexed parts of cooperatives' service areas; eleven stated that acquisition had taken place with TVA assistance, four reported such action without TVA assistance, and two said that the cooperatives had been allowed to continue service. Several municipal officials expressed dissatisfaction with TVA's arbitration, alleging that the Authority favored the cooperatives. TVA personnel are fully aware of this hazard, which no doubt explains their reluctance to be drawn into such disputes. A district manager stated that they usually satisfy neither party, and he also indicated that properties subject to transfer are more valuable to a cooperative because they will produce a higher rate of return at the cooperative's higher rate level.[30]

---

[29] The TVA board chairman advised that "TVA will be happy to continue to assist in the administration of such agreements by furnishing a member of the arbitration committee as indicated and by taking such official action on each of these agreements." Letter from A. J. Wagner to Herbert J. Bingham, April 21, 1964 (in the files of the Tennessee Municipal League).
[30] Interview with Jack W. Eakin, Dec. 18, 1964.

The Franklin Case: TVA Backs a Cooperative

TVA has adopted a distinctly unfavorable policy toward one of its privately owned distributors. Following an annexation by Franklin in 1964, the Middle Tennessee Electric Membership Corporation, which served the annexed area, took steps to keep the Franklin Power & Light Company, which distributes TVA power, from extending its service into the area. The cooperative was unsuccessful in its effort to persuade the Tennessee Public Service Commission to revoke the certificate of convenience and necessity that had been issued to authorize the company to so extend its service. TVA tried to aid the cooperative, in the form of a letter from a district manager to the president of the company, calling his attention to a provision in the company's contract with TVA which prohibited extension of service into the cooperative's service area "without reaching a satisfactory agreement *with such distributor* [emphasis added] and Authority concerning such service." The letter continued:

> This provision of the power contract prohibits the company from offering or furnishing service to any of the cooperative's existing customers, or to any new consumers which may be located within the service area of the cooperative, either within or outside the corporate limits of the Town of Franklin, without reaching a satisfactory agreement with the cooperative and TVA concerning such service. In applying this provision of the contract, the service area of the cooperative will be determined from the facts.[31]

Thus, TVA attempted to give the cooperative an effective veto over an extension of the company's service area—by only declining to reach any agreement the cooperative could preserve its existing service area. By this device TVA undertook to guarantee a part of a cooperative's service area and to supersede the jurisdiction of the State Public Service Commission to determine such matters for private electric companies.[32] TVA's position in

---

[31] Letter from Jack W. Eakin to Lawrence B. Howard, Jr., July 8, 1965 (copy in files of the Tennessee Municipal League).

[32] The first contract (May 15, 1939) with the Franklin Power & Light Company, which was superseded by the 1948 contract, limited the company to "the existing area actually served . . . and it shall in no event offer service in any location now served by the Tennessee Co." The

this case contrasts sharply with its stand in the dispute with the Volunteer Electric Cooperative, discussed later in this chapter, in which the Authority argued, and was sustained by a federal district court, that the cooperative had no service area but simply a contract to buy power from TVA for resale.

A chancery court dismissed a suit brought by the cooperative against the Franklin Power & Light Company, holding that the company had the only valid franchise to serve the annexed area. The court held that a 1956 service area agreement between the two parties, providing that the cooperative would transfer its properties in any annexed areas, had no bearing on the company's rights. The provision in TVA's power contract forbidding service to any customer in the cooperative's service area was ruled inapplicable, on the grounds that "service area" meant the cooperative's "legal service area," which could not include territory within the city limits. The suit was brought despite the company's willingness to pay the TVA appraisal of $108,000 on the properties in question, which were carried on the cooperative's records at a depreciated value of $36,900.

On appeal the Tennessee Court of Appeals modified the chancellor's decision.[33] Although it was conceded that the cooperative's "long continued service to the area and permission from the county and state to use the public roads and highways" did not constitute a franchise to serve within the corporate limits of Franklin, the court viewed a "taking away of such rights without just compensation" as a violation of "both the spirit and the letter of Article 1, Section 21 of the Constitution of Tennessee," which prohibits taking of property for public use without just compensation.

The appeals court reaffirmed the chancellor's holding that the provision in the TVA contract with the Franklin Power & Light Company purporting to preserve the cooperative's service area meant "an area in which electric service is being furnished under an existing franchise" and therefore was inap-

---

original contract (Feb. 1, 1939) with the only other privately owned distributor of TVA power (the Bells Light & Water Company) contained no territorial limitation, but its present contract (Jan. 22, 1959) includes the same provision as in the 1948 contract with the Franklin Power & Light Company.

[33] *Middle Tennessee Electric Membership Corp.* v. *Franklin Power & Light Co.*, unreported opinion filed Jan. 15, 1968.

plicable because the cooperative had no franchise. A provision in Section 6-604, *Tennessee Code Annotated*, prohibiting any "county, utility district, municipality or public utility agency" from extending its services "into sections of roads or streets already occupied by other public agencies rendering the same service" was held to be applicable only to a "utility owned or operated by a county, a utility district, or municipality" and therefore could not be relied upon to protect "an electric co-op against competition from an investor owned public utility."

In a lengthy opinion, necessitated by the fact that this case was one of first impression in Tennessee, the court reached this conclusion:

> It appears to us that by weight of authority from other jurisdictions, and in accordance with the principles of equity and justice prevailing in this State, the co-op should be allowed to continue to serve from distribution lines constructed in the newly annexed areas prior to November 2, 1964, which was the date of annexation, such persons who were its members on that date and who desire to continue their membership and to receive service from the co-op.
>
> We also hold that it may add transferee members, but only insofar as they may be substituted as transferee members where pre-annexation members have resigned, moved away or have, for some other reason, discontinued their membership in the co-op, provided, however, that only subsequent occupants of those houses or places of business actually connected to the co-op lines as of date of annexation would be eligible as such transferee members.

The Franklin Power & Light Company took the case to the Tennessee Supreme Court, which overruled the appeals court and held that the company's franchise from the city gave it exclusive rights to serve all areas within the city. In addition to the franchise basis, the court pointed to Section 6-318 of the *Tennessee Code Annotated* (part of the annexation statute) as clear indication of legislative intent to give cities exclusive power to control utility services within city limits. Portions of the law governing cooperatives which require permission from a city to serve within its limits were also cited. The constitutional objection of taking property without just compensation was dismissed by noting that the company was willing to pay

TVA's appraisal of $108,000. The court concluded that "the effect of their [the Court of Appeals'] opinion was to substitute their judgment for that of the Legislature."[34]

However, the company realized no benefits from its victory. After the city of Franklin declined its requests for authority to serve annexed areas and a franchise extension to 1999 to make bonds more marketable, the company sold the system to the city on July 1, 1969.

Conflict in Cleveland

In another case the city of Cleveland and the Volunteer Electric Cooperative each claimed the right to serve a new subdivision a "considerable distance" from the city's boundary. The area, known as Mouse Creek Valley, about two miles wide and four and one-half miles long, was bounded on three sides by territory served by the cooperative and on the fourth side by territory served by the municipal system. Service by the city had been requested by the developers, according to the mayor, because of superior maintenance capabilities as well as lower rates. The cooperative saw this move as the beginning of a general invasion (which the mayor also indicated was a possibility) of its territory. Although conceding that its franchise from the county was nonexclusive, the cooperative undertook to establish an exclusive right on the grounds "that it has validly developed an electrical distribution system in the area and . . . the fact it has previously provided electric services . . . within the area." The chancellor recognized the equitable basis of the complaint:

> It is quite understandable that complainant is offended by the alleged encroachments on territory which it had assumed would be exclusive to it. The fact of the initial entry of the complainant into this unserved area and the expenditure of large sums of money for the development of said area has challenged the serious consideration of the Court. The Court has given great consideration to the philosophy that since complainant entered said territory and made tremendous investments that equity might demand that complainant's efforts in this connection should be protected.

[34] *Franklin Power & Light Co.* v. *Middle Tennessee Electric Membership Corp.*, 434 S.W. 2d 829 (1968).

The chancellor concluded, however, that the legislature had authorized municipal systems to serve areas outside city limits, that "the word, non-exclusive, means just what it says," and that the cooperative had to be "well aware of the risk . . . of competition and possible loss thereby in the acceptance of the said non-exclusive franchise." The Court of Appeals sustained the chancellor, holding that the cooperative was "not entitled to injunctive or other relief to prohibit the defendants from distributing electricity to the undeveloped areas of Bradley County."[35]

The precedent in this case, as suggested by the language used by the Court of Appeals, might apply only to "undeveloped areas," but it could by extension permit pirating of existing customers of a cooperative. The mayor (a lawyer) indicated that the city was making plans to serve other suburban areas, and that the city's legal position would enable it to duplicate the cooperative's facilities instead of paying "four times the value of their properties" as had been done in the past.[36] Until passage of an act in 1968, mentioned below, the laws of Tennessee have permitted this kind of competition in suburban areas. Whether a city, having in the past refused to serve its rural hinterland when TVA urged it to do so, should later undertake to invade a cooperative's territory, is an issue involving a question of fair dealing. Although threats such as the one by the Cleveland mayor have been issued, no instances of such cutthroat action have actually occurred.

A Legislative Solution

The cooperatives made another move in the 1967 General Assembly in identical bills introduced in both houses[37] that would have empowered a cooperative to "continue to exercise its rights to provide electric service within such area [any annexed area] to the same extent as if such annexation had not taken place," provided its rates were at the same level as the municipal system. The proviso as to rates would have required most cooperatives to give lower rates to customers in annexed

---

[35] Unreported opinion filed Dec. 5, 1966; certiorari denied by Tennessee Supreme Court, March 20, 1967.
[36] Telephone interview with Mayor William K. Fillauer, Aug. 30, 1965.
[37] House Bill No. 500 and Senate Bill No. 472.

areas than in other parts of their service areas. Seeing this as being in conflict with the directive in the TVA Act that TVA must sell its power "without discrimination as between consumers of the same class," municipal leaders made three efforts by correspondence to determine TVA's position on this issue.[38] TVA's three equivocal replies avoided the issue.[39] However, House committee questions put to Paul S. Button, TVA director of power marketing, and Robert H. Marquis, TVA solicitor, evoked more specific answers.[40] When confronted with the facts of an actual case—annexation by Tullahoma of 85 customers of the Duck River Cooperative, which also serves the cities of Manchester (pop. 6,038) and Decherd (pop. 1,771)—both conceded that the cooperative could not, because of the TVA act, make its charges to these 85 customers lower than its charges to customers of the same class in the other two cities.[41]

The cooperatives' bill became the most serious threat to municipal interests in the 1967 legislative session. At the behest of municipal leaders, who wanted to avoid a vote on the bill, the legislature adopted a resolution calling on the Legislative Council Committee to make a comprehensive study of the problem. The study was made, and a report[42] was filed shortly before the recessed session reconvened in February, 1968. In the meantime, negotiations between municipal and cooperative leaders were undertaken to arrive at a solution acceptable to both parties, and on December 15, 1967, they presented to

---

[38] Letter from Herbert J. Bingham to Paul S. Button, Dec. 12, 1966; letter from J. F. Perry to Aubrey J. Wagner, March 25, 1967; letter from J. Travis Price to Aubrey J. Wagner, March 31, 1967 (in the files of the Tennessee Municipal League).

[39] Letter from Paul S. Button to Herbert J. Bingham, Dec. 19, 1966; letter from Aubrey J. Wagner to J. F. Perry, March 31, 1967; letter from G. O. Wessenauer to J. Travis Price, April 5, 1967 (in the files of the Tennessee Municipal League).

[40] Hearing before the House Public Utilities and Transportation Committee, April 26, 1967.

[41] Notes taken by Austin Adkinson, information director of the Tennessee Municipal League (in the files of the league). But note that at Sparta, in 1960, the highest officials of TVA gave assurances that the Caney Fork EMC would give city customers lower rates if the city would sell its system to that cooperative.

[42] *Study on Electric Service Rights of Rural Electric Cooperatives and Municipalities, 1968* (State of Tennessee, Legislative Council Committee, Jan. 19, 1968).

the Legislative Council Committee a bill on which they had agreed.[43]

The bill moved through the 1968 session without controversy and without any change and became law on March 6, 1968.[44] It gives an annexing city two options: purchase of a cooperative's properties in an annexed area, or the granting of a franchise to the cooperative for not less than five years, which may be extended for like periods. If the option to buy is exercised the city must pay a cash consideration determined as follows:

> (a) the present-day reproduction cost, new, of the facilities being acquired, less depreciation computed on a straight-line basis; plus (b) an amount equal to the cost of constructing any necessary facilities to reintegrate the system of the cooperative outside the annexed area after detaching the portion to be sold; plus (c) an annual amount, payable each year for a period of ten (10) years, equal to the sum of (i) twenty-five per centum (25%) of the revenues received from power sales to consumers of electric power within the annexed area, except consumers with large industrial power loads greater than 300 kilowatts, during the last twelve (12) months preceding the date of the notice provided for in (1) above, and (ii) fifty centum [sic] (50%) of the net revenues (gross power sales revenues less wholesale cost of power including facilities rental charge) received from power sales to consumers with large industrial power loads greater than 300 kilowatts within the annexed area during the last twelve (12) months preceding the date of the aforesaid notice.

Upon expiration of a franchise period the city may exercise the option to buy on the same terms, and during the period of any such franchise the city may serve only the customers or locations actually served on the date of annexation.

The act should also put an end to competitive activities, by a provision that establishes legal service areas for both municipal systems and cooperatives:

> Provided further the territorial areas lying outside municipal boundaries served by municipal and cooperative electric systems will remain the same as generally established by power facilities already in place or legal agreements at the

[43] Ibid., pp. 55–57.
[44] Public Acts of Tennessee, 1968, ch. 413.

time of the passage of this Act and new consumers locating in any unserved areas between the respective power systems shall be served by the power system whose facilities were nearest at the time of the passage of this Act, except to the extent that territorial areas are revised in accordance with the provisions of this section [codified as TCA 6-320].

In this squabble TVA found itself in the middle between two sets of customers: municipal systems and cooperatives. In a statement[45] filed with the Legislative Council Committee, the Authority subscribed to the general principle that "municipal annexation of highly urbanized adjacent areas necessarily accompanies sound overall growth and development," but the main thrust of the statement was sympathetic to the cooperatives' side. Reflecting TVA's traditional concern for rural customers, the statement noted that continued intrusion into a cooperative's service area by annexations could make it unfeasible for the cooperative to sell power "at rates in keeping with those available elsewhere in the rural areas of the Valley."

An Ultimate Solution?

Finally, as an "ultimate solution in some areas," TVA's statement to the Legislative Council Committee recommended "the consolidation of municipal and cooperative systems" and cited the merger of the Fayetteville and Lincoln County Electric Membership Corporation accomplished in 1963. In a similar vein, Herbert J. Bingham, executive secretary of the Tennessee Municipal League, in 1962 suggested that "ultimately it may become essential that TVA, municipal and state governments, and the rural cooperatives engage in an effort to create a new type of electric distribution system that will serve a larger territory."[46] Bingham's testimony before the Legislative Council Committee in 1967 included the following:

> If the studies of this Council and others concerned indicate that present municipal and cooperative instrumentalities are no longer adequate to the task of providing electric service, then methods of consolidating and reorganizing these municipal and cooperative electric enterprises should be pro-

[45] *Study on Electric Service Rights, op. cit.,* pp. 31–32.
[46] Letter from Herbert J. Bingham to Charles M. Kneier, University of Illinois, March 21, 1962 (in the files of the Tennessee Municipal League).

vided by the General Assembly. . . . Specifically, consideration should be given to enabling legislation authorizing cooperative and municipal electric distribution systems to consolidate and reorganize their administrative and territorial jurisdictions.[47]

DIRECT TVA SERVICE TO LARGE INDUSTRIES

An issue provoking bitter controversy at times is the question of whether TVA or a distributor (municipal system or cooperative) should serve large industries locating in the Valley. This battle with TVA has been fought primarily by power system personnel, with municipal officials, except in cities without power boards, sitting on the sidelines.

In the early years, when acquisition of the private power systems was proceeding slowly, rather than waste the power being produced, TVA decided to sell it to large industries and to nearby utilities. Contracts were made with the Monsanto Chemical Company at Columbia (May 15, 1936), the Aluminum Company of America at Alcoa (July 17, 1936), the Victor Chemical Company at Mt. Pleasant (July 2, 1937), and the Electro Metallurgical Company at Sheffield, Alabama (August 17, 1937). Others followed, and in the fiscal year ending June 30, 1939, TVA reported that 55 per cent of its total sales were to directly served industrial customers. TVA grounded its policy on the following provision of Section 11 of the TVA Act: "sale to and use by industry shall be a secondary purpose, to be utilized principally to secure a sufficiently high load factor and revenue returns which will permit domestic and rural use at the lowest possible rates and in such manner as to encourage increased domestic and rural use of electricity."

The Authority came under some criticism for this policy, on the grounds that the benefits of low-cost power were being diverted to the large corporations. TVA's justification was that such contracts provided revenue to help finance transmission lines to serve distributors, opened up the only market for interruptible power produced by the then predominantly hydroelectric system, and would not diminish the distributors' power

[47] Testimony on Joint Resolution 70 before the Tennessee Legislative Council Committee by Herbert J. Bingham, Aug. 3, 1967 (mimeographed copy in files of the Tennessee Municipal League).

supply because industrial contracts were for staggered periods and would not be renewed if the power were needed by preference customers.[48] This policy was reviewed in the course of the 1938 congressional investigation of TVA, and a federal district judge, referring to that investigation, noted that "express approval of defendant's programs in this respect has been voiced by Congress through a joint committee."[49]

Chattanooga versus *TVA*

A skirmish between the city of Chattanooga and TVA took place in 1941, in connection with service to a government-constructed plant for production of TNT, operated by the Hercules Powder Company under contract with the War Department. The city's power board rejected TVA's contention that the War Department's contract made the plant a federal customer entitled to direct service, on the grounds that a private company was the operator. Power board spokesmen took a view that the Authority had recognized the board's "exclusive rights" in the area and that TVA was "muscling in" by proposing to serve the plant. Power Board Chairman L. J. Wilhoite saw this development as an indication of possible "plans in high and responsible quarters in the TVA for the Authority to gradually take over all the systems of the municipalities and cooperatives now engaged in the distribution of electric energy in the Tennessee Valley."[50]

The Chattanooga power board's first protest brought a reply from TVA that "the War Department expects to take service . . . directly from the Authority as another agent of the Federal Government . . . in order that the costs to be borne by the Federal Government may be minimized."[51] The city pressed its case vigorously in Washington, and subsequently it was disclosed that its bid, based on its regular industrial retail rate schedule, was less than half of TVA's proposal: $318,240 per year as compared with TVA's $780,000, or a difference of $461,-

---

[48] *TVA Annual Report for the Fiscal Year Ended June 30, 1938* (Washington, D.C.: U. S. Government Printing Office, 1939), p. 71.
[49] *Volunteer Electric Cooperative* v. *T.V.A.*, 139 F. Supp. 22, 26 (1954).
[50] *Chattanooga News-Free Press*, Sept. 29, 1941.
[51] *Ibid.*

760.⁵² A statement issued by the power board chairman asserted that there was

> "an evident policy upon the part of TVA agents to sell the TVA's proposal to the war department by convincing officials of the department that the board's proposal was merely another scrap of paper." TVA agents were reported by Mr. Finley [power system manager] as telling war department officials that the board could not guarantee delivery of power when needed, and that on the other hand, if the TVA's proposal was accepted delivery of power would be guaranteed.⁵³

The Chattanooga power board made a formal demand for the additional power required to serve this load, which it was entitled to do under its contract with TVA. According to a journalist's account, the city simply out-maneuvered TVA and won the skirmish:

> Chairman Lilienthal had undertaken to have the war department promulgate a "power policy" which had as its purpose the elimination of the power board from the contest. Chairman Lilienthal revealed this much of his plans to Chairman Wilhoite in Knoxville when the fight was at fever pitch. Chairman Wilhoite responded to that threat, if it could be called that, by going directly to the policy-making official of the war department, Undersecretary Robert M. Patterson. Mr. Patterson advised him that the only policy the war department would promulgate was to purchase the power from the "lowest and best bidder." Wilhoite, again sensing the value of maintaining good public relations on the home front, immediately announced from Washington the assurances that had been received from the undersecretary. According to Chairman Wilhoite, the TVA responded to that announcement by reducing its bid from the one cent per kilowatt hour rate to the four mills rate which had been proposed by the power board.
>
> It did not take the TVA long to realize that it was headed for serious trouble if it continued to pursue the [TNT plant] contract in the face of that development. The ultimate end of such a policy was acknowledged by Chairman Lilienthal

⁵² Letter from Representative Estes Kefauver to Undersecretary of War Robert P. Patterson, partially quoted in *ibid.*, Nov. 2, 1941.
⁵³ *Chattanooga Times*, Oct. 27, 1941.

and Senator Pope [TVA director] in their joint statement here Nov. 3.

Noting that the TVA and the power board had proposed to sell the current at identical rates, Chairman Lilienthal and Senator Pope said:

"The negotiations, however, have indicated that the war department regards the TVA and the Chattanooga Electric Power Board, in a sense, competitors, for this contract. Such a condition of competition would violate the fundamental relations which have existed from the outset between the TVA and the wholesale distributor. To prevent such a condition of competition between TVA and the electric power board from arising, the TVA board today concluded that it would withdraw entirely its proposal to render service."[54]

The city's victory was short-lived, however, as a result of the outbreak of World War II. Chattanooga consummated its contract with Hercules Powder Company the day after the attack on Pearl Harbor (December 8, 1941), but on the same day the War Department wrote a letter asking TVA to supply power to all of its plants in the TVA service area, which TVA agreed to do in a letter of December 15, 1941. A three-party contract of September 29, 1942, between the War Department, TVA, and the city of Chattanooga cancelled the city's contract, gave TVA the entire power load, and provided that TVA would pay for using the city's lines for delivery to the ordnance plant (a monthly minimum payment of $750 to the city was specified).

An Emerging Policy

Until the rise in industrial rates in 1952, made necessary by increased costs of steam generation, TVA had not covered the matter of direct service in its contracts with distributors. It handled such cases on an individual basis, apparently taking for granted that public understanding of its general policy would develop from information disseminated through publicity channels. The criteria applied in reaching such decisions, according to the manager of power, were "the magnitude of the load, any unusual characteristics of the load, the most economical manner of serving the load in view of the available

[54] Fred Hixson, in *ibid.*, Nov. 16, 1941.

transmission and distribution facilities, the risks associated with supplying the load, and any other pertinent factors involved in that particular case."⁵⁵

The 1952 industrial rate increase necessitated amendments to the power contracts, and these amendments included a provision that TVA and the distributor would

> consult one another as early as feasible in the consideration of service to large new industrial loads in the area served by Distributor, and that standard arrangements be available for normal application, so that only in unusual cases, where the loads are of disproportionate size, or involve unusual service conditions, or where direct service by TVA would make possible substantial economies through coordination of the TVA system with the customer's facilities, would service by TVA, or by Distributor under special arrangements with TVA, be called for.

The Volunteer Cooperative Goes to Court

The location of a paper plant by the Bowaters Southern Paper Corporation at Calhoun, on the Hiwassee River in eastern Tennessee, led to a bitter dispute between the Volunteer Electric Cooperative and TVA that was finally settled by the federal courts. Bowaters' representatives in 1944 first discussed with TVA personnel a possible location in the Valley, but specific planning for the chosen site was not undertaken until 1951. Bowaters needed 17,000 kilowatts of firm power and 10,000 kilowatts of standby power for use if one of its two 10,000-kilowatt generators should be out of service because of a breakdown or for maintenance. For obvious reasons the company preferred to deal with TVA rather than with a rural cooperative that had a demand for its entire system of only about 32,000 kilowatts and had never served a load larger than 696 kilowatts.

When the planned location of the Bowaters plant became known, Volunteer made several moves in an effort to secure the plant as its customer. After having executed the industrial rate

---

⁵⁵ Affidavit of G. O. Wessenauer, *Answers of the Defendant, Tennessee Valley Authority, to the Interrogatories Served upon it by the Plaintiff*, in the case of *Volunteer Electric Cooperative v. Tennessee Valley Authority*, Docket number 2161 in the U. S. District Court for the Eastern District of Tennessee, Southern Division, Dec. 9, 1953, p. 26.

increase contract on April 14, 1952, the cooperative's manager on April 22 by telephone requested return of the contract, but by that date it had also been executed by TVA. The next move was a letter of July 16, 1952, requesting TVA to construct an additional delivery point and to increase its demand load by 17,000 kilowatts to serve the plant, acting in accordance with a contractual provision authorizing such requests. TVA advised the cooperative on July 29, 1952, that its contract with Bowaters was in draft form, and on January 27, 1953, that the matter would be further discussed after a study, then underway, was completed. On April 1, 1953, TVA contracted with Bowaters to supply all of its power needs and advised Volunteer by letter of April 20, 1953, that this had been done.

Volunteer, in October, 1953, filed suit against TVA in federal district court, assailing the Authority as "ruthless and selfish" and charging that TVA's action violated "both the spirit and letter of its contractual relationship" because the cooperative had "the right to distribute such power."[56] The cooperative asserted that the preference clause of the TVA Act gave it preference over the industrial plant as a customer, that it had exclusive rights to distribute power within its service area, and that TVA by contract was required to furnish sufficient power to meet its entire requirements. TVA argued that the cooperative had no requirement for 17,000 kilowatts without a contract with Bowaters, and that there could be no such contract with the cooperative because the company had already contracted with TVA.

The TVA manager of power answered an interrogatory "Whose interest is paramount in planning sales to large industrial customers?" by saying, "The public interest has been the paramount factor." He justified this policy on grounds that only through direct service can the profits from such large customers be distributed throughout the TVA system. Permitting local distributors to serve large industries would result in low rates to domestic and rural customers in some systems but unusually high rates in other systems, as TVA would have no choice but to raise its wholesale rate to all distributors to offset the loss of such revenue. He cited the specific case of a Rey-

[56] *Knoxville News-Sentinel,* Oct. 15, 1953.

nolds Metal Company plant in the Sheffield-Muscle Shoals area, which at regular industrial rates would produce a profit of about $800,000 annually, more than eight times the gross revenues of the Muscle Shoals municipal system and $65,000 in excess of Sheffield's gross revenues. Direct service was the only means, in his view, whereby TVA could comply with the act of Congress directing "sale to and use by industry" in such a manner as to serve "domestic and rural customers at the lowest possible rates."[57]

The federal district court, deciding the case in favor of TVA, concluded that such direct sales to large industry were necessary to carry out the intent of the TVA Act and were "in complete harmony" with the preference clause. The court also upheld the Authority's contention that the power contract did not purport "to define a specific area in which plaintiff is to do business" but was "simply a contract . . . to sell power to plaintiff wholesale for resale at certain specified prices."[58]

TVA's Negotiations with Distributors

The Volunteer case triggered a protracted, and at times acrimonious, series of negotiations between TVA and representatives of the Tennessee Valley Public Power Association. Soon after the industrial rate increase of 1952, and while the Bowaters matter was pending, TVA's manager of power advised: "TVA is in agreement with the basic principle that as nearly as possible TVA should serve directly only a minimum of industrial loads in the Distributors' service areas. Therefore, the matter of whether service to new large industrial loads in a Distributor's service area will be by the Distributor in that area, or by TVA directly, will be made a matter of mutual agreement between them."[59]

The leader in this battle with TVA for the next several years was the late Thomas H. Allen, president of the Memphis Light, Gas & Water Division. In the early stages he expressed a hope that the matter could be handled without any "ill-feeling or

[57] Wessenauer, *Answers to Interrogatories, op. cit.*, pp. 24–25.
[58] *Volunteer Electric Cooperative* v. *T.V.A.*, 139 F. Supp. 22, 27 (1954); affirmed, per curiam, 231 F. 2d 446 (1956).
[59] Letter from G. O. Wessenauer to S. R. Finley, July 17, 1952 (in the files of TVPPA).

rancor . . . in a broad and liberal fashion . . . [so that] TVA has all the liberty it should have in the matter without taking from the contractors the first call on any load in their area."[60] However, discussions with personnel of TVA's Office of Power failed to resolve the matter, and in May, 1953, Allen, as chairman of TVPPA's rate committee, presented the distributors' case to the TVA board of directors in a letter which included the following:

> Early in 1951, the Tennessee Valley Public Power Association appointed a committee to consider the proposed revision of [industrial rate schedules]. . . . The committee also considered other related matters which representatives of Tennessee Valley Authority agreed to in principle, but in the opinion of the committee and some of the contractors this agreement has not been fully carried out by the TVA in dealing with some of its contractors.
>
> . . . .
>
> Relying entirely upon TVA's assurance that policies of the Power Department would conform to the wishes of the Committee, no provisions were written into the contract signed prior to July 1, 1952, putting into effect the new Wholesale Rate and the revised Large Lighting & Power Rate.
>
> . . . .
>
> It is the opinion of the Rate Committee and substantially the whole group of contracting municipalities and cooperatives that TVA's primary function is that of a wholesaler, that the individual municipalities and cooperatives should decide whether or not they desire to serve any prospective industry or other load that locates within their service area, and that TVA should serve only those loads which, in the opinion of the local unit, cannot be advantageously served by them and that final decision should rest not with TVA but with the municipality or cooperative.
>
> . . . .
>
> Further, it is the opinion of the members of the Rate Committee that TVA should not serve direct power customers in any distributor's service area. Substantially all of the contractors have expressed themselves about this, and we feel

[60] Letter from Thomas H. Allen to J. Wiley Bowers, July 23, 1952 (in the files of TVPPA).

that TVA's Board should clarify this problem by recognizing this as a principle.[61]

TVA's response was to document its case in what came to be known as the "Green Book."[62] Some of its highlights were: on January 1, 1953, TVA served only 28 out of a total of 3,886 large lighting and power consumers, but such sales (including federal agencies) took about one-half of TVA's power output; these sales produced revenues of 5.08 mills per kilowatt-hour, as compared with 4.26 mills on power sold to its distributors, and without such direct customers TVA would have had to increase its wholesale rate about 10 per cent, thereby lowering the net income of all distributors about 25 per cent; TVA and the entire region profit from coordination of the TVA system with facilities of such large industries, which makes possible such economies as interruption rights, peak shaving rights, interchange of power, standby power, and supplemental power; "to avoid financial windfalls to a few distributors which are derived from TVA's investment in generation and transmission facilities and in the long run paid for by the remainder of the distributors, TVA must assume the responsibility for direct service to such loads"; TVA must make the entire investment (approximately $2 million for a customer needing 10,000 kilowatts) to provide the generation and transmission facilities to deliver the power at the industrial plant site, and a distributor would have no investment to serve such a load.

The Green Book proposed that 15,000 kilowatts be the breaking point (5,000 kilowatts had previously been the general rule), except that a distributor could serve a load up to 30,000 kilowatts if it was all firm power taken through a general delivery point; that TVA serve all federal agencies supplied through special delivery points; that the distributors make a guarantee of 90 cents per kilowatt of contract demand under certain conditions; and that special arrangements be made for construction of certain types of substations.

[61] Letter from Thomas H. Allen to TVA board of directors, May 8, 1953 (in the files of TVPPA).
[62] TVA Office of Power, "Arrangements for Providing Service for Large Power Consumers in the Tennessee Valley Region" (duplicated, Aug. 7, 1953). TVA sent this to all of its distributors.

The contents of the Green Book and the distributors' point of view were debated at a day-long meeting on September 10, 1953, in Gatlinburg, attended by members of TVPPA's rate committee and executive committee, high officials of the power systems in Tennessee's four largest cities (Memphis, Nashville, Knoxville, and Chattanooga), and from TVA the three directors, general counsel, and ranking officials of the Office of Power. Although a few voices on the distributors' side gave some support to TVA's position, the minutes show that "the general opinion of the group as a whole, however, was unmistakably to the effect that TVA was a wholesaler and that the distributors should serve all loads in a resale capacity." The minutes continued: "the final conclusion was that the Rate Committee would again seek an answer to these problems and re-study the whole contractual relations with TVA, and after so doing, would again report their findings to the TVPPA for discussion by the Valley through the medium of regional meetings."[63]

Continued negotiations failed to produce a satisfactory settlement. The TVPPA rate committee, on March 16, 1954, reiterated its position that TVA should not make a contract in any service area until after thorough discussions with the distributor, which should be given first choice of serving the customer. TVA's manager of power, answering complaints about lack of consultation, gave assurances that "it is our intent and practice to consult with each of our distributors as early as feasible in the consideration of service to large new industrial loads."[64] The chairman advised members of the TVPPA rate committee: "TVA has been told that there is one principle set out in the 'Green Book' that will be absolutely unacceptable to the distributors, the principle being that of TVA taking over a customer whenever the customer grows out of the 'size limitation' through expansion of its facilities and increased use of power. . . .

---

[63] Minutes signed by Thomas H. Allen, chairman of the rate committee (in the files of TVPPA). At that time the Valley was beginning to feel apprehensive over the hostile attitude of the Eisenhower administration, and one power system manager commented, "With the adequacy of our future power supply so uncertain, we are about like men arguing about dividing the milk while the cow is going dry."

[64] Letter from G. O. Wessenauer to Thomas H. Allen, May 5, 1954 (in the files of TVPPA).

Briefly, TVA was informed that once a customer is served by a distributor, he will remain the distributor's customer regardless of size."[65] As noted below, this view did not prevail.

Beginning in 1953, and until the matter was resolved in 1956, TVA included the following provision in its power contracts with distributors:

> The supply of power by TVA to Municipality for resale to any consumer requiring in excess of 5,000 kilowatts, and service by Municipality to any such consumer, shall be in accordance with written arrangements negotiated in each instance by Municipality and TVA, and Municipality shall not have the right to serve any consumer requiring in excess of said amount unless and until such arrangements have been agreed upon by Municipality and TVA.
>
> . . . .
>
> It is the desire of the parties that insofar as possible Municipality rather than TVA will serve all power consumers except those which are very large, or which involve unusual service conditions, or where direct service by TVA would make possible substantial economies through coordination of the TVA system with the consumer's facilities. It is recognized that TVA and the municipal and cooperative distributors of TVA power are in the process of developing a policy defining conditions under which a large industrial load may be served through a distributor. Upon completion of the development of such a policy, the parties agree to amend the provisions of this contract to conform to all of the provisions of said policy as so developed.

In May, 1955, TVPPA put its case in the form of a "Gray Book," which covered other grievances as well as this issue. It asserted the right of a distributor to serve any industry, "unless, in the opinion of the distributor, it is desirable that the load be supplied directly by TVA," with financing for such service to be arranged by the distributor and the customer, and TVA to be reimbursed for the cost of special facilities not useful for other purposes. A local system should not lose a customer because of a load increase, and there should be no restriction on the overall load served by a distributor. TVA should contract with

---

[65] Letter from Thomas H. Allen to members of the rate committee, July 1, 1954 (in the files of TVPPA).

the distributor and there should be no relationship "contractually or otherwise" between TVA and the customer. Instead of minimum demand charges and monthly bills, it proposed that a guaranteed amount per kilowatt of demand be fixed for the entire TVA system, such amount to be prorated among all distributors. It called for elimination of subnormal rates in some areas to provide more funds for improvements, salaries, and the like. It proposed that interruptible power be made available through distributors and that large customers be required to sign contracts for five years or longer. Finally, TVA was urged to adopt a uniform contract for all distributors.

Over a period of about four months a small group selected from the TVPPA rate committee, in seven meetings with members of the TVA staff ranging from one to three days in length, hammered out a compromise agreement which was ratified by the full TVPPA rate committee on January 18, 1956. The agreement permitted distributors to serve loads ranging from 15,000 to 25,000 kilowatts of demand, or up to the total of residential sales through the same delivery point, which would enable some distributors to serve loads as high as 100,000 kilowatts of demand, but the wholesale rate for such loads would be adjusted upward to reduce their profits. Customers would be transferred if changes in customer loads or distributor's residential sales place them within the claim of either TVA or a distributor. Distributors were given federal loads under 5,000 kilowatts served from general delivery points. Large loads using other than firm power or requiring a guaranteed rate over a period of years would be served by TVA. Distributors would determine minimum bills and charges for exceeding contracted demands, but those serving loads larger than 5,000 kilowatts (nine at that time) would compensate TVA for the risks involved by making "insurance payments"; each distributor's minimum monthly bill would be the highest demand charge during the preceding twelve months ("only about one-half dozen distributors are likely to be affected . . . and the amounts involved will be very small"). TVA's wholesale rate would be adjusted according to the power factor of large customers with loads in excess of 5,000 kilovolt-amperes. All loads in excess of 5,000 kilowatts would be served at 44 kilovolts, and other minor changes would be made so that all distributors would provide industrial power on the same basis, except that service could be at 13 kilovolts with compensating payments to TVA for the portions of loads in excess of 5,000 kilowatts. The range of coal prices requiring no change in TVA's wholesale rate was narrowed from 16–20 to 17–19 cents per million Btu of all coal delivered to TVA, and instead of 1/8 of a mill for each 1 cent (or major fraction thereof) change above or below the old limits the billing adjustment would be .01 mill per kilowatt-hour for each .1 cent change above or below the new limits.

The foregoing provisions have been included in power contracts made since 1956, with some slight revisions attendant on the 1967 and 1969 wholesale rate adjustments. An indication of some continuing concern on the part of distributors was activation in November, 1963, by TVPPA of an enlarged and more representative "rates and contracts committee" to replace the former rate committee. This action apparently followed a suggestion from the executive manager of TRECA that "there has been considerable increase in the capabilities of our systems and some increase in loads served should be permitted. . . . [after committee consideration] negotiations along this line with TVA would naturally follow."[66] However, no moves have been made toward such negotiations.

[66] Letter from J. C. Hundley to J. Wiley Bowers, April 8, 1963 (in the files of TVPPA).

5 FINANCE: THE PROBLEM OF PROFITS

ELECTRIC UTILITIES are profitable enterprises, and the problem of profits—how much and how to dispose of them—has been a cause of continuing concern to TVA. The Authority's policies and means of control, which have generated sparks at times, are examined in this chapter.

TVA CONTROL OF REVENUES

TVA carefully controls the use of power revenues to guard against any "milking" of an electric system for general municipal purposes. The specter of a "taxless town" haunts TVA, and its alert personnel are especially aggressive in blocking any tendencies in this direction. This was a threat in TVA's early years, as many cities used the argument of lowered taxes to induce their citizens to vote for public power. Chattanooga even considered construction of its own generating plant after TVA refused to include a contractual provision to permit transfer of profits to the city government. A state senator from that area reported that it had been a "part of the campaign itself that the acquisition by the city of Chattanooga of its electric distribution system would go a long way toward relieving the tax burden upon real estate."[1] That general practice in those days encouraged such views is indicated by the results of a 1936 survey by the Federal Power Commission: publicly owned utilities provided 26.8 per cent of their base revenues in the form of taxes, net contributions, and free services, as contrasted with 14.4 per cent paid in taxes by privately owned utilities.[2]

[1] F. R. Morgan, quoted in *Electrical World*, CXVIII, No. 18 (May 4, 1940), 67.
[2] *Knoxville News-Sentinel*, March 29, 1939.

The issue was put to a vote in Tullahoma, following a period during which the city purchased power from TVA without a long-term contract. TVA gave notice in 1946 that it would not increase the power supplied unless the city accepted its standard contract, but the city held out for a contract with no restrictions on the use of revenues. Rather than submit to TVA's terms, the city's board of aldermen asked the voters to approve a $600,000 bond issue for a generating plant. They indicated in advance of the election that an adverse vote would be viewed as a "mandate to renew the power contract" with TVA, and this they received by a lopsided majority: 1,147 to 49. The vote was hailed as a victory for the "people's power systems protected by the TVA contract which requires that profits be used to reduce rates and extend services."[3]

The use of revenues was not the sole issue in the Tullahoma vote. The higher costs of generation in a small plant and the certainty of lower TVA rates, later estimated to save 37 per cent for home owners and 43 per cent for small commercial users, were significant influences.[4] It was a decisive victory, however, for a TVA linkup as opposed to an independent municipal plant.

Interest in the use of power revenues for general municipal purposes has not been entirely dispelled by TVA's excellent information program on the evil effects of diverting revenues. Ten years after TVA's beginning, E. H. Crump of Memphis still had the notion that eventually revenue from city-owned utilities would replace taxes entirely.[5] Union City's mayor urged municipal ownership of utilities as "a lucrative source" of revenue.[6] Views of this sort were expressed on questionnaires returned in 1965. A city commissioner thought that a new contract "should allow certain surpluses to come into the General Fund of the City." A mayor asserted the right of a city "to use profits as desired." Several other officials, and even a few power board members, wrote similar comments.

A TVA district manager, discussing the activities of a district staff, said, "There seems to be an endless variety in the situations which arise to harass contractual agreements and press

[3] *Chattanooga Times,* May 24, 1947.
[4] *Ibid.,* Jan. 4, 1949.
[5] *Commercial Appeal,* Feb. 20, 1944.
[6] *Chattanooga Times,* Oct. 3, 1944.

the interpretation of the contract to its very limits."[7] The root difficulty usually giving rise to such situations is the need for money; as the TVA board chairman has observed, "There is constant pressure for local units of government to find new sources of tax revenues. It is not surprising, I suppose, that they sometimes turn in one way or another to power revenues...."[8]

The outlook of the municipal official is understandable. He must bear the brunt of demands of citizens for more and better services, which are made more costly by the growth of his city and the inflationary spiral; he usually must work in an old city hall; he encounters strong resistance against tax increases or new taxes; and periodically he must face the electorate to keep his job. Yet he sees a power system with a well-defined service responsibility, assured income, a modern and attractive building, no political liabilities, and so financially well-heeled that it can pay high salaries and sometimes curry public favor by granting rate reductions. Why shouldn't this affluence be shared?

The basic justification for TVA's policy, as expressed by its board chairman before a congressional committee, is that "it would be rather improper for an agency of the United States Government such as TVA to bend every effort and make use of every proper device in order to sell power as cheaply as possible and at as small a margin as possible, and then have some community sell it at a rate which would permit them to wipe out all of the necessity for city taxes. . . ."[9] The rejoinder by Congressman John Phillips (California) pointed up the issue of federal control versus local democracy:

> you and I must have a fairly different interpretation of representative government, because this depends entirely upon the opinion of the local people. If . . . the board of trustees, or

---

[7] Jack W. Eakin, in an address before an assemblage of selected personnel of the Office of Power, Chattanooga, Oct. 16, 1964 (MS furnished by TVA director of power marketing).

[8] A. J. Wagner, "Objective: Low-Cost Power," address before a meeting of the Accounting Section of the Tennessee Valley Public Power Association, Knoxville, Nov. 13, 1961 (MS in TVA Technical Library, Knoxville).

[9] U. S., Congress, House, Subcommittee of the Committee on Appropriations, *Hearings, Public Works Appropriation for 1957* (Tennessee Valley Authority), 84th Cong., 2d Sess., 1956, pp. 310–11.

commissioners or whatever you call them in Tennessee . . . added a levy or a supplementary tax upon the people through the power costs that was excessive, or for some purpose the people did not agree with, I give you one guess as to what would happen to the city trustees in the next election. That is what is known as representative government, and I believe in it, and I do not see that the TVA has authority to come in and say that the city trustees and the city council or whatever you choose to call it may or may not do that.[10]

Over the years, however, the TVA policy has been accepted by the people of Tennessee, and no concerted effort has been made to sell the opposing point of view. Municipal officials, too, have acquiesced in the policy as a cardinal point insisted upon by TVA even though some hold strong contrary opinions.

PRIORITIES IN USE OF REVENUES

The statutory basis for controlling the disposition of revenues is found in the following part of Section 10 of the TVA Act, added in 1935 at the request of the TVA board:[11] "The board is authorized to include in any contract for the sale of power such terms and conditions . . . and to provide for such rules and regulations as in its judgment may be necessary or desirable for carrying out the purposes of this Act, and in case the purchaser shall fail to comply with any such terms and conditions, or violate any such rules and regulations, said contract may provide that it shall be voidable at the election of the board."

It should be noted that policy on this point is TVA-made—the congressional act authorized but did not determine the policy. One of the four points in the Plan of Action adopted by the TVA board on August 22, 1933, required a "municipal utility to stand on its own bottom (i.e., to be wholly self-supporting)

[10] *Ibid.*
[11] Section 4(g) of the original act granted the Authority "such powers as may be necessary or appropriate for the exercise of the powers herein specifically conferred upon the Corporation." Section 10 also "empowered and authorized [the board] to sell the surplus power . . . according to the policies hereinafter set forth." But nowhere was there any mention of terms and conditions for wholesale power contracts with public agencies, which seems a little surprising in view of the development of this concept in New York, where Gov. Franklin D. Roosevelt had advocated the contract as a superior device of regulation.

Finance: The Problem of Profits 149

and (on the other hand) not to be a source of tax relief, at the expense of the rate payers, beyond a fair return to the city's general fund on the city's utility investment."[12]

The first draft contract approved by the board included this provision:

> Revenues will first be used for operating expense, depreciation, payment to the general fund of the City of taxes at rates equivalent to the taxes and assessments a private system would have to pay, interest on bonds or other indebtedness applicable to the electric system, the amortization of such bonds and other indebtedness, reasonable reserves for new construction and contingencies, and a return on the City's equity of not more than six per cent per annum. After the above items have been taken care of out of revenues, the City hereby agrees that any and all surplus sums available shall be applied toward reductions in rates to consumers.[13]

TVA's first power contract, with Tupelo, Mississippi, bound the municipality to apply its electric system revenues in the following order, according to the first TVA annual report:

> operating expenses;
> interest on electric-system bonds or other indebtedness;
> amortization of electric-system bonds or other indebtedness;
> reasonable reserves for new construction or contingencies;
> payments in lieu of taxes at rates equivalent to the taxes assessed against other property of a similar nature;
> a return on the equity of not more than 6 per cent per annum;
> after all of these items have been covered, the contractor agrees that all remaining revenues shall be applied to reduction in rates.

Low Priority of Tax Equivalents

A significant difference between the board-approved draft contract and the Tupelo contract was the priority accorded to payments in lieu of taxes. The former placed this item near the

---

[12] "A Plan of Action for Carrying Out the Power Program" (Exhibit 8-22-33b in the files of TVA), p. 4.

[13] David E. Lilienthal, memorandum on "Basic Provisions for Contracts between the Authority and Municipalities for Power," approved Oct. 16, 1933 (in the files of TVA).

head of the list, whereas the latter placed it near the bottom where it has remained except as noted below. The former is in accord with tax law, which gives the highest priority to tax claims. Since the priority was "in the order named," and later contracts prefaced each item "from remaining revenues," this is significant, because if the money doesn't hold out the city fails to get a full tax equivalent, and there have been many instances when power boards have cited insufficient funds as the reason for not paying full tax equivalents.[14] Just what happened to cause this switch in policy within such a short time is not known.

In the Kentucky contracts, where state law requires payments in lieu of taxes, these payments are listed in the first category as part of "operating expenses." Two other exceptions were noted: a 1934 contract with New Albany, Mississippi, which included "taxes" as an operating expense and tax equivalents in the fourth priority; and the 1937 contract with Chattanooga, which ranked reimbursement for taxes lost by city acquisition of the private utility in third place, following operating expenses and debt service requirements.[15]

[14] This statement is based on information brought to my attention during fifteen years of contacts with municipal officials of the state. Three specific instances come to mind. Mayor Kiser of Greeneville, in the early fifties, told me that power system officials cited insufficient funds as the reason for not paying more tax equivalents, largely because of expenditures on rural electrification. Alcoa officials in 1964 stated that this was the reason cited by that city's power system for not paying more tax equivalents. The mayor (and chairman of the power board) in Lenoir City, another city making very low tax-equivalent payments, in 1965 told me that the power system had even had to borrow money to meet a payroll. Such situations may involve an element of discretion as to use of revenues; TVA might say that funds would be sufficient if the power systems would borrow money for expansion and improvement of their plants instead of using a pay-as-you-go policy. There is ample evidence that many systems have not paid adequate tax equivalents, though perhaps not always for this reason.

[15] The Chattanooga contract did not conform with the requirements of state law; ch. 455 of the *Private Acts of Tennessee, 1935*, from which the city derived its contracting authority, placed tax-loss replacements in second position, and debt-service payments in third position, the reverse of the order in the contract. This private act also contained a unique provision that "such part [of surplus revenues] as the parties may agree cannot practicably be used for rate reductions may be used in payment of the general obligations of the City." The provision of course was meaningless—it is unimaginable that TVA would agree that revenues "cannot practicably be used for rate reductions."

Power boards at times have used electric system revenues for construction or early redemption of bonds, or lowering rates, and have failed to pay the full amount of tax equivalents authorized in the power contract. This is a violation of the spirit, and probably the letter, of the contract, because such uses are accorded lower priority in the power contract. The point can also be made that the Municipal Electric Plant Law[16] provides that the "supervisory body *shall devote* all moneys" (emphasis added) for the same purposes set out in the TVA power contracts but without any qualification as to sufficiency of funds for the last-named items. This may be construed to mean that rates must be maintained at levels to produce revenues sufficient to meet all such obligations.

Revisions in Contract Terms

Contracts in the early years provided that if the full investment return or tax equivalent was not paid in any year, the amount not paid would be added to the municipal investment. Such a stipulation seems to have been uniformly included until about 1940, usually with the qualification "to the extent such amounts are needed by or used in the system," but it was unqualified in three 1935 contracts with Memphis, Dayton, and Somerville.

Except for the use of surplus revenues and elimination of the investment return, power contracts have continued to specify generally the same priorities on use of revenues as in the first contract with Tupelo. Until 1939 use of the word "shall" with respect to payments of investment returns and tax equivalents would seem to indicate a mandatory intent; beginning in that year this was changed to "may," and this word appeared in the 1952 edition of the standard power contract. The provision introduced in the 1954 Tupelo revision is still in use. It gives first priority to operating expenses, including salaries, wages, cost of materials and supplies, power at wholesale, and insurance, and places interest and principal retirement in second place. Third on the list are reserves for renewals, replacements, and contingencies, and cash working capital adequate to cover operating expenses for a reasonable number of weeks. Next, "from any revenues then remaining," tax equivalents

[16] *Tennessee Code,* sec. 6–1530.

may be paid into a municipality's general fund. Any revenues left over after meeting these "requirements" are declared to be "surplus revenues" which may be used for new construction or early debt retirement, subject to the following proviso: "that resale rates shall be reduced from time to time to the lowest practicable levels considering such factors as future circumstances affecting the probable level of earnings, the need or desirability of financing a reasonable share of new construction from such surplus revenues and fluctuations in debt service requirements."

Policy respecting the disposition of "surplus revenues" has varied. The 1934 contracts with Knoxville, Dayton, and Pulaski referred to rate reductions only. From 1935 to 1938 early retirement of debt was mentioned first, followed by rate reductions. Beginning in 1939, rate reductions were to be given first consideration, with a proviso that the municipality could, "subject to the consent of Authority," pay off indebtedness before maturity.

Uses Which Might Justify Rate Increases

A few early contracts provided that if existing rates were not sufficient under economical and efficient management to maintain the system on a self-supporting and financially sound basis, upon application by contractor, the Authority would consent to changes in rates to provide increased revenues. This provision reserved to TVA the prerogative of making a judgment as to whether there had been economical and efficient management. It is not difficult to imagine the extent of intrusions into local management that would be necessary to arrive at such judgment, and this probably explains why the provision was soon dropped.

The standard contract provides for agreement of the parties on rate increases if required to place the power system "on a self-supporting and financially sound basis, including requirements for interest and principal payments on indebtedness." Nothing is said, however, about a rate increase to permit payment of authorized tax equivalents.[17] A power system manager

---

[17] The 1939 Nashville contract was an exception by including investment return and tax equivalents as bases of possible rate increases. However, that city's 1957 contract included the standard provision on this point.

in the early 1950's stated that allowable tax equivalents could not be paid because TVA would object on grounds that rate reductions should be accomplished instead. A city official involved in negotiations in 1965 for a contract renewal and under pressure to reduce rates, stated that he raised this point and was told that the question had never arisen before and so had not been decided. Only Kentucky cities receive assurance, which is required by state law, that tax equivalents are to be included in the standard of "self-supporting and financially sound basis." Contracts since the 1954 revision have implied that there should be no rate reduction unless revenues are more than sufficient for purposes listed in Section 6, which includes tax equivalents.

PROHIBITION OF CHARITABLE CONTRIBUTIONS

Curbing donations was described by a TVA district manager as a specific duty of a district office staff.

We are continually slapping the wrists of our power distributors in connection with donations. I cannot stress too strongly that such a simple matter of saying "no" to a local group is not simple at all. If done properly, it is a most demanding task. From the viewpoint of those to whom we say "no," it involves contact between a federal agency with the large power of big government and the powerless individual or small group trying to promote a worthy cause for his community. On our part we must prepare well enough to persuade them that the ultimate success of their community and of TVA in providing power at the lowest possible cost is involved even in so small a matter as a donation to a worthy cause. Donations and other violations of the power contract are like leaks in a dam. Held in check, the damage is minor and can be repaired. Unchecked they would destroy.[18]

In the course of interviews, several power board members mentioned such surveillance as an advantage of being linked to TVA by a power contract. They said that they probably could not resist the pressures of their fellow townsmen and neighbors for contributions to worthwhile projects. Letting TVA say "no" takes them off the spot, and eventually everyone learns that

[18] Eakin, Oct. 16, 1964, *op. cit.*

such requests may as well not be made. As in cases of unpopular rate decisions, this may represent the majority view of municipal power system officials. However, a few comments indicated resentment against TVA's tight controls. For example, a power board member remarked, "We could do with a little more leeway in performance of civic obligations."

As reported on questionnaire returns, requests have included aid for a Babe Ruth Little League and to crippled and mentally retarded children, donation of labor and materials on various civic projects, and participation in special street lighting for Christmas. One power board chairman reported in an interview that power system personnel erect and install Christmas lighting decorations for the Christmas season. The manager of another system reported "Christmas decorations for town and Christmas baskets for employees" as an example of joint action with other city agencies. The Knoxville Utilities Board bears up to $2,500 of the annual expense for downtown Christmas lighting.

When Chattanooga entered the TVA system, the chamber of commerce was unhappy that the power board did not continue the membership fee of about $5,000 annually previously paid by the power company. An alderman of another city, on his questionnaire return, mentioned failure of the power system to join the chamber of commerce. However, a power board chairman in still another city reported that the power system regularly pays $25 annually to the chamber of commerce, as membership dues for the power system manager. One power board maintains a $500 annual membership in the chamber of commerce, justified as part of its industrial promotion program.

Sometimes indirect means have been attempted to give small contributions to a municipality, according to questionnaire comments. One question asked was whether there had been occasions to make "choices between the policies or preferences of TVA and those of the city governing body." An alderman reported that TVA has prohibited power system participation "in city projects that would benefit the electric department." In another city, the Authority took exception to the expenditure of funds "on what the power board considered a progressive and needed local service for the public." Power system managers reported requests for loan of personnel for

Finance: The Problem of Profits 155

nonelectric purposes, failure of a city to pay the costs of relocating street lights on a closed street, and a proposal to charge the power system for use of city streets and lands.

A contribution of $3,000 by the Johnson City power board for a Memorial Hospital expansion program elicited from TVA the following discourse and a request for assurance that similar contributions would not be made in the future.

> We appreciate fully the strong pressures on your Board for a contribution to the hospital expansion program. Private businesses generally support campaigns for funds for such purposes. It must seem to the Board that it would be derelict in its responsibility as a "citizen" of the community if it made no contribution. However, there is an essential difference between private business and a publicly-owned and operated electric system managed by the Board. The earnings from a private business can be used for any purpose the owners wish because those earnings belong to them and are not dedicated to any particular use. The revenues from the electric system, however, do not belong to the Board; they are public funds in the custody of the Board for particular public purposes. The Board is in a very real sense a trustee of the funds and can properly dispose of them only for the purpose authorized by section 17 of the Municipal Electric Plant Act under which the Board was created.
>
> . . . .
>
> Once the Board starts making contributions of this kind it becomes increasingly difficult for it to refuse to make similar contributions to other worthwhile projects and they are legion. The failure of many municipal electric systems in this country is evidence of the frequently fatal results of diversion of funds to non-electric system purposes.[19]

The Authority made no protest, however, against contributions by power systems to Citizens for TVA, an organization formed in 1953 to support TVA's requests for funds from Congress during the lean years of the Eisenhower administration. From 1953 to 1964, twenty Tennessee municipal power systems contributed a total of $15,534 to this organization, ranging from Chattanooga's $5,750 to $39 from Somerville; 1954 was the year

[19] Letter from C. Wilson House, manager of TVA's eastern district, to Charles Stine, manager of the Johnson City power system, as reprinted in the *Johnson City Press-Chronicle,* Oct. 20, 1957.

of largest contributions—$6,523, followed by $2,300 in 1953, $1,509 in 1955, and $1,062 in 1960; $700 was received from five systems in 1964.[20] In 1959 an appeal was made for contributions from the Nashville power system in a letter which stated: "The Tennessee Valley Authority, which audits electric systems and in effect controls the purposes for which the revenues can be spent, has not objected to use of electric system funds for this purpose."[21] (An attempt might be made to distinguish these contributions from the others on the grounds that they went to support an organization that had joined in the effort to provide electric power at the lowest possible rates, but this stretches the imagination a bit.)

DEBT SERVICE ON GENERAL OBLIGATION BONDS

Soon after Paris became a TVA distributor in 1940, the city council by a resolution imposed on the power system the debt-service liability for $40,000 in general obligation bonds. This resolution was later repealed because, according to a press report, "the TVA, which manifests a degree of control over the local Board of Utilities, has repeatedly insisted that the city had violated its contract with the TVA in placing the $40,000 worth of bonds in the hands of the Utilities Board. Authorities explained Wednesday this was the cause of the action."[22]

A similar case was not so easily settled, and TVA had to go into a federal district court to nullify a commitment of power system revenues made by Lenoir City to amortize a general obligation bond issue. An ordinance was adopted in 1941 and validated by a special act of the legislature,[23] pledging power revenues and guaranteeing that the city would charge sufficient rates to meet the debt service requirements, thus implying that rate increases might be made for this purpose. The court, viewing the essential question as being whether the ordinance and validating act were "unconstitutional, because if enforced as properly construed they would impair the obligation of the

[20] Records of Citizens for TVA, Nashville.
[21] Letter from Herbert J. Bingham, executive secretary of the Tennessee Municipal League, to Ben West, mayor of Nashville, July 7, 1959 (in the files of the league).
[22] *Commercial Appeal*, Feb. 12, 1942.
[23] *Private Acts of Tennessee, 1941*, ch. 357.

contract" with TVA, reached this conclusion: "By this ordinance the City undertook new and substantial duties in opposition to those contained in the contract and provided for their performance. This ordinance therefore constituted an impairment of the obligation of the power contract between TVA and Lenoir City. For the same reason, Chapter 357 . . . impaired the obligation of the power contract. . . ."[24] TVA's general counsel, Joseph C. Swidler, hailed this decision as being "of utmost importance, for it gives assurance to the consumer that any profits from resale of TVA power will be passed on in the form of lower rates and not diverted to other purposes."[25]

Most of the newspapers of the state strongly supported TVA on this issue. The *Knoxville Journal* was virtually a lone voice in decrying "almost absolute power over lesser governmental subdivisions" and the power to "dictate in detailed terms the manner in which a wholesale product is to be retailed and the uses to which the profits from these retail sales can be put."[26] An editorial in the *Nashville Tennessean,* soon after the suit was filed in 1943, typifies the general reaction and provides some insight into the reasons for the broad base of public support that TVA has enjoyed over the years:

> This suit is important. It is important to Nashville and every other user of TVA power, and to the whole idea of TVA itself. It is important because the "TVA Contract" is the thread upon which the whole service of TVA power distribution is strung. It is the charter that links—and to a large degree shapes—the power policies of the numerous communities attached to the TVA system. The contract is the only guarantee to the people themselves that they will continue to be able to buy power at going standard TVA rates or better.
>
> . . . the truth is that, despite low TVA rates and the lugubrious predictions of the opponents of TVA, all the municipal systems distributing TVA power have "come out"—that is, they have made money up to and above the amount required for all operational purposes and the discharge of bond obligations. They are building up surpluses in special funds and in war bonds. Money like this, substantial money, just cannot lie around without attracting ideas as honey attracts flies.

[24] *T.V.A.* v. *City of Lenoir City,* 72 F. Supp. 457 (1947).
[25] *Electrical World,* CXXVIII, No. 1 (July 5, 1947), 66.
[26] Quoted in *Southern City,* VII, No. 7 (July, 1943), 10.

Also in several of the municipalities there always have been men who prefer to regard municipal power operations as a business rather than a service, and in the back of their heads these men always have nursed the thought that some day the burden of municipal upkeep could be shifted to the "profits" of the power system.[27]

JOINT OPERATIONS WITH OTHER CITY AGENCIES

Under the "arm's length" policy, if TVA had its way completely, a power system would be wholly independent of other city departments and agencies, but the Authority has consented to some cooperative arrangements.

Industrial Promotion

Attracting new industry, which is given high priority by municipal officials, increases the consumption of electricity and is therefore a legitimate concern of municipal power systems. Cooperative efforts of cities and power systems in this field began in the mid-fifties. As early as 1942 the Electric Power Board of Chattanooga set up an industrial promotion department to help local industries solve problems involving national defense production and to encourage new industries to locate in that area. This department was authorized to seek assistance from the legal, financial, and operating departments of the power board.[28]

One of the first Tennessee municipalities to undertake a joint industrial promotion program was Johnson City, and TVA registered no objection. Although TVA has no firm policy respecting cooperation by its distributors in such programs, it has expressed a preference for the organization of such efforts through regional associations which would include power systems, as has been done in Alabama and Mississippi. To a specific proposal that electric funds be used to acquire industrial sites, TVA's answer was negative.

One city manager, after negotiating an agreement with a power board to pay two-thirds of the costs of such a program, received an indication that TVA planned to lodge a protest. As

[27] *Ibid.*
[28] *Chattanooga News-Free Press*, Jan. 26, 1942.

a tactical maneuver to improve his bargaining position, the next year he proposed that all costs be paid by the power system. During the ensuing negotiations, TVA indicated its desire to eliminate any participation by the power system, but the final compromise was a 50–50 split of the costs.

Herbert J. Bingham, executive secretary of the Tennessee Municipal League, after a conference in 1961 with the TVA board and other high officials, reported that clearance had been given "for a municipal electric system to participate on any reasonably equitable basis with a municipality and a county in the financing of an industrial promotion or development staff and office." TVA was asked specifically whether the Pulaski power system could contribute $4,000 to such a program (the city and county each would also pay the same amount). Bingham stated that assurances were given by the TVA board and staff that "this was perfectly legal, and that the question of whether it was a wise expenditure is one to be made locally by the governmental agency controlling the expenditure of electric department funds."[29]

Municipal and cooperative distributors in four of TVA's districts, with TVA encouragement, have formed district nonprofit corporations to engage in industrial promotion activities. Each corporation has employed a small staff for this purpose, and the costs are apportioned among the distributors according to a formula that reflects numbers of customers and revenues. No such organization has been formed in TVA's eastern district, but many of the distributors in this district have joined with other local agencies in carrying on such activities.

Operation of Other Utilities

The operation of other utilities by a power board sometimes borders on diversion of electric revenues, because of the necessity of allocating common expenses and shared facilities. Of forty-five power managers who responded to questionnaires, seventeen reported various combinations of power, water, gas, and sewer systems operated under a single board. The TVA general manager has reported that "new problems are constantly created by the rapid growth of the distributors and an

[29] Letter from Herbert J. Bingham to Dr. Aymett Garner, mayor of Pulaski, Jan. 8, 1962 (in the files of the league).

increasing number of joint services or operations involving the electric system and other municipal departments."[30] TVA is fully aware of the possibilities and always on the alert for any instances of excessive charges to the electric system. Just how complex this problem can become is indicated by the following excerpt from a report on the Shelbyville Electric Power and Water Board:

> The salaries of the Accountant and Office Manager and the Engineer and Treasurer are split 1/3 paid by the Water Department and 2/3 paid by the Electric Department. Three clerks are on the Electric Department payroll and two clerks on the Water Department payroll, although all five clerks work on both operations. Separate crews of service men and construction crews are employed by each department and their salaries are kept separate. The water plant operator also takes care of the electric substation, and $75.00 of his salary is charged to the Electric Department each month. The Electric Department pays the office electric bill and the Water Department pays the office water bill. The Water Department also pays the Electric Department $25.00 a month for office space. Insurance and office supplies are split between the two departments. In some cases furniture such as desks and files are owned by one or the other department. In respect to the present office and warehouse building, the Water Department owns the land and the Electric Department owns the building.[31]

TVA would prefer a completely separate operation of an electric system, partly because it would avoid such sticky problems of allocations. Contracts through the 1952 edition of the standard power contract pledged a municipality "to administer its electric system as a separate department" but authorized charging "an equitable portion" of the pay of shared employees to the electric system. Since 1954 the requirement of a separate department has been essentially unchanged but the following has been added: "In the interest of efficiency and economy, Munici-

[30] Letter from Aubrey J. Wagner, general manager, to Frederic H. Smith, General Accounting Office, July 3, 1956 (in the files of TVA).
[31] Memorandum for the files, by E. W. Meisenhelder, consultant of the Municipal Technical Advisory Service, The University of Tennessee, reporting on a field visit to the system, Aug. 18, 1952 (in the files of the Municipal Technical Advisory Service, The University of Tennessee).

pality may use property and personnel jointly for the electric system and other operations, subject to agreement between Municipality and TVA as to appropriate allocations, based on direction of effort, relative use, or similar standards, of any and all joint investments, salaries and other expenses, funds, or use of property or facilities."

An amendment in 1960 to the power contract with Oak Ridge recognized that overall savings in costs can be accomplished through joint use of employees and claimed for the electric system a fair share of such savings. It provided that this would be accomplished by allocations of "joint salaries and expenses . . . in accordance with sound cost accounting principles as mutually agreed upon." At the end of the first year's operation and at any time thereafter at the request of either party, actual costs experienced in providing joint services were made subject to review and adjustments to insure an equitable division of these costs.[32]

In one city accumulated electric revenues were used to construct a new building for the water, gas, and electric systems. TVA asserted that rent should be paid by the water and gas systems on a basis of relative floor space. The power board contended that this was a local matter that lay within its discretion and that the allocation would be made on a basis of relative investments in and revenues of the three systems. A compromise was reached after the power board threatened to move the water and gas systems back into a vacated building. In another city an effort by the power board to sell an office building (that it had outgrown) to the city government at a nominal price ("we wanted to help the city because we are a part of the city") was blocked by TVA insistence that the building be sold at its appraised value because it had been built with electric system funds.

Joint Buildings

Joint buildings have been constructed in some cities for the power system and other utilities and in a few instances to house both utilities and the municipal government. TVA discourages such arrangements, especially the latter type, but they are

[32] Letter from G. O. Wessenauer, TVA manager of power, to A. K. Bissell, mayor of Oak Ridge, June 1, 1960 (in the files of TVA).

usually approved if local officials are persistent. TVA carefully checks the details of such ventures and the use of electric system funds must be specified with exactness.

Plans for a cooperative building may provide that: (1) the city government construct and maintain the building and rent space to the electric system; (2) the city government and the electric system each finance and maintain a designated part of the building; or (3) the electric system construct and maintain the building and rent space to the general city government and other utilities.[33] If the electric system is to be housed with other agencies, TVA sees separate financing as the best means of preserving separateness and properly accounting for funds. The Authority's next choice is rental from the municipal government, giving the electric system an option to go elsewhere, especially under a short-term lease. Finally, TVA has approved a joint occupancy building financed with electric funds on the grounds that the electric system will ultimately need the space rented "temporarily" to other agencies. Construction for permanent rental to a city government would be considered a diversion of electric funds or credit for the benefit of the city government. One can easily foresee a time of troubles if a general city government or other utility were to be evicted against its will.

Continuing opposition by TVA to joint buildings is indicated by two recent cases. At a 1964 conference a TVA district manager emphasized the desirability of a separate electric building and mentioned that one advantage from the city's viewpoint would be collection of a tax equivalent on the value of the building. He also urged establishment of a power board, based on arguments for separating the electric system from other city departments, and suggested that separate billing and collecting would be to the advantage of the utility and consumers. The

[33] These plans were examined in some detail in Victor C. Hobday, "Municipal-Utility Buildings: Three Tennessee Plans," *Tennessee Town & City*, III, No. 11 (Nov., 1952), 13–17, and in greater detail in Hobday, *Financing Electric-Municipal Buildings in Tennessee* ("Technical Bulletin No. 20" of the Municipal Technical Advisory Service; Knoxville: The University of Tennessee, Aug., 1953). A number of such arrangements have been instituted since that time, but the differences do not seem to be substantial.

other case occurred in 1965. A small town (with no power board) decided to move the electric department from a separate location into the city hall to realize economies in office operations, but, according to the mayor, the move was consistently opposed by TVA.

TVA's opposition to joint building arrangements is largely based on a view that it places electric system personnel too close to politicians in the general city government. TVA is not alone in holding such views. William C. Ross, a member of the Knoxville Utilities Board, gave the following objection to the mayor's proposal to construct a new civic center to house all city agencies:

> Everybody knows political appointments the world over are often made on the ability of the one appointed to get votes, rather than on his ability to do his job well. Everybody also knows that if this practice is indulged in to any great extent it is not conducive to efficient operations, and I simply do not believe KUB should be in an atmosphere where that condition could ever prevail. . . .
>
> I have been surprised at the large number of reputable men who have held high executive and councilmanic positions in former city administrations who have called me to say they think I am 100 per cent right. So why take an unnecessary chance?[34]

Attitudes toward joint housing of the power system and the city government appear to be evenly balanced, if we use our questionnaire responses as evidence. Favorable responses by city government officials were somewhat more than offset by unfavorable responses from power board members and power system managers. The replies are tabulated in Table 8. Considering only the replies from cities where the general city government and the power system are housed in the same building, approval was expressed by 87 per cent of general city government officials and 63 per cent of power system officials. Negative answers were given by 80 per cent of the general city officials and 81 per cent of the power system officials to a question as to whether there had been "any problems or difficulties from joint use of the same building."

[34] *Knoxville News-Sentinel,* June 21, 1950.

TABLE 8

QUESTIONNAIRE RESPONSE: ATTITUDES OF CITY AND POWER SYSTEM OFFICIALS TOWARD JOINT USE OF BUILDINGS*

	General city government officials		Power system officials	
	No.	Per cent	No.	Per cent
Strongly approve	34	24	8	6
Approve	38	26	20	14
Neutral	18	12	20	14
Disapprove	28	20	41	30
Strongly disapprove	14	10	45	33
No reply	12	8	4	3
Total	144	100	138	100

* Questionnaire Item: "Please indicate your attitude toward the power system and the general city government being housed in the same building: ☐ Strongly approve ☐ Approve ☐ Neutral ☐ Disapprove ☐ Strongly disapprove."

Joint Activities

Power system managers were asked by questionnaire to indicate any joint activities of the power system and the general city government. Replies on this item were received from twenty-six power systems. Of this number fifteen reported "none," ten checked "billing," three checked "purchasing," three indicated "accounting," and two reported joint use of equipment. One of the last two specified "transportation and office equipment for the Light, Water and Sewer System," and the other named postage machine, safe and thermofax, and two-way radio equipment.

One city effected substantial economies by assigning the same employees to read water, gas, and electric meters and by doing the billing for the power board. This made possible acquisition by the city of modern accounting and billing equipment which probably could not have been justified if the electric system had not been included.[35] TVA has called on the city

---

[35] This is the evaluation of Inslee Burnett, consultant on finance and accounting, Municipal Technical Advisory Service, The University of Tennessee, who has studied these arrangements in some detail.

several times to justify the arrangement, and each time it has been shown that the cost to the power board is less than other alternatives available. An alderman of that city stated that he objected "especially to TVA's continuing insistence that we separate our meter readers and employ central service to do the billing on separate bills—regardless of the economies we effect by our local billing." His reference to "central service" meant the Central Services Association, a nonprofit corporation serving TVA's municipal and cooperative distributors and water utility districts. Meter readings made in the field are mailed to branch offices of this organization, which prepares the bills and mails them to customers. Members of the association's board of directors are managers of cooperative and municipal distributors of TVA power (two from each of TVA's five districts).

RETURN ON MUNICIPAL INVESTMENT

All power contracts until the mid-fifties contained provisions respecting payment of a return on the municipal investment. However, this has been a meaningful provision only for municipalities that had invested general funds in a power system. In Tennessee only municipalities owning electric plants prior to TVA, and Oak Ridge, have received returns on the valuation of their plants at the time they entered the TVA system. These systems subsequently, and other municipal systems from the time of their acquisition, have been financed by revenue bonds which created no municipal investment.[36]

A policy statement of TVA in 1935 specified the basis for payment of such an investment return:

> The amount of the CITY's investment in the ELECTRIC SYSTEM shall be determined as of the initial date of delivery and shall be adjusted subsequently at the end of each fiscal year.
>
> The CITY shall receive a return on this investment not to exceed one-half (1/2) of one (1) per cent per month, computed on the basis of the investment as of the last day of the month next preceding.... Except as limited in this statement, the board of aldermen or other governing body of the

[36] Memphis issued general obligation bonds, but these became revenue bonds in effect when the electric system assumed the debt-service requirements.

municipality shall determine the rate of return on the CITY's investment and/or the interest rate on loans and advances.[37]

Contracts with several cities up to the year 1936 gave their governing bodies the power to determine the rate of return, but thereafter the provision was simply stated without specifying which agency of a city would make the determination.

As mentioned previously, early contracts contemplated an increase in the municipal investment equal to the amount of any unpaid tax equivalent or unpaid investment return. Beginning in 1940 and continuing until 1954, when a new policy of liquidation was initiated, this policy was applied only to unpaid investment returns if "funds" or "revenues" were insufficient.[38] A municipality was given an option of not withdrawing the return, thereby increasing its investment "to the extent such amount is needed by and used in the operation of the electric system." Withdrawals of such funds were permitted "only at such times and in such amounts as will not interfere with the efficient operations of the electric system, including requirements for expansion."

A change of policy by TVA in this respect was signaled in the 1950 contract with Union City, which limited the municipal investment to $200,000 and required the city to accept payment, from the proceeds of electric revenue bonds, for the value of its system above this amount. TVA decided that paying a 6 per cent return to the owner-city was an unnecessary burden on electric revenues, especially when money could then be borrowed on electric revenue bonds at 3 per cent or less. The liquidation of all municipal investments was required as contracts came up for renewal, beginning in 1954.

The special situation at Oak Ridge, following its incorporation in 1959, may be regarded as an exception to the "no municipal investment" policy. All public facilities at Oak Ridge, including the electric system, had been constructed with federal funds. Nevertheless, after these facilities were transferred to the newly incorporated city, the power contract with TVA

---

[37] "Statement of Financial and Accounting Policy Proposed for Adoption by Municipalities Owning Electric Systems for Purchase of Power from the TVA," presented by David E. Lilienthal and approved by the TVA board, March 18, 1935 (in the files of TVA).

[38] "Funds" was used until about 1943; thereafter "revenues" was used.

gave the city credit for a municipal investment of $2,425,000, to be amortized over a twenty-year period with a 3 per cent annual return to the city on the unamortized balance. Since federal assistance was directed by Congress only to the extent necessary to supplement local revenues, this arrangement, by increasing local revenues, operates to reduce federal assistance payments and places an added burden on the system's electric ratepayers. In the words of the city manager who came on the scene later and had the advantage of hindsight, "the citizens of Oak Ridge are purchasing the electric utility from the AEC rather than receiving it by gift."[39] Officials of Oak Ridge inadvertently contributed to this result by asking TVA for the investment return as an exception, which was viewed at the time as quite an accomplishment.[40]

ACCOUNTING STANDARDS PRESCRIBED BY TVA

The Plan of Action adopted by the TVA board of directors in 1933 required the keeping of accounts according to uniform practices to be prescribed jointly by TVA, utility managers, accountants, and representatives of the cities concerned.[41] This provision, with little change, was incorporated in the 1934 contract with three cities (Knoxville, Pulaski, and Dayton), pledging each municipality:

(a) To administer its electric system as a separate department, and not to mingle funds or accounts with those of any other of its operations.

(b) To keep the general books of accounts of its electric system according to a system of accounts to be prescribed by AUTHORITY after conference with BOARD, which system of accounts will so far as possible be uniform with other systems prescribed and applied in other municipalities purchasing

[39] Letter from C. E. McMullin, city manager of Oak Ridge, to Paul Noland, chief administrative officer, Los Alamos County, New Mexico, printed in the *Oak Ridger*, Nov. 29, 1962.
[40] The mayor of Oak Ridge sought help from the executive secretary of the Tennessee Municipal League in persuading TVA to this view, and I was also asked to assist. My response was that "TVA would probably resist to the last kilowatt" any move to set up a municipal investment when in fact none existed, so I was very much surprised by TVA's action.
[41] "A Plan of Action . . . ," *loc. cit.*

electrical energy from AUTHORITY. AUTHORITY agrees at its own expense to render advisory accounting service in the setting up and administering of such accounts.

(c) To furnish promptly to AUTHORITY such operating and financial statements relating to electric system operations as may be requested by AUTHORITY.

(d) To allow the duly authorized agents of AUTHORITY to have free access to all books and records relating to electric system operations.

Minor changes in the foregoing language were made in 1935. In 1938 the last paragraph was amended to provide that if the municipal system failed to furnish financial reports promptly, TVA could collect data for such reports and charge the municipality for the costs. These basic provisions still constitute the core of this part of the standard power contract, but in 1954 the section was considerably lengthened by refinements and additional qualifications. Certain prohibitions were spelled out: furnishing, advancing, lending, pledging, or otherwise diverting electric system funds, revenues, credit, or property to other operations of a municipality; purchase or payment of, or providing security for, indebtedness or other obligations applicable to such other operations; and payment of greater than standardized or market prices for property or services from other departments of a municipality. Fiscal year reports were required by August 15, "in such form as may be requested." The words "in all respects" were added after the requirement that the electric system be administered as a separate department.

Considerable attention has been given to accounting controls. An authority outside TVA viewed "a uniform system of accounts and a uniform report" as being "indispensable and therefore . . . appropriate subjects of centralized control."[42] TVA's comptroller in 1941 listed the principal requirements of the agency's distributor accounting policies: an arm's-length relationship with other departments of a municipality; uniform accounts; uniform financial reports; and access by TVA

---

[42] E. W. Morehouse, "The New Administrative Problems of Municipal Electric Plants and Rural Cooperatives," *Proceedings: Southern Institute on Local Government*, The University of Tennessee *Record, Extension Series*, Vol. XVII, No. 1 (May, 1941), p. 22.

representatives to the books of every distributor-contractor at any time. He said the primary objective of the last requirement was not "to interfere in any way . . . [but] rather to make periodic inspections possible that will prevent difficulties arising at a later date through mistaken interpretations of the uniform accounting plan."[43] A manual of accounts published by TVA in 1942 and subsequently revised was used as a guide until 1961, when it was replaced by the Federal Power Commission's *Uniform System of Accounts Prescribed for Public Utilities and Licensees (Class A and Class B)*.

A procedure which must be fairly common practice where a power board or city government has responsibility for other utilities was approved for use by the Knoxville Utilities Board. The board's general manager explained their practice of placing billings for electricity, gas, and water on the same bill, of having one cashier collect and deposit the whole amount in a single bank account, and of maintaining separate accounting records for each utility service. The TVA board approved these procedures, both in the form of a letter[44] and in the subsequent 1948 contract, with a proviso that "strict accounting be kept of the amounts to be credited from such receipts to the electric funds, the water funds, and the gas funds, and that no payments are to be made from credits to the electric funds except on account of electric operations."

THE ROLE OF THE FIELD ACCOUNTANT

The power contracts refer to "advisory accounting service" available from TVA, but as is often the case with governmental "service" a more accurate description would be "accounting supervision." Through some fifteen central office and field accountants in the Division of Finance, TVA exercises a large degree of management control over distributors' accounting operations.

The official description of a field accountant's duties in the

[43] E. L. Kohler, "Accounting Problems," *Proceedings: Conference for Electric Distributors,* The University of Tennessee *Record, Extension Series,* Vol. XVII, No. 2 (June, 1941), pp. 20–21.

[44] Letter from Gordon R. Clapp, general manager, to Max C. Bartlett, general manager of Knoxville Utilities Board, Nov. 15, 1940 (in the files of TVA).

Distribution Accounting Section clearly indicates his key role. He reviews and analyzes accounting methods and financial practices of distributors and develops improved accounting systems, better reporting techniques, more effective systems of internal control, and "more efficient operating procedures in order to give the distributors better administrative control of their fiscal affairs." He "makes technical accounting interpretations" and "advises and consults" in the preparation of monthly and annual statements and reports. He is also assigned a key role in contract enforcement: "He analyzes power contracts and interprets them for the distributors. He will spend a considerable part of his time in analyzing accounting and financial transactions for contract violations—violations which would undermine the financial structure of the distributor or load the electric distribution system with expenses properly chargeable to other functions."

The General Accounting Office in 1955 suggested that TVA consider reducing or discontinuing the activities of this section and charging distributors for services primarily for their benefit. TVA's reply is reproduced in part below:

... field accountants are serving more and more as assistants to management in distributor relationships and contract administration rather than as accounting technicians.

... The Distributors Accounting Section discharges another important responsibility—that of reviewing compliance with the financial provisions of the distributors' contracts with TVA. ...

... Inasmuch as the work we are doing falls within the area relegated to management by the auditor, it seems clear that annual audits do not provide a substitute for the activity of TVA's field accountants.

With regard to reimbursement for accounting services, TVA is required by its power contracts to furnish such services, and it has always been understood that the distributors were paying for these services in their wholesale power bills. The alternative you suggest would require a segregation of the work between that primarily for TVA's benefit and that primarily for the distributors' benefit, a distinction that would be extremely difficult to make in specific cases and also one that would have little real significance. Both TVA and the distributors have the same aim—the widest possible distribution of electricity at the lowest possible cost—and the assurance that adequate measurements are available to determine how well this aim is being accomplished is of mutual benefit to both parties.[45]

Appendix 4, "Functions of the TVA Distributors Accounting Section," was an internal TVA memorandum prepared as a basis for writing the above letter. It conveys quite clearly the important role that this section plays in TVA's plan of contract administration. As stated in the concluding paragraph, "Perhaps their main value lies in the fact that their familiarity with the distributors' accounts, personnel, office procedures, etc., enables them to act as the eyes and ears of TVA's District Managers."

[45] Letter, Wagner to Smith, July 3, 1956, *op. cit.*

6 CONTROVERSY OVER TAX EQUIVALENTS

PAYMENTS IN LIEU OF TAXES, commonly referred to as "tax equivalents," is one of the most controversial aspects of TVA power service. Tax equivalents provide the only means of channeling any part of power revenues to general municipal purposes and consequently have been a point of prime concern to municipal officials, especially as underpayments have been common. Showers of sparks have flowed from contacts on this issue.

EARLY POLICY

When the Norris bill of 1928 for government operation of Muscle Shoals properties was being considered, Senator Black unsuccessfully tried to amend it to provide for replacement of the Alabama tax on hydrogenerated power, arguing that "the states own the streams that flow through them, and should receive taxes whenever such streams are developed."[1] The 1930 Norris bill, vetoed by President Hoover, provided for payment of 5 per cent of hydroelectric power revenues to the states of Alabama and Tennessee. A TVA staff member tells us that Senator Norris, by exempting properties used for national defense, navigation, or flood control, "successfully defended the section as a payment in lieu of the taxes that the states would collect from the power development if it were in private ownership."[2]

Senator Norris, at one point during the 1933 debate, summed

---

[1] Hershal L. Macon, TVA economist, "Payments in Lieu of State and Local Taxes," *The Southern Economic Journal*, VIII, No. 4 (April, 1942), 494.
[2] *Ibid.*

up the kind of cross-fire that he had encountered on this issue:

> Every time we have ever proposed to do anything in the way of generating electricity by any governmental instrumentality—the Federal Government, State government, county government, municipality—we have had hurled in our teeth, to begin with, "That is not fair. You do not pay taxes." That has been the argument against a bill similar to this for 12 years. "It is the Government going into business. You do not pay taxes. It is not right to come in competition with private parties," who have robbed their stockholders as well as the consumers. "You must not interfere with these men because you do not pay taxes."
>
> When we say, "We will pay what is equivalent to taxes," then the same kind of people come back, as they have today, and take just the other side, and kick because we are going to pay taxes. So it is a case of being damned if we do and damned if we don't.[3]

States and local governments were dependent upon Congress for any tax equivalents from TVA. Efforts to apply reciprocally the doctrine of taxable proprietary functions, imposed on the states by superior federal power in *South Carolina v. United States*,[4] have been unsuccessful because the federal courts refuse to recognize federal "proprietary" functions. "The general rule that the states may not hamper or control the activities of the national government is too well settled to be questioned, and is based on the latter's constitutionally declared supremacy."[5]

TVA Favors Private Utility Standard

Spokesmen for TVA in its early years echoed the views expressed by Senator Norris. Speaking to the Memphis Rotary Club prior to the referendum in that city, Lilienthal was reported as saying that the Tennessee Valley project "is not to be a government subsidy, but is to be a self-sustaining enterprise

---

[3] U. S., *Congressional Record*, 73d Cong., 1st Sess., 1933, LXXVII, Part 3, 2682-83.
[4] 199 U. S. 437 (1905). This case held that state-owned liquor stores were subject to taxation by the federal government.
[5] "State Taxation and Regulation of the Tennessee Valley Authority," *Yale Law Journal*, XLIV, No. 2 (Dec., 1934), 334.

whose operating expenses will include all of the costs to which a privately operated utility is subjected, even to taxes and interest, although no bonds are to be issued against its construction. In that way the Authority hopes to make the public operation a yardstick by which to measure the fairness of electric rates."[6]

On another occasion Lilienthal stated that "electric consumers in their rates pay into the general treasury an amount equivalent to every kind and description of taxes, property taxes, sales taxes, etc."[7] Appearing before the Alabama Public Service Commission, he said that "the Authority would not pay State and local taxes but would pay equivalent amounts, not as taxes but as a matter of 'policy.'"[8] Before a congressional committee, he testified: "Interest was figured at 3½ per cent. Taxes were figured at 12½ per cent of gross revenues, 'because this was the percentage of gross revenues paid in taxes by private utilities throughout the country.'"[9]

The 1938 congressional investigation of TVA disclosed that the Authority's planned tax provision "of 12½ per cent of the cost of power, when added to the provision in the retail rates, will give tax costs to ultimate consumers of approximately 13.74 per cent of the gross revenues provided by these consumers, as compared to 13.84 per cent for the 15 private companies operating partially or entirely within the Tennessee Valley in the year 1936."[10] Lilienthal, in the course of this investigation, after defending the 3½ per cent rate of interest used by TVA in its rate calculations against the utility industry's average cost of 5½ per cent, commented "about the question of taxes": "I should not say that that is in the same class with cost of money or interest. It seems to me that taxes are something that are

[6] *Wall Street Journal*, Oct. 18, 1933.
[7] David Lilienthal, "Figures Show TVA's Electricity Plan Works," address before a joint meeting of the American Society of Mechanical Engineers and the Society for Promotion of Engineering Education, Norris, June 22, 1935 (MS in TVA Technical Library, Knoxville).
[8] *New York Times*, Oct. 11, 1934, p. 35.
[9] *Electrical World*, CX, No. 5 (July 30, 1938), 41.
[10] U. S., Congress, Special Joint Committee, *Report of the Joint Committee on the Investigation of the Tennessee Valley Authority*, 76th Cong., 1st Sess., 1939, Senate Doc. 56, Part 3, Appendix B, *Report of Chief Engineer*, pp. 227, 233.

going to have to be paid. The cost of government goes on and my view would be that as nearly as possible the rate computations should include some effort to equate that difference."[11]

TVA Opposes Private Utility Standard

A different tack was taken, however, as the congressional climate changed—as the need for politically justifying the creation and existence of TVA gave way to the urgent need for appropriations to expand and operate the power system. During congressional consideration of a bill to provide funds for purchase of the Tennessee Electric Power Company, an amendment was offered to replace Tennessee's annual tax loss, estimated by the Tennessee Taxpayers Association at over $3.5 million. Speaking on the proposed amendment, William C. Fitts, Jr., TVA general counsel from 1939 to 1944, objected to "the rule that these properties shall pay the same tax as they paid in private ownership" as being "fundamentally wrong." His view was that since the TVA power system "has been financed by the Federal taxpayer [he] has a right to expect that part of that, at least, shall be paid back to him from the revenues which will be produced by the power sold."

Fitts estimated that "revenues from the sale of power will be sufficient to pay all of the power cost, including interest and depreciation on that part of the investment that is allocated to power, and leave over and above that a margin of approximately 20 per cent of the total receipts." With 5 per cent of that margin going to the states of Alabama and Tennessee, he saw the primary question as being "simply this: How much, if any, of that remaining 15 per cent margin is to be taken from the Federal Treasury and paid to the States and local communities." He considered this point critical because the entire improvement had been financed by the federal government, and "we all know that those funds have come from the Federal taxpayers."[12] (The 1959 TVA self-financing act required pay-

---

[11] U. S., Congress, Special Joint Committee, *Hearings, Investigation of the Tennessee Valley Authority*, 75th Cong., 3d Sess., 1938, Part 2, p. 947.

[12] U. S., Congress, House, Subcommittee of the Committee on Military Affairs, *Hearings, on S. 1796*, 76th Cong., 1st Sess., 1939, pp. 312–13, 317. Hereinafter referred to as *1939 Hearings*.

ment into the federal treasury of both principal and interest on the appropriated power investment.)

Tennessee Governor Prentice Cooper, appealing for more time to study the problem and expressing confidence that TVA would take proper action, gave some support to the views expressed by Fitts: "I think that the various benefits that the Tennessee Valley Authority is rendering the people over and above what is possible to be rendered by or has been rendered by any private utility, should be considered, because there is a benefit being paid for by the taxpayers of the Nation and I think those things ought to be weighed and carefully considered, and that they ought to enter into any equitable adjustment of the tax problem."[13]

At the direction of the board of directors, Chairman H. A. Morgan wrote to the *New York Times*, in response to one of its columnists, "the fact is that the consumers are now paying in their rates a sum equivalent to the taxes previously assessed against these [distribution] systems" and explained that the theory of the TVA Act was to use power profits to liquidate a part of the cost of the navigation and flood-control program.[14] A year later two TVA officials, writing on the conduct of federal business enterprises, asserted that "even though the activity is one which produces substantial revenues, the proper measure of payments to be made to the states may or may not be the amounts which they would have received by way of taxes had the enterprise been privately conducted. Against tax losses should be balanced, to some extent at least, benefits which may result to the region through the federal enterprise."[15]

Such arguments against full payment of state and local taxes,

---

[13] *Ibid.*, p. 75.

[14] *Nashville Tennessean*, Dec. 31, 1939. The "theory" proved to be an unsound one. The federal government has done well to provide for recovery of the appropriated power investment; repayments of principal began in 1948, and the first interest payments were made in 1961. Recovery of federal funds committed to the other phases of the TVA multiple-purpose program would not be good public policy, considering the expenditures of the federal government for similar projects in other parts of the country, but it was apparently thought necessary to attempt such a justification for TVA in those days.

[15] David E. Lilienthal and Robert H. Marquis, "The Conduct of Business Enterprises by the Federal Government," *Harvard Law Review*, LIV, No. 4 (Feb., 1941), 599–600.

based on the premise that federal taxpayers had provided funds for the TVA experiment, contrast sharply with the later, frequent assertions of TVA spokesmen that the TVA power system is completely self-supporting and has received no tax subsidy. Interest alone on the power investment in 1961 was over $41 million, the first year of a payment to the federal treasury equal to the average rate on marketable U.S. debt obligations. The cumulative (unpaid by TVA) interest on the power investment for the preceding quarter of a century would amount to a much larger sum. Federal funds for TVA were obtained either by borrowing or taxation; hence the former interest on the TVA power investment was borne, not by revenue collected from TVA power customers, but by federal taxpayers. (TVA has tried to refute this argument by pointing to the "return earned on the power investment," but prior to 1961 not a cent of this was paid into the federal treasury to ease the aforementioned financial burden—all was retained by TVA and used for its own purposes.)

TVA and Power Agencies as Tax Collectors

Fitts, at one point during the 1940 hearings, conceded that there was some merit in the states' position that TVA was only a tax collector and that the taxes included in the rate base, admitted by TVA's own spokesmen, should be remitted to the states rather than being retained as profits by TVA.[16]

Following a suggestion by the chairman of the Wisconsin Public Service Commission that it would be desirable "if publicly owned utilities were brought into the tax fold and required to bear their share of the cost of government the same as privately owned utilities," *Electrical World* editorially asserted that the issue was not whether "government projects should pay the same as privately owned properties" but was that customers should not be discriminated against. Since utilities simply collect taxes for governments, "the Knoxville customer, for instance, . . . has no right to escape the payment of his share of the cost of government no matter how assessed."[17]

---

[16] U. S., Congress, House, Committee on Military Affairs, *Hearings, on H. R. 5068, H. R. 3822, H. R. 2741, H. R. 4640, and H. R. 4094*, 76th Cong., 3d Sess., 1940, p. 210. Hereinafter referred to as *1940 Hearings*.
[17] CXXII, No. 22 (Nov. 25, 1944), 82.

At one time the TVA board of directors declared that this was "clearly a matter for local determination" and that the "question as to whether the states and counties should recapture their portion of these payments is one of state policy that can be solved only by state legislation." The TVA board saw this as "clearly . . . neither a TVA nor a Federal problem."[18]

The Tennessee governor, Prentice Cooper, likewise suggested that the state "could save two-thirds of the situation by passing our own proper legislation to tax the municipalities and other governmental subdivisions . . . and we think that we will be entirely safe in taking that view."[19] In the same vein, Fitts declared that this was "purely a question of State public policy" and that "it would be improper for Congress to assume to legislate on that subject."[20]

Thus, the issues were further confused by the attempt to pass the buck back to the states. If the taxes were in the rates, why should TVA have objected to acting voluntarily as the collecting and paying agency? One reason given for not doing so was that the federal government should share in the profits. However, Congress took another look at the problem and undertook to deal realistically with state and local tax claims.

THE SECTION 13 AMENDMENT

In 1940, when the issue was tax replacement alone instead of the preceding year's prime issue of appropriating funds to purchase the private utility systems in the state, Governor Cooper sang a different tune from the one he had sung in 1939:

> We have been deriving something in the neighborhood of $700,000 a year from the utilities, from privilege taxes. . . . this bill as written requires that we give up every penny of our privilege taxes. . . . It is going to cost the State of Tennessee more to educate the new families that come in; they have to pay more for police protection, and all of the multiple services delivered by the State government will increase. . . .
> We are hard pressed to try to find some source of revenue,

[18] Letter from H. A. Morgan, chairman of the board, to the *New York Times*, reprinted in part in the *Nashville Tennessean*, Dec. 31, 1939.
[19] *1939 Hearings, op. cit.*, p. 82.
[20] *Ibid.*, p. 309.

and here this bill comes along and proposes to take away 100 per cent of our revenue that we have heretofore derived from public utilities which were always regarded as a legitimate source of tax, and you take them all from us. And, as head of the State Government of Tennessee, I ask that the Congress and this committee restore half of the lost revenue.[21]

Fitts replied to the governor by pointing out that "57 per cent of the properties we are talking about . . . are owned by State agencies [municipalities and cooperatives] that are still subject to State taxation." Previous spokesmen for TVA had said such taxes were in the rates, but he said such payments to the states would require "Congress to authorize the T.V.A. to pay that out of its revenues that it derives from the sale of power."[22]

Lilienthal also retreated from his earlier position that TVA would pay amounts equivalent to state and local taxes. When asked whether the full national average of private utility taxes used in rate construction would be a better standard than the proposed sliding scale, beginning with 10 per cent of power revenues and dropping to 5 per cent after eight years, he responded:

it is obviously a question of policy for the committee as to whether it desires to pay back such an amount to the States. Our position in dealing with the States has been that the surplus of the T.V.A. ought to be divided equitably between the States and the Federal Government. . . . the purpose of the bill . . . is an effort to replace, in part, revenues which have been received by local bodies from private property, either land or public-utility structures, which have been subject to taxes.[23]

The House Military Affairs Committee refused to approve the amendment but it was enacted by Congress as a rider to the Emergency Relief Appropriation Act for 1941.[24] The only significant change from the original TVA proposal was a requirement of direct payments to counties equal to "the two-year

---

[21] *1940 Hearings, op. cit.*, pp. 38, 47, 48.
[22] *Ibid.*, pp. 210, 212.
[23] *Ibid.*, pp. 441, 447.
[24] U. S., *Statutes at Large*, LIV, Part 1, 626-27, amending Section 13 of the TVA Act. The committee chairman was Andrew Mays of Kentucky, who vigorously opposed TVA as a threat to his state's coal industry.

average of county ad valorem property taxes (including taxes levied by taxing districts within the respective counties) upon power property and reservoir lands allocable to power," but such amounts are deducted from total amounts due the states. The amount due each state was fixed at a percentage of gross power proceeds, starting with 10 per cent in 1941 and decreasing each year to 5 per cent for 1949 and each year thereafter. "Gross proceeds" was defined to exclude "power used by the Corporation or sold or delivered to any other department or agency of the Government of the United States for any purpose other than the resale thereof." Each annual payment is allocated among the states, one-half in proportion to the location of power property and one-half in proportion to power sales by states. A minimum annual payment of $10,000 was fixed for any state in which the Authority "owns and operates power property." Lilienthal testified that "the point in decreasing that percentage was to maintain the estimated tax payment at a constant level."[25]

TVA OPPOSITION TO TAXES ON ITS POWER

The early TVA position that the taxation of municipal electric systems was a state matter and not a TVA problem was keyed to the Authority's need to gain political acceptance. As the political climate became more favorable, the policy shifted to one of keeping taxes on TVA electricity as low as possible. Any tax is viewed as a threat to low-cost power, and largely as a result of TVA insistence electricity has enjoyed a special tax status. Power consumers have received the benefits of both low power rates and low taxes. In many areas of the country utility services have been considered legitimate objects of taxation, but TVA argues that electricity, as a precious commodity for development of the Valley,[26] should be favored to keep its price low. TVA has used its influence to modify or defeat state

---

[25] *1940 Hearings, op. cit.*, p. 443.
[26] TVA's assumption that low power rates are decisive in industrial development, except for industries that use great quantities of electric power, is questionable. See: John R. Moore (ed.), *The Economic Impact of TVA* (Knoxville: The University of Tennessee Press, 1967), pp. 4–9, 74–75, 129, where two economists and a political scientist question the validity of the assumption. An article, "Bank Deposit Growth and Income Changes in the Southeast," in the *Monthly Review* (published by the

tax programs and to keep many local tax equivalents below adequate levels.

In 1950 the Tennessee Stream Pollution Study Commission recommended that municipalities be required to construct sewage treatment plants and listed fourteen cities where such action was needed within the next five years, at an estimated cost of $29 million. To finance such undertakings the commission recommended that the state grant to its municipalities, "subject to the approval of the voters in each community," the right to impose three types of taxes: "(1) an increase in the sales tax, (2) a utilities tax, and (3) a gross wage tax."[27] The Tennessee Municipal League "agreed to lend its full support to . . . the Commission's recommendations."[28]

A proposal to authorize a 5 per cent tax on utility bills grew out of the recommendations. An outcry was immediately heard from power interests. The proposal was seen as something which "might imperil the whole Tennessee Valley Authority program of cheap power." A spokesman for TVPPA, vowing a fight "to the last ditch" against any tax on power bills, saw it as compromising "the whole basic structure of TVA rates and TVA's contractual [sic] relations with state and city governments and REA co-operatives." He asserted that it was inconsistent with the basic TVA theory that "raising the economic level of our region is based upon the lowest possible charge for electric power" and characterized the proposal as "silly business."[29]

The chairman of the joint legislative council representing all organized labor groups in the state said the tax would help to achieve the objective of private power companies to cripple TVA, and that in effect "a tax on power bills would simply amount to an increase in power rates charged the consumer."[30]

Federal Reserve Bank of Atlanta), April, 1969, pp. 50–52, shows that among six states (Alabama, Florida, Georgia, Louisiana, Mississippi, Tennessee) Tennessee has been near the bottom in growth of personal income and bank deposits since 1946.

[27] Quoted in *Tennessee Town & City*, I, No. 12 (Dec., 1950), 2.
[28] *Ibid.*
[29] *Nashville Tennessean*, Dec. 15, 1950. Although most of the opposition here reported came from sources outside TVA, they reflected TVA's views. Part of the genius of TVA has been inducing others to fight its battles.
[30] *Ibid.*, Jan. 5, 1951.

State Representative-elect Harry Mansfield declared that "eternal vigilance" must be kept "lest those who would sacrifice TVA and the public power movement to satisfy their lust and greed, will sneak in under the guise of an innocent straggler and strangle TVA and its allied agencies before they know it."[31]

Advocates of the utilities tax didn't have a chance and the proposal never received any serious legislative consideration.

The outcome was different when extension of the state's 3 per cent sales tax to electricity sales was proposed in 1963. The urgency was greater and the political support was stronger. After four years of Governor Buford Ellington's "no new taxes" program, the state had to find new revenues to meet its expanding needs. Governor Frank Clement recommended that the 3 per cent tax be extended to charges for lodging, most personal services, and all utility bills. The reaction of power interests ran true to form. The executive secretary of TVPPA, noting that his organization continuously during its existence had "been preaching low rates and high usage of electricity," declared that "the imposition of a sales tax on electric bills is the same thing as raising our rates 3 percent."[32] A columnist wrote, "The private power trust could not have done better than did Governor Frank Clement, to strike a blow at TVA with his plan to put a sales tax on electric power."[33]

TVA registered a mild protest, apparently bowing to the inevitable: " 'We are conscious of the problems involved in raising the tax revenues necessary to support continued progress and services in the state,' [Chairman Aubrey J.] Wagner said. He added: 'However, we regret the necessity for recommending extension of the sales tax to the cost of electric energy, since low-cost electricity is in itself a vital factor in the economic progress of the region.' "[34] TVA Director Frank Smith later stated that there would have been a determined effort to block this extension to electric bills if such a tax had not already been in effect in other states.[35]

[31] *Chattanooga Times*, Dec. 22, 1950.
[32] *Nashville Tennessean*, Feb. 2, 1963.
[33] Joe Hatcher, in *ibid.*, Jan. 31, 1963.
[34] *Ibid.*
[35] At a conference in TVA's Knoxville office, Feb. 24, 1965, which I attended.

The *Nashville Banner*, however, sounded a different note: "Those who advocated treating valid revenue sources, from 'TVA power' up or down, as untouchable sacred cows, were engaging in political sophistry of the same character as those contending that it was possible to defray expanding costs without altering the tax structure."[36] Claiming that a surplus of state funds was being built up, the *Nashville Tennessean* a year later editorially declared that the "state's utility customers . . . have been soaked with an onerous tax for no reason at all." The newspaper labeled it "punitive taxation" and an "unwise precedent" of taxing TVA electricity.[37]

Many senators and representatives elected in 1964 had pledged themselves to repeal of the tax on electric bills. However, after looking at the state budget, they gave no consideration to several bills introduced in the 1965 legislative session for this purpose. In retrospect it seems strange that there would be opposition to nondiscriminatory taxation from the beneficiaries of a federal program that gives them, even with the 3 per cent tax, power rates that are less than half the national average. Far from being punitive, as charged by the *Nashville Tennessean*, this was a tax applying equally to nearly all goods and services sold in the state, and what that newspaper was really saying was that electricity should not carry its share of the tax burden. Kentucky levied a tax of 3 per cent on electricity sales, including those of TVA distributors, from 1936 until 1968, when it was increased to 5 per cent. TVA consumers have paid a similar tax in Mississippi since the exemption of municipal and cooperative systems was removed in 1958 (that state also increased its sales tax rate from 3 to 5 per cent in 1968). No reports of dire results such as predicted for Tennessee have been heard from those states.

TVA was more successful in opposing another 1963 bill, which as originally written would have authorized cities and counties to levy 1 per cent sales taxes on the same basis as the state tax. A state representative (Bill Leader) charged that exemption of TVA electricity was "a deal" made by the Clement

[36] Feb. 21, 1963.
[37] May 31, 1964.

administration to get the bill passed. He added, "if the TVA strongly opposed this bill its chances of passage would be very dim indeed." A municipal spokesman (W. C. Keaton) said the agreement on exemption was reached "after the TVA had advised us that this would violate its contractual arrangement with local distributors of its electric energy."[38]

Charles J. McCarthy, general counsel of TVA, appeared personally and argued for the exemption (a collateral effect was exemption of competitive fuels). McCarthy, when asked about the matter, stated that he had gone to Nashville at that time, at the direction of the TVA board, and had opposed inclusion of electricity on grounds that application of the bill to sales of electric power would be unconstitutional as an impairment of the obligation of contract because the power contracts prohibited municipalities from levying any taxes other than the tax equivalents prescribed in the contracts.[39] In other words, TVA's general counsel ran a very good bluff; if the bill as originally drawn had passed, existing contracts would have continued to be valid and binding, and only *future* contracts would have been affected.

In 1969 negotiations (discussed later in this chapter) TVA reversed itself by proposing removal of this exemption. However, it was opposed by the state administration and city and county leaders made no effort in this direction in the 1969 session of the General Assembly—not even introduction of a bill—because they viewed it as a hopeless cause in a legislature already on record against any new taxes. One may wonder whether TVA also gauged the political climate in the same way and thought it was safe to make the proposal.

The fiscal advantages of the 1 per cent sales tax exemption to a municipal power system are illustrated by the example of Clarksville. Montgomery County, in which Clarksville is located, in 1964 adopted the 1 per cent sales tax and reduced its property tax rate by 70 cents per $100 of assessed valuation. Clarksville concurrently reduced its property tax rate from

[38] *Chattanooga News-Free Press,* March 6, 1963.
[39] Telephone interview with McCarthy, March 26, 1965. He refrained from saying that the bill would have been unconstitutional *per se* but said only that the application of its provisions by a municipality would have been an impairment of contract. This doctrine would of course have prevented any such application under existing contracts.

$2.80 to $1.80. (It is fair to say that this is the purpose and effect of the sales tax in every case, as the property tax is the only other source of substantial revenue subject to discretionary adjustment by cities and counties.) The power system's allowable city tax equivalent was reduced by more than $24,000, and the authorized amount based on the county tax rate was diminished by more than $16,000, or a combined saving to the power system of over $40,000 for the one year. If the 1 per cent sales tax had applied to the power system revenues the tax bill would have been $15,000, which would have decreased the system's net tax savings to $25,000. And this comparison takes no account of the possibility that, without the sales tax, property tax rates could have been increased. Other municipal power systems paying full tax equivalents, as the Clarksville system was, have likewise enjoyed substantial savings by the transfer of part of their tax burden to other taxpayers.

This TVA-lobbied exemption is depriving Tennessee's cities and counties of more than $3 million annually on electricity sales alone in the seventy-seven counties and eight cities that had adopted a local sales tax by the end of June, 1969.[40] (The local rate was 1 per cent in sixty-six counties and seven cities. Eleven counties and one city, containing 37 per cent of the state's population, had adopted the higher rate of 1½ per cent authorized in 1968.) Since these estimates do not reflect the power rate increases of 1969 nor increasing power usage, the potential loss statewide at the 1½ per cent rate would exceed $6 million—at least $4.5 million on electricity sales and more than $1.5 million on competitive fuels also exempted. TVA personnel, with their single-minded concentration on lowest possible rates, no doubt view these figures as substantial savings to electric customers resulting from their efforts. The same people might also deplore the adverse effects of inadequate revenues on local governmental services, but they have stoutly opposed the idea that their product should be a taxable resource that could help to alleviate such conditions.

Questionnaire responses, summarized in Table 9, indicate

[40] This estimate of loss is based on 1967–1968 sales of electricity, except for street and outdoor lighting, by Tennessee municipal systems and cooperatives (and the two privately owned companies) serving areas wholly or substantially covered by local sales taxes.

TABLE 9
QUESTIONNAIRE RESPONSE: PROPRIETY OF EXEMPTING ELECTRICITY
SALES FROM LOCAL OPTION SALES TAX*

Respondents	No Opinion No.	Per cent	Agree No.	Per cent	Disagree No.	Per cent
General city government officials	17	12%	72	50%	55	38%
Power system officials	14	10%	94	68%	30	22%
Totals	31	11%	166	59%	85	30%

* Question: "The 1963 Local Option Revenue Act exempted electric power from imposition of a 1% local sales tax by vote of the people. In your opinion was this exemption justified? (Please try to confine your opinion to whether *the exemption* was justified—not your opinion as to whether a 1% local sales tax is desirable; in other words, assuming that such a tax is voted by the people, do you think that electricity should be exempted?)"

that 50 per cent of municipal officials and 68 per cent of power system officials approved exempting the power systems from the local sales tax. For the two groups of officials combined, 41 per cent were either opposed to the exemption or expressed no opinion.

COMPARATIVE TAX DATA

Sensitive to the criticism that TVA power is not taxed equally with private power, the Authority has used various comparisons in attempts to counter such arguments. For a number of years tax equivalents were compared with the dollar amount formerly paid in taxes by power companies. Commenting editorially on a TVA release that the agency and its distributors in 1955 had paid in tax equivalents "approximately $6,960,000 more than former property taxes on all reservoir lands and on all privately owned power properties acquired by TVA and the distributors," the *Knoxville Journal* pointed out the fallacy in this type of comparison: it overlooks general increases in the assessment level of all real estate and improvements that unquestionably would have occurred under private ownership in the intervening years.[41]

Hershal Macon years ago suggested that a "percentage of

[41] *Knoxville Journal*, June 4, 1955.

gross revenues appears to afford a practical method for relating such a payment to the extent of the operations in question and for shifting the charge to the consumers."[42] This has come to be the measure most used by TVA for comparative purposes.

The measure is sometimes applied to sales of distributors only—e.g., this statement in a TVA report: ". . . the distributors' customers paid a total of $29.4 million in their electric power bills, or 7.9 cents out of every dollar paid for electricity. By comparison, the state and local taxes paid by the customers of privately owned electric systems bordering TVA ranged from 3.9 to 10.3 cents of each dollar paid for electricity, and averaged 8.3 cents."[43]

A more comprehensive comparison can be made, based on total sales of TVA power except to federal agencies, including TVA's sales directly to industries which are subject only to the Authority's tax equivalents at the rate of 5 per cent of gross sales. On this basis the total for the entire TVA system in fiscal year 1968 was 7.1 per cent[44] and for Tennessee alone was 8.0 per cent. In the calendar year 1967, twelve privately owned companies[45] serving the area surrounding TVA paid in state and local taxes an average of 8.3 per cent of their gross revenues. Although the spread for these twelve companies was 3.9 to 10.3 per cent,[46] only two of these (both Kentucky companies at 3.9 and 4.0) were under 6.7 per cent, six exceeded 8.8 per cent, and the remaining four fell in the range of 6.7 to 8.4 per cent.[47]

TVA likes to use the gross revenues basis because its extremely low rates produce lower revenues as compared with

[42] Macon, "Payments in Lieu of . . . Taxes," op. cit., p. 500.
[43] Tennessee Valley Authority, *1968 Operations: Municipal and Cooperative Distributors of TVA Power* (Knoxville: Tennessee Valley Authority, 1968), p. 9.
[44] Tennessee Valley Authority, *Power Annual Report 1968* (Knoxville: Tennessee Valley Authority, 1968), p. 6.
[45] Alabama Power Company, Appalachian Electric Power Company, Arkansas Power & Light Company, Carolina Power & Light Company, Duke Power Company, Georgia Power Company, Kentucky Utilities Company, Kingsport Power Company, Louisville Gas & Electric Company, Mississippi Power Company, Mississippi Power & Light Company, and South Carolina Electric & Gas Company.
[46] Tennessee Valley Authority, *Power Annual Report 1968*, op. cit., p. 6.
[47] From a compilation of data supplied by C. M. Stephenson, TVA Regional Studies Staff, Knoxville.

deliveries of comparable power by the twelve private companies. TVA's retail rates for residential uses are estimated to be roughly one-half of the rates charged by neighboring private companies;[48] therefore, an equal percentage of gross sales in the TVA system represents delivery of double the quantity of electricity delivered by the private companies. In terms of standards of living—conveniences of washing and drying clothes, the comforts of home heating and air conditioning, cooking, freezing foods, etc., which surely are the considerations that really matter instead of the amount of money that changes hands—the TVA consumer is paying only half as much in taxes as his privately served neighbor *if the percentages of gross sales are the same.*

The factor of TVA's unusually low rates can be eliminated, and the real benefits of electric power reflected, by making comparisons on a basis of taxes paid per kilowatt-hour. (TVA always uses this basis for comparing power rates.) In 1967 customers of the twelve private companies paid an average of .99 mill per kilowatt-hour in state and local taxes. The comparable average in fiscal year 1968 for all of TVA's customers except federal agencies was .54 mill. Customers of all TVA municipal distributors paid an average of .73 mill, and customers of municipal systems in Tennessee only (excluding the three county-owned systems) paid an average of .80 mill. Applying the 1969 settlement for Tennessee municipal systems except the four largest to 1968 fiscal year data indicates .92 mill per kilowatt-hour with minimum payments in effect and only .78 mill without minimum payments.

It should also be noted that these policies have the effect of giving a tax subsidy to large industries served directly by TVA. Such sales, subject only to the Authority's 5 per cent payment, constituted 23.4 per cent of TVA's total sales in fiscal year 1968. The difference between 5 per cent and the private companies'

---

[48] This was the comparison made by H. N. Stroud, Jr., chief, Distributor Marketing Branch, Office of Power, at a meeting in Clinton, June 15, 1965, which I attended. TVA news releases on the 1967 rate hike and the pending rate increases announced in Oct., 1968, also stated that residential rates would continue to be less than half of the national average. Commercial and industrial rates are relatively somewhat higher—possibly about two-thirds of the private companies' rates.

average of 8.3 per cent, on TVA's direct industrial sales of $84.2 million in that year, is $2,778,600.

MUNICIPAL TAX EQUIVALENTS

Initially, TVA contracts with distributors, reflecting the emphasis on comparisons with private power systems, provided "for taxes at rates equivalent to the taxes assessed against other property of a similar nature." Various pronouncements indicated that this would be the general policy to be followed by TVA. Lilienthal reported that the municipal system of Athens, Alabama, had 20 per cent more total revenues and 4.5 per cent lower rates in May of 1935 compared with May, 1934, after paying all expenses, including "every nickel of taxes which a private utility would pay.... These taxes the municipal utility is required to pay under its contract with TVA under a specific formula set out in that contract."[49] This statement came very soon after the TVA board had adopted, on March 18, 1935, a "Statement of Financial and Accounting Policy Proposed for Adoption by Municipalities Owning Electric Systems for Purchase of Power from the TVA," which included the following:

(a) The prevailing city property tax rate shall be applied to the value of the property used in electric operations.
(b) If the electric operations of the city are not subject to county and state taxation, the tax equivalent paid to the city under (a) above shall be increased by application of the county and state tax rates to the value of the electric system....
(c) If there is in effect in the state in which the municipality is located a sales tax applicable to privately owned electric systems, and such tax is not applicable to municipally owned electric systems, an amount equivalent to the application of such sales tax to the revenues of the municipal electric system may be paid to the city in addition to the tax equivalent payments set forth above.

TVA in 1938 reported that each "electric system also contributes to the cost of local government in the same manner as

[49] Lilienthal, "Figures Show TVA's Electricity Plan Works," *loc. cit.*

if the city were served by privately owned public utilities."[50] The 1938 congressional investigating committee likewise found that "wholesale power contracts with municipal electric systems . . . provide that municipal electric departments shall make 'in lieu' payments to the municipal treasury . . . by applying the ad valorem tax rates for the city, county, and State," and that in "some cases additional items such as State sales taxes are also included."[51] By 1940, however, Lilienthal had shifted to a view that this was not a binding contractual obligation but was a matter to be dealt with by state law.[52] The use of "shall" in the power contracts with respect to such payments was also discontinued about 1940, and "may take" was substituted.

TVA has pointed out that the book value of electric properties, under its prescribed accounting system, is higher than the general level of property assessments determined by local assessors for other types of property. It has at times conceded that this higher level is justified to compensate for nonproperty taxes customarily paid by utilities. TVA advanced the argument in 1952 that its power contract "permits a tax base averaging more than twice as high as the 36.7 per cent assessed valuation of the privately owned power companies" and that this "more than compensates for the franchise and other miscellaneous State and local taxes paid by private companies."[53]

It is important to note that in the foregoing comparison TVA used "maximum" amounts based on a "tax base" which the TVA power contract "permits" but does not require. In actual practice, payments have been below this level. Average payments by all Tennessee municipal systems fell from 73 per cent of the maximum level in 1961 to 68 per cent in 1964. The average increased to 76 per cent in 1966 and 74 per cent in 1967, largely the result of an extremely low maximum imposed on Memphis, which re-entered the TVA system in 1965. Adjusting

[50] *TVA Annual Report for the Fiscal Year Ended June 30, 1938* (Washington, D. C.: U. S. Government Printing Office, 1939), p. 64.
[51] *Investigation*, Senate Doc. 56, *op. cit.*, p. 227.
[52] *1940 Hearings, op. cit.*, pp. 452–53.
[53] TVA Office of Power, "State and Local Taxes Paid by Electric Systems in the Tennessee Valley," pp. 4–5 (in the files of the Tennessee Municipal League).

the Memphis maximum to the standard basis of county and city tax rates applied to book value produces averages of 66 per cent in 1966 and 64 per cent in 1967.[54]

When the Tennessee Municipal League requested that the level of authorized tax equivalents be established under a new formula at 5.5 per cent of net plant value (the average maximum for all Tennessee municipal distributors in 1964), TVA refused to go above the 1960 average of 5 per cent, for reasons expressed by the TVA manager of power: "As you know, the effective ad valorem tax rate of Tennessee municipal property is generally less than 2 per cent. To allow a margin for other taxes which the electric consumer might properly bear, the upper limit could conceivably be as high as 4 per cent. Thus, it was only with considerable reluctance that TVA was willing to work with your committee in developing a solution to this problem which raised this upper limit to 5 per cent."[55]

In recent years TVA has shifted on various occasions to use of property taxes only as a standard of comparison. When the small town of Newbern (pop. 2,033) reassessed its property at 100 per cent of actual value, TVA strictly applied the tax-rates formula and lowered the town's maximum tax equivalent from $7,405.86 in 1966 to $1,481.17 in 1970.[56] It appears that in this instance TVA took advantage of a small town; obviously the change eliminated any equivalence for nonproperty utility taxes.

Cleveland faced a loss of about $130,000 annually under the tax-rates formula, as a result of reductions in county and city tax rates following a countywide reassessment in 1966 at 50 per cent of full value. To avoid this loss the city governing body (the city has no power board) ordered payment at 5 per cent of the system's book value, on a basis that this was the level previously agreed to by TVA. TVA threatened suit against the city because the payments exceeded an amount arrived at

[54] Data specially prepared for the Tennessee Municipal League by the TVA Office of Power (in the files of the league).
[55] Letter from G. O. Wessenauer to Herbert J. Bingham, Aug. 6, 1964 (in the files of the Tennessee Municipal League).
[56] Letter from L. J. Van Mol to Mayor E. A. Nichols, Dec. 14, 1966, approved as contract amendment by TVA board Feb. 9, 1967 (in the files of TVA).

by applying the lowered tax rates. It is an open question whether the system's book value exceeded 50 per cent of its "full value" (involving all the difficulties of determining "full value" of an electric utility), but any excess certainly would have produced less than the customary nonproperty taxes paid by electric utilities.

Knoxville's charter empowers the city's director of finance to fix an assessment for payment of a tax equivalent by the power system. A journalist reported that the city's practice has been to "first apply the local assessment rate to the book value and then apply the tax rate, making the utility payments at the same rate as payments on other property."[57]

Which Municipal Agency Is Responsible?

In many cases power boards have unilaterally determined the amounts of tax equivalents to be paid by power systems. Sometimes they have consulted with and have been influenced by municipal officials, but the decisions have been theirs. The standard power contract simply specifies that "municipality may take" and does not mention which agency is to act for the municipality, which is proper because the powers of municipal agencies should be determined by state law. Provisions of the general law (prior to 1969), to which most private acts conform, is the basis of the following analysis.

Such unilateral action by power boards has apparently developed from a liberal construction of the provisions empowering the "supervisory body [to] make all determinations as to improvements, rates and financial practices . . . [and to] disburse all moneys available in the electric plant fund hereinafter established. . . ."[58] However, there is another provision of the same law that may be construed as specifically vesting this authority in the governing body of a municipality. This section directs the supervisory body to distribute money in the electric plant fund for certain purposes, and "if the governing body of the municipality shall by resolution so request, payments to the municipality in lieu of ad valorem taxes on the property of the electric plant within the corporate or county

[57] Dudley Brewer, in the *Knoxville Journal*, May 31, 1960.
[58] *Public Acts of Tennessee, 1935*, ch. 32, codified in *Tennessee Code*, secs. 6–1514 and 6–1515.

limits of the municipality not to exceed the amount of taxes payable on privately owned property of a similar nature."[59]

Under a resolution by a municipal governing body requesting tax equivalent payments equal to the amount of taxes on the property if it were privately owned, it seems that the power board would have been required to make such payments providing sufficient revenues are available. The law clearly directed payment "to the municipality" and not to taxing jurisdictions (as in the Kentucky law). The nub of the question is whether a power board possessed statutory powers to resist such a resolution and to unilaterally exercise discretionary power to determine the amount to be paid and the availability of funds for this purpose.

The law did not unequivocally empower a specific municipal agency to make this determination. However, application of collateral facts and general principles of municipal law would seem to support the case for the governing body of a city. At the time the law was enacted (1935), TVA spokesmen, state legislative leaders, and municipal officials almost with one voice were emphasizing that the publicly owned systems that were replacing the privately owned systems would pay the same amounts in tax equivalents as would be paid under private ownership. The obvious intent of the legislature was to delegate to each municipality the determination of policy in this respect. If this be so, to which agency would the legislature logically delegate such authority—to the governing body elected by the voters and traditionally responsible for policy-making, or to an appointive power board with a specialized interest?

A provision of the act, "corporate or county limits of the municipality," could have limited the application of city and county tax rates to power property within a municipality. This issue was raised in a suit filed in 1959 by Washington County as a customer of the Johnson City power system, which had been paying tax equivalents to the city based on county tax rates, but the case did not come to trial.[60] The argument against

---

[59] Ibid., codified in *Tennessee Code*, sec. 6–1530.

[60] Probably because the city attorney pointed out that even if the county should be successful it would only reduce the amount that could be paid to the city, because there is nothing in the act to require any payments to

such payments was that the act defines "municipality" to mean any county or city, that "corporate" refers to a city-owned system and limits the base to properties within the city limits, and that "county" refers to a county-owned system. Such an interpretation would be contrary to the concept of payments to the municipality equal to the "taxes payable on privately owned property of a similar nature." Even an excessively literal interpretation, though, could have excluded only property outside city limits, because both city and county ad valorem property taxes apply to property within a city, and the law most certainly did not specify *municipal* ad valorem taxes as a maximum. TVA attorneys, however, in 1967 filed a brief in a lower court against the city of LaFollette contending on the basis of this law that the upper limit is the municipal tax rate applied to a system's book value within a city; the point was not judicially settled, as the case was dismissed after an out-of-court compromise was reached.

At a conference of city, county, and TVA officials in 1965 to consider a proposed new formula for tax equivalents, the TVA board chairman seemed to assume that a power board should determine amounts but suggested remedial action if necessary:

> Hobday [the author]: How can TVA give any assurances on tax equivalents to be paid when determination of amounts is discretionary with local power boards?
> Wessenauer [TVA manager of power]: That is a local matter.
> Wagner [TVA board chairman]: We will get nowhere if we sit here and act like antagonists. We must undertake to work out a reasonable formula, and we cannot sit here and master-mind this for everybody. If a local power board is paying tax equivalents that are too low, the remedy is up to the electorate.[61]

The chairman did not elaborate as to just what "remedy" the electorate has over an appointive power board that is insulated from politics and kept at arm's length from the politicians.

A 1935 general law, enacted after adoption of the Municipal

---

the county. Finally, in 1966 by agreement of the parties the case was dismissed.

[61] From my notes on the conference.

Electric Plant Law of 1935, empowers "any municipal corporation, county, city or town" to enter into contracts with TVA and specifically allocates to governing bodies the authority to determine major policies. It authorizes a municipality "to stipulate and agree to such convenants, terms and conditions as *the governing body thereof may deem appropriate* [emphasis added], including but without limitation, covenants, terms and conditions in respect to the resale rates, financial and accounting methods, services, operation and maintenance practices and the manner of disposing of the revenues, of any such system. . . ."[62]

The first draft of a bill prepared by TVA in 1962, at the request of the Tennessee Municipal League and the Tennessee County Services Association, included provisions that the amounts in lieu of taxes were to represent, "in the judgment of the supervisory body [power board], the fair share of the cost of government properly to be borne" by the electric system, and that "the total amount to be actually transferred to municipality's general funds for each fiscal year shall be determined by the supervisory body." In a second draft TVA added the words "and municipality" after "supervisory body," but requiring such a joint decision would still have given a power board effective control. Several subsequent drafts of the bill, prepared by the Tennessee Municipal League, simply provided that "the municipality" would make such determinations, the effect of which would probably have been to give this power to a municipality's governing body only. In 1969 TVA, in a redraft of the bill, again inserted "in the judgment of the supervisory body and the municipality's governing body." As a part of a compromise settlement the final language as enacted into law by the 1969 General Assembly[63] was: "in the judgment of the municipality's governing body, after consultation with the municipality's supervisory body." This act also removed the doubtful point mentioned above by affirming that the plant value of a power system lying outside of a city's corporate limits will be included in the base for tax equivalents.

---

[62] *Public Acts of Tennessee, 1935*, ch. 37, codified in *Tennessee Code*, secs. 6-1535–6-1537.
[63] *Public Acts of Tennessee, 1969*, ch. 237.

Tax-Equivalent Base

TVA's standard power contract provides for a tax equivalent representing "a fair share of the cost of government properly to be borne by such system." One might wonder how such a nebulous standard can be applied. However, TVA's chief power attorney has stated that it is not a "meaningless phrase" and that a case may arise where the Authority would argue that the tax-rate formula produces tax equivalents in excess of a "fair share," measured by comparisons with taxes paid by other utilities, and under such conditions TVA would go into court if necessary to enforce the standard.[64] This argument was made in a 1967 TVA brief in the LaFollette case, which was settled out of court.

The first contracts provided for tax equivalents equal to taxes that would be paid on the systems if privately owned. Beginning in 1935 book value was established as the base for computing authorized tax equivalents, and until 1944 the contracts defined book value as "the actual historical cost of the property then in use or useful in the distribution of electricity as shown on the books, including reasonable spare capacity for expansion and reasonable quantities of materials and supplies less accrued depreciation, plus property under construction and a reasonable amount of cash working capital." These contracts further provided that to determine the amount of tax equivalents "the tax rate shall be applied to the value of the property as determined above plus additions, less the depreciation reserve."

Beginning about 1945, the provisions were changed to call for the application of the "property tax rate to the value of the property used in electric operations," which was defined to mean "the book cost of the tangible plant attributable to the system . . . less the proportion of the depreciation reserve properly allocable thereto." This base persisted through 1952.[65] The

---

[64] Telephone conversation with C. A. Reidinger, June 18, 1965.
[65] Chattanooga's charter (*Private Acts of Tennessee, 1945*, ch. 53) until 1968 included an unusual provision requiring annual changes on Jan. 1 equal to "75% of the net plant additions" during the preceding year, which were defined as "the book cost of gross additions less the original cost of property retired." Thus, all of its property went on the books

1954 revision and subsequent contracts have provided that the maximum amount of tax equivalents shall be "calculated by applying the prevailing municipal, county and State property tax rates to the depreciated original cost of tangible property used in electric operations within the respective taxing jurisdictions at the beginning of the taxable year."[66]

The change to "book cost of the tangible plant" had the effect of eliminating materials and supplies and working capital from the tax-equivalent base. The interpretation given by TVA to the provision currently in use, "the depreciated original cost of tangible property," is also that materials and supplies and working capital are excluded. There can be no question that this language excludes working capital as intangible property, but materials and supplies certainly fall within the meaning of "tangible property." With the exception of some items of equipment, TVA limits the valuation for tax-equivalent purposes to the installed plant and claims that regulations of the Federal Power Commission sustain this interpretation. However, such regulations would not seem to override specific provisions of contracts nor obscure the fact that systems have variable amounts of tangible property in the form of materials and supplies which should be in the tax-equivalent base. The exclusion of these properties lowers the tax-equivalent base below the standards used by the Tennessee Public Service Commission, which assesses private companies for their materials and supplies.[67]

The total value of materials and supplies held by municipal electric systems in Tennessee in 1968 was $10,832,777—2.4 per

---

initially, for tax-equivalent purposes, at a depreciated figure (75 per cent) but was not subject to further depreciation no matter how long retained in the system. This act was repealed by ch. 310 of the *1968 Private Acts*.

[66] It is worthy of note that few municipal systems actually keep their plant accounts in a manner to reflect the plant values within each taxing jurisdiction, e.g., within the owner-city, within any other city served, and in a county outside of the owner-city. When the need arises for such breakdowns, TVA uses various estimating factors which are considered to be reasonably valid. The TVA accounting staff checks especially thoroughly the plant accounts, and the breakdown as between city and county areas, of a municipal system that is paying full amounts of authorized tax equivalents; as payments fall below the authorized amounts, this becomes less critical.

[67] Telephone interview with Stanley J. White, Nov. 1, 1966.

cent of the total book value of these systems.[68] Inclusion of materials and supplies in the tax-equivalent base was authorized in nine contracts signed from 1937 to 1950; eight of these fixed the maximum for materials and supplies (and working capital in a few cases) at amounts ranging from $6,565 to $50,000.[69] Chattanooga scored a minor success by incorporating in a 1968 private act[70] a requirement that materials and supplies be included in the tax-equivalent base. Perhaps TVA made this concession because it had encountered opposition to other provisions of the act (this matter is discussed in Chapter 2).

Of forty-five power system managers who answered our questionnaires circulated in 1965, four reported that the tax-equivalent base included materials and supplies, and working capital (three gave the amounts: $100,000, $35,000, and $10,000), thirty-one said these were excluded, and ten failed to answer this item. In answer to another question, an additional five indicated that an allowance existed for materials and supplies only and that cash working capital was excluded. To a question designed to determine whether items of equipment are included, affirmative answers were received from twenty-six for motor vehicles, and twenty-four for tools; ten stated that such equipment was not included and eight made no reply.

The 1969 act (discussed later) resolved this matter by specifically including materials and supplies in a part of the tax-equivalent base.

Another point of concern for municipal officials has been that the tax-equivalent base may shrink to a low level as depreciation accrues. TVA's answer to such objections is that "a stable plant, with replacements, will average having a book value of 60 to 65 per cent of its original cost."[71] This estimate is borne out by the data in Table 10, which compares book values with original plant costs for forty-two Tennessee municipal distributors in the TVA system in 1940 (except Spring-

[68] *1968 Operations, op. cit.*, pp. 17–29.
[69] Winchester (1944), $7,000; Sevierville (1944), $6,565; Jackson (1944), $74,208; Dickson (1945), $19,000; Springfield (1945), $10,000; Tullahoma (1947), $20,000; Columbia (1949), $35,000; and Maryville (1950), $50,000.
[70] *Private Acts of Tennessee, 1968*, ch. 310.
[71] From my notes on a conference of TML and TVA officials in Knoxville, Jan. 29, 1953, which I attended.

Controversy Over Tax Equivalents 199

field, which entered in 1941). The years selected for this table show the level near the time most cities came into the TVA system (1940); the effect of the shortages caused by World War II (1945); the results of the period of rapid postwar growth (1953); and the level after ten years of sustained growth at a slower rate (1963). Since economic activity and the general

TABLE 10

RELATION OF BOOK VALUES TO ORIGINAL COSTS FOR
42 TVA MUNICIPAL DISTRIBUTORS IN TENNESSEE*
1940, 1945, 1953, AND 1963

Year and class of system	Average	40–49%	50–59%	60–69%	70–79%	80–89%	90–99%
\multicolumn{8}{l}{Book value as percentage of original cost}
\multicolumn{8}{l}{Number of systems}
Urban systems (18)							
1940	93	—	2	—	—	2	14
1945	65	2	1	10	5	—	—
1953	78	—	—	5	8	5	—
1963	72	—	1	4	12	1	—
Urban and rural systems (24)							
1940	96	—	—	2	2	5	15
1945	85	—	2	11	10	1	—
1953	78	—	—	—	14	10	—
1963	74	—	—	14	9	1	—
All systems (42)							
1940	95	—	2	2	2	7	29
1945	83	2	3	21	15	1	—
1953	78	—	—	5	22	15	—
1963	74	—	1	18	21	2	—

* *Urban systems*: Athens, Brownsville, Clarksville, Cleveland, Etowah, Fayetteville, Gallatin, Humboldt, Lewisburg, Maryville, McMinnville, Murfreesboro, Newbern, Ripley, Somerville, Springfield (1941 data, its first year in TVA system), Trenton, Winchester. *Urban and rural systems*: Bolivar, Chattanooga, Clinton, Columbia, Dayton, Dickson, Harriman, Jackson, Knoxville, LaFollette, Lawrenceburg, Lenoir City, Lexington, Loudon, Milan, Mt. Pleasant, Nashville, Newport, Paris, Pulaski, Rockwood, Sevierville, Shelbyville, Sweetwater.

level of prosperity have significant effects on the expansion and replacement of electric plants, predictions as to future trends necessarily depend on such factors.

Tax-Equivalent Rates

Most municipal power contracts authorize tax equivalents computed by applying state, county, and city property tax rates to book values of the electric system. There have been exceptions to this rule.

An employee of TVA in its early period has reported a plan conceived by the TVA power staff to achieve a lower and more stable payment, based on their belief "that the payments were generally higher than they would be on a strictly tax-equivalent basis, and . . . that tax rates were manipulated by local officials to obtain a still higher payment." The plan was to stabilize the tax equivalent by using the last year or an average of recent years as a base, with variations only for "changes in plant value." These provisions were "intended to block any possibility of defeating the contract by manipulation of tax rates and assessments." He reports that the provisions were "accepted by the Board of Directors through approval of the specific contracts" but were removed subsequently by contract amendments.[72] Such a provision in Sevierville's 1939 contract was replaced by the standard formula in a 1944 amendment. Six other municipal contracts contained this type of provision for periods ranging from five to twenty years.[73]

Another type of exception resulted from low plant investments and declining book-value bases during World War II. The Murfreesboro contract of 1944, retroactively effective to 1943, specified a book-value base of $290,345, to be used until such time as the current book value would exceed $253,545, and then the excess above the latter figure would be added to the $290,345, with allowance for reductions only in case of plant disposal. Under a 1944 contract the amount of the Sevierville tax equivalent was frozen at $4,441 until such time as

[72] Ormond C. Corry, "TVA Contractual Regulation of Electric Distribution Systems" (unpublished MS, 1942, in the writer's office at the University of Tennessee, Knoxville).
[73] Springfield, 1940–1945; Clarksville, 1941–1947; Dayton, 1941–1955; Jellico, 1940–1949; Humboldt, 1942–1958; and Newport, 1939–1960.

application of the standard provision would result in a higher payment, but proportionate reductions were to be made in the event of plant disposal or tax-rate reductions. Contracts with four other municipalities in 1944 and 1945 contained a provision fixing minimum tax equivalents.[74] A 1950 contract with Maryville provided that for five years "no monthly installment shall be less than $1,800." TVA did not extend this type of provision to all distributors but added it in response to specific requests.

The 1937 contract with Trenton contained a provision not found in any other Tennessee municipal contract: "So long as the Federal Government imposes a sales tax upon private electric utilities from which MUNICIPALITY is exempt, MUNICIPALITY may take from its electric department revenues for its general funds the equivalent of such sales tax."

The 1954 revised contract required a deduction from the maximum tax equivalent of "any refunds or other benefits accruing to Municipality's non-electric operations as a consequence of any State or Federal taxes or charges upon Municipality's electric operations." In negotiations concerning a new tax-equivalent formula (discussed later) TVA agreed that this provision would be inapplicable to the portion of the state sales tax which is distributed to municipalities on a per capita basis. The receipt of this revenue in addition to full tax equivalents would be a technical violation of the contract, but TVA agreed to waive the requirement because the amounts are small and difficult or impossible to trace.

A restrictive provision still in use made its first appearance in a 1950 contract with Union City:[75]

> Municipality agrees that it will not impose any tax or other charge not expressly provided for in this contract upon the property or operations of its electric system, or upon the sale, purchase, use or consumption of electric energy supplied

[74] Jackson, at 1942 level; Winchester, $2,445; Dickson, $9,778; and Springfield, $7,323.

[75] Possibly as a result of a suggestion made by me, as a consultant to the city's officials, that enabling legislation might be obtained as a private act to permit the city to levy an excise tax on sales of electricity to consumers, which legally would not have been within the previous prohibition against taxes on the power system. A 1969 act (see n. 63) makes this restriction inapplicable to a local sales tax levied on all utilities and fuels.

thereby. In the event Municipality should impose such a tax or charge the tax equivalent which Municipality would otherwise be permitted to take under this section shall be reduced each year by the aggregate amount of the tax or charge so imposed; provided, however, that no such reduction in tax equivalent payments shall in any way prejudice the rights of Authority to enforce, by whatever means available to it, said agreement and any other provision or provisions of this contract which may be violated by the imposition of said tax or charge.

Such a levy became an issue between TVA and Tupelo, Mississippi, in 1961, when TVA served notice that it would file suit and cancel that city's contract if the proceeds from the city's sales tax were not deducted from the contract maximum. The reported response of the mayor was that "he wasn't worried and the next move was up to TVA.... the TVA contract requires a four year notice before Tupelo can be dropped off the public power system."[76] The press reported that the dispute was settled by agreement of the city to make sales tax deductions of $8,040, which were offset by a corresponding increase in tax equivalents by adding the value of warehouse and supply rooms to the electric plant value.[77] Mississippi in 1968 increased the state sales tax rate from 3 to 5 per cent, which superseded city sales taxes, but the state returns a portion to the cities which, in the case of Tupelo, exceeds the amount that had been realized from the city's own tax. TVA has not required an offset of the state-shared portion against the power system's tax equivalent paid to the city of Tupelo.

Retroactive Tax-Equivalent Payments

Tax-equivalent payments differ from taxes in that there is no concept of back taxes. Any owner of property is liable for all taxes due every year, tax liens enjoy the highest priority, and delinquent taxes for past years, with penalty and interest, are subject to collection by suit and by sale of the property if necessary. The policy is quite different for electric system tax equivalents—no matter how small the payment in any one year,

[76] *Chattanooga News-Free Press,* June 24, 1961.
[77] *Nashville Tennessean,* May 25, 1962.

TVA says that amount is final, and no collections for past years may be made.

The early policy was different, when the political climate made expedient a policy of tax equivalents equal to the taxes that private companies would pay. The 1935 contracts with three Tennessee cities provided that if the city failed "at any time" to withdraw the full amount due by reason of a return on its investment or tax equivalent, that part not withdrawn "shall be added" to the municipal investment. Contracts from 1936 to 1940 permitted such amounts to be added to the municipal investment if "needed by and used in the operation of the electric system." Beginning in 1941 and persisting through 1952, the following contract provision was inserted with respect to tax equivalents:

> In the event funds ["revenues" in some contracts] . . . for the payment of said tax equivalents are not available, the portion of the computed amount not paid shall be accrued in a separate non-interest-bearing account and shall be paid to the general funds at such time as the funds of the electric department will permit. In no case shall such accrued tax equivalents be added to Municipality's investment or in any way subjected to the payment of a return or interest.

Any claim for back payment was limited to amounts actually "accrued" as a matter of record. Otherwise, there could be no basis for making a claim under this provision. Many systems have failed to follow the admonition of TVA's comptroller: "Taxes should be accrued strictly in accord with the basis provided by the distributor's contract."[78] A 1942 contract revision with Humboldt specified that "payments in lieu of taxes or on Municipality's investment shall not be retroactive beyond January 1, 1942." A new power board in Harriman voted in 1947 to pay the city $45,174.88 in state and county replacement taxes that had not been paid for the past six years. Representatives of TVA questioned the legality of the payments as being in excess of the contract allowance and indicated that a lawsuit might be filed; the press account also reported:

[78] E. L. Kohler, "Accounting Problems," *Proceedings: Conference for Electric Distributors,* The University of Tennessee *Record, Extension Series,* Vol. XVII, No. 2 (June, 1941), p. 22.

The city council and the power board maintained that the payment was allowable under the contract and was in keeping with practices followed by other municipally-owned systems.... (The utility board has paid the city replacement tax of approximately $5000 per year ever since the TVA-Tennessee Electric Power Co. transfer and last year paid into the city treasury not only the city tax but the county and state tax as well, amounting to about $12,000. Payment of the city, county and state tax replacement into the city treasury is allowable under the TVA contract). The TVA officials maintained that the system's tax payments should be on a current basis and each payment of $5000 in previous years should be considered as "payment in full."

Mayor Harry Dillard . . . maintained that the city had continuously asked for complete tax replacement payments from the electric system and the "TVAers" asked for some documentary proof to that effect.

The TVA representatives advised the group that the electric board's system of computing the back tax payments was incorrect and the amount paid was about $6,000 in excess of that allowed under terms of their contract. Board Manager J. W. Love said he arrived at the tax on the basis of figures supplied by the TVA, though the Authority's representative denied the statement.[79]

The 1954 revision and subsequent contracts have contained this provision: "Determination of the amount to be taken in lieu of taxes for each year shall be made as early in each year as practicable and shall become final at the end of such year."

Tax Equivalents Below the Authorized Amounts

Payments by municipal power systems of less than authorized tax equivalents are partly the result of TVA efforts.[80] Table 11 shows the percentages of authorized amounts actually paid by Tennessee municipal systems, 1962–1968.

A spokesman for TVA, commenting on the payment of only 42 per cent of the authorized amount by one municipal system, argued that the authorized level might be challenged as violat-

---

[79] *Harriman Record*, April 24, 1947.

[80] Ray F. Bowen, supervisor of the distributor accounting section, in an interview March 31, 1965, stated that TVA personnel in many cases had recommended lower tax equivalents because power system book values were higher than the general level of locally assessed property.

ing the concept of "fair share of the cost of government."[81] He recommended instead a payment equal to 3.7 per cent of book value, which was the average level for all Tennessee municipal systems in 1964. The manager of TVA's eastern district on the same occasion stated that his staff had been fairly successful in encouraging agreements between governing bodies and power boards fixing tax equivalents at less than authorized levels.

It is evident that TVA, taking note of the wide differences in county and city tax rates across the state, has tried to establish some degree of equalization of tax equivalents, using as a standard the existing statewide average of amounts paid. The success it has enjoyed has largely resulted from the persuasive

TABLE 11
DISTRIBUTION OF TENNESSEE MUNICIPAL SYSTEMS
BY PERCENTAGES OF STANDARD MAXIMUM
TAX EQUIVALENTS PAID, 1962–1968

Percentage range of payments	Number of systems						
	1962	1963	1964	1965	1966	1967	1968
10–19	4	4	3	4	3	3	1
20–29	2	1	4	2	3	3	4
30–39	2	3	4	3	3	2	2
40–49	7	7	5	6	4	3	4
50–59	8	6	7	5	3	7	5
60–69		3	4	2	4	2	5
70–79	6	5	2	8	4	7	6
80–89	6	5	3	2	7	3	2
90–99	8	13	9	14	13	18	20
100 and over	15	11	17	12	15	11	10
Totals	58	58	58	58	59*	59*	59*

* Total increased by re-entry of Memphis into TVA system.
Source: Special tabulations prepared by the TVA Office of Power for the Tennessee Municipal League.

[81] H. N. Stroud, Jr., chief, Distributor Marketing Branch, Office of Power, at a joint meeting of the board of aldermen and the power board of Clinton, June 15, 1965, which I attended. A rate reduction was also recommended, estimated to save power consumers $160,000 annually. A city official stated that this was not mentioned until after the city had asked for a more adequate tax equivalent.

arguments and subtle pressures of its field staff on municipal officials and personnel of power systems.

The presentation has been different when cities were considering entry into the TVA system. TVA's feasibility reports to the cities, showing the fiscal effects of entering the TVA system, have been based on calculations showing the full amount of county and city tax rates applied to book value going into a city's general fund.[82] The former general counsel of TVA has described this practice (in connection with the Murfreesboro litigation—discussed in a subsequent section):

> TVA shares responsibility for the plight in which most of the TVA distributors in Tennessee will find themselves and cannot conscientiously remain aloof.... In many cities the decision whether to acquire an electric system to distribute TVA power ... or whether in the case of an existing system to secure power from TVA or from other sources under contracts which would not restrict payments into the city's general fund, has been based upon the availability of full tax equivalents, including that derived from the county rate.[83]

Many power boards have violated the spirit, and probably the letter, of the contract by using revenues for expansion of plant, which is assigned a lower priority in the TVA power contract, and then pleading insufficient funds to pay the authorized tax equivalents. The Greeneville system, which serves a large rural area, paid the city only $3,751 as a tax equivalent in 1951, in comparison with an authorized amount of $67,310 computed by applying city and county tax rates to the book value of plant. In 1963 this system paid $109,691 as a tax equivalent to the city.[84]

The Alcoa system's financial report for 1964 showed net earnings of $190,701, additions to electric plant of $355,430,

---

[82] Reports for Union City, Dyersburg, and Covington, cities that entered the TVA system from 1950 to 1958.

[83] Letter from Joseph C. Swidler to Herbert J. Bingham, July 30, 1959 (in the files of the Tennessee Municipal League).

[84] I consulted several times with former Mayor Clark M. Kiser (now deceased), who was chiefly responsible for the change in policy. He told me that he had considerable difficulty in persuading the power board to increase the amount and that he failed to make any real progress until he used the threat of nonappointment on incumbent members and obtained prior commitments before appointing new members to the power board.

and tax equivalents of only $22,000.[85] According to data from the TVA Office of Power, the system was authorized to pay a total tax equivalent for the year of $74,506. Prior to 1965, requests of Alcoa city officials for higher tax equivalents were declined on the grounds of insufficient funds. This has been particularly objectionable because the city of Alcoa and its county (Blount) have relatively low tax rates, and TVA in the original contract forced a rate reduction to take effect eighteen months after TVA service began.[86] In 1965 the Alcoa power board directed payment of $72,000, approximately the amount authorized by the contract, to the city.[87] However, the payment was frozen at that figure for the next three years, which, by 1968, was only 75 per cent of the contract-authorized amount of $96,444.

Nashville also took belated action to bring its tax equivalent up to the authorized amount. The city received $593,487 in 1957–1958. In the following year $1,235,207 was received, as a result, according to the press, of the city assessor's exercising his powers under the city charter to fix "the tax equivalent to be paid to the City on the basis of all the Power Board properties used in operation of the power distribution system."[88]

[85] Tax-equivalent data from the city of Alcoa; other data from the "Annual Audit Report for the Year Ended June 30, 1964," by Gillespie & Sherrod, Certified Public Accountants, Maryville.

[86] Interview with A. B. Smith, Nov. 14, 1955 (Smith was city manager at the time the contract was made). He said TVA was anxious to show immediate savings because the system owned by the Aluminum Company of America was selling power at slightly less than a nearby TVA distributor was selling to rural customers, with its added $1.00 per month amortization charge.

[87] City officials reported that the data and justification presented by Inslee Burnett, a consultant of the Municipal Technical Advisory Service, at a joint meeting of the power board and the governing body of the city were the major determinants in reaching this decision.

[88] *Nashville Banner,* July 30, 1958. The city assessor of one other city— Knoxville—also possesses such authority. Athens' charter (*Private Acts of Tennessee, 1953,* ch. 455) provides that the power board "may pay" sums equal to the taxes that would be paid if privately owned, based upon assessments made by the director of finance; the language "may pay" makes relatively meaningless the fixing of the assessment. The charter of Maryville (*Private Acts of Tennessee, 1955,* ch. 176) places the valuation function in the hands of the municipal governing body and provides that the power board "shall pay" tax equivalents—but the amount is limited to "city real and personal property taxes on the . . . electric . . . properties within the city limits."

However, increases in subsequent years were not proportionate to increased book values of the Nashville system, and by 1963 the system was paying only 80 per cent of the authorized amount. As a result of applying the tax-rates formula for the newly established Nashville-Davidson County Metropolitan Government $3,324,960 was paid in 1964 (raising the system's total payments to all taxing jurisdictions to 89 per cent of the authorized amount), but payments were frozen at that amount from 1965 to 1968, resulting in a decline to 77 per cent of the authorized amount in 1968. In these years an average of about $1 million annually from current revenues was used for capital construction. When asked by Metro officials late in 1968 to apply again the tax-rates formula, the power system's officials expressed apprehension that TVA would not permit them to do so, and indicated a desire to continue the practice of using current revenues for capital expansions. (Use of the full tax-rates formula was especially justified because the Metro government for years has assessed property at 40 per cent of full value.) Subsequently the power board proposed a compromise amount which was rejected. Metro officials pressed their case, and the power board finally agreed to pay $4,131,104 (an increase of $806,144) for 1969—about $125,000 less than the contract-authorized amount.

In 1966 new officials in Jellico found that tax-equivalent payments unilaterally determined by the power board had been about one-third of the authorized level. When the city's mayor and aldermen requested payment of the amount authorized by the power contract, which they considered especially justified because of the low level in past years, TVA sent its personnel in to try to defeat this move. According to the power board chairman, they even threatened "that when the Jellico contract expires in three years, T.V.A. would not renew the contract, but would sell power on an interim basis at a much higher figure than heretofore."[89] The mayor and aldermen held their ground, however, and, with the assistance of a new appointee who filled a vacancy on the three-member power board, successfully insisted on payment of the amount that they had

---

[89] Letter from J. W. Bealle to Mayor A. B. Foreman, July 15, 1966, published in the Jellico *Advance-Sentinel*, July 29, 1966.

requested (7.5 per cent of plant value—the authorized level was 7.9 per cent).

Fireworks at Memphis

A real hassle developed at Memphis following that city's decision to re-enter the TVA system. A power contract was entered into on January 1, 1963, providing for initial delivery of TVA power two years later and stipulating that "all obligations relating to tax equivalents shall commence with the calendar day January 1, 1965." After the city commission on June 2, 1964, voted by 3 to 1 to establish the tax-equivalent base at 90 per cent of original plant cost (which had been the basis before Memphis left the TVA system in 1958), a heated exchange of views took place in telegrams and by personal visits of the highest TVA officials to Memphis. The city correctly insisted that their action violated no provision of the power contract, but TVA vigorously maintained that it was a "breach of faith" and contrary to "assurances" that had been given by the city at the time of making the contract. TVA cited tax-equivalent data in the city's bond prospectus, and both the bond company's attorney and the lawyer for the Light, Gas and Water Division asserted that the city could assess the electric system no higher than other property, which averaged about 50 per cent of full value. After four weeks of extreme pressure, on June 29 the city commission unanimously reversed its previous action and agreed to hold to 51.4 per cent of original cost, the level of the previous "assurances."

This was especially detrimental to Memphis because its charter provides that the annual tax equivalent may not exceed the city tax rate applied to the value of the system within the city. Nearly all Tennessee city distributors, in addition to an amount thus calculated, may also take an amount based on the county tax rate applied to the countywide value of the system (sometimes shared with the county). As a result, the total tax equivalent accrued by the Memphis power system in fiscal year 1968 was only 1.3 per cent of its book value, as compared with 1968 accruals of 2.8 per cent by Knoxville, 3.4 per cent by Nashville, and 5.6 per cent by Chattanooga.

During the 1964 argument, G. O. Wessenauer, TVA manager of power, stated that the primary cause of their concern was whether TVA rates would be feasible under costs prevailing in Memphis. TVA no doubt counts it a great success that as a result Memphis has rates, under the 1969 rate adjustments, that are two levels lower than in Knoxville and Nashville and one level lower than Chattanooga's general power rate.

When Memphis faced a financial crisis early in 1968, the new thirteen-member city council, which took office in January of that year under a mayor-council charter amendment, asked for assistance from the Light, Gas and Water Division. This division determined that three years of operations and a sound financial position would justify breaking away from the 51.4 per cent level and basing the tax equivalent strictly on the power contract, which resulted in an increase of $294,995 for fiscal year 1968 over the amount that would have been paid at the 51.4 per cent level. TVA at this stage offered no objections. Whether this level can be continued is questionable, as a provision in the power contract (the only contract in Tennessee to contain such a provision) that payment of tax equivalents cannot reduce "the ratio of operating income to operating revenue below 10 per cent" may impose a lower limitation. To permit payment of only a city tax equivalent, TVA granted a one-year waiver of this limitation for the 1969 tax year. At Nashville's and Knoxville's rate level this limitation would probably not be a factor.

This is the situation if the Memphis system simply tries to pay a *city property tax equivalent only* (city and county tax rates for many years have reflected assessments at 50 per cent of full value). *Not a cent is being paid in lieu of county property taxes.* Application of the county's 1967 property tax rate of $2.21 per $100, authorized by the city's contract with TVA (subject to the 10 per cent limitation), to the system's book value of approximately $100 million would have yielded an additional $2.2 million tax-equivalent payment.

TAX EQUIVALENTS FOR COUNTIES

Except for a few private acts, until 1969 Tennessee law did not require that municipal power systems pay tax equivalents to counties or to other cities. In congressional debate prior to enactment of the TVA Act, it was assumed that distribution of tax equivalents was a state matter: "Mr. Hill: So far as counties, municipalities, and school districts are concerned, that will be a matter that the State will have to adjust and determine when the money is paid over to the State."[90]

This issue, at least partially resolved by 1969 legislation, was first raised in 1938 by the county judge of Madison County, who proposed that the city of Jackson be required to pay tax equivalents to the county. He said the law was needed because the TVA power contract authorized the city to keep "every penny the county and state have been receiving as taxes from this source."[91] The mayor of Jackson countered with the argument that city taxpayers in several respects pay county taxes for the benefit of people residing outside and that to pay tax equivalents on the power system "would either wipe out or materially reduce the amount which might be paid to the city's general fund as a tax equivalent."[92] A bill was introduced for the counties in the 1939 session, but it died in committee.

Failing to secure state legislative action, delegations of county officials placed pressure on Congress to require tax-equivalent payments to counties. Responding to this pressure, the 1940 amendment to Section 13 of the TVA Act required TVA to pay directly to counties an annual payment equal to the two-year average of county and district property taxes on TVA-purchased power company properties and reservoir land allocated to power. Congress, however, refused county demands for legislation to compel cities to pay tax equivalents to the counties, and we have an explanation from the father of the TVA Act—Senator George Norris—as to the reason:

> it was the intention of Congress, I take it, when it passed the law, or it was the intention of the T.V.A. when it made the contract to sell the power to that municipality A, that it should really be in lieu of taxes, and therefore it should be divided up when it was paid to the city, just the same as though they would have divided it up if it had been privately owned. Some of it would have gone to the State, some to a school district, and some to other subdivisions. But, as I

[90] U. S., *Congressional Record*, 73d Cong., 1st Sess., 1933, LXXVII, Part 4, 3598.
[91] *Jackson Sun*, Dec. 9, 1938.
[92] *Ibid.*, Jan. 15, 1939.

understand it, the State never passed any law requiring that division, and the Municipality, naturally, keeps it all.... While we cannot legislate on that, being a State matter, we have gone so far as to state in here that . . . it is the intention of Congress to do that very thing.[93]

The expression of intention to which Senator Norris referred was embodied in the following provision, a part of the 1940 amendment, later to become the basis of prolonged litigation between cities and counties:

Nothing herein shall be construed to limit the authority of the Corporation in its contracts for the sale of power to municipalities, to permit or provide for the resale of power at rates which may include an amount to cover tax equivalent payments to the municipality in lieu of State, county and municipal taxes upon any distribution system, or property owned by the municipality, or any agency thereof, conditioned upon a proper distribution by the municipality of any amounts collected by it in lieu of State or county taxes upon any such distribution system or property; it being the intention of Congress that either the municipality or the State in which the municipality is situated shall provide for the proper distribution to the State and county of any portion of tax equivalent so collected by the municipality in lieu of State or County taxes upon any such distribution system or property.[94]

A determined effort was made by county interests in 1941 to secure state legislation to require municipalities to share tax-equivalent payments with the counties. At the behest of the Tennessee County Judges Association a bill was introduced which also drew support from the Tennessee Taxpayers Association and organized agricultural interests. Responding to this threat, the president of the Tennessee Municipal League argued that this issue should not be considered singly and instead "a thorough study should be made of the present general inequalities of state, county and municipality [sic] taxation, and

[93] U. S., Congress, Senate, Subcommittee of the Committee on Agriculture and Forestry, *Hearings, on S. 2925*, 76th Cong., 3d Sess., 1940, p. 33.
[94] U. S., *Statutes at Large*, XIV, Part 1, 627, amending Section 13 of the TVA Act.

provisions made for remedying such inequalities."[95] The league also countered with a bill to share with municipalities the revenue from the gasoline tax of two cents per gallon distributed to counties only (at that time about $5.5 million per year). The judges' bill was labeled discriminatory because it exempted systems owned by municipalities prior to 1934 and was opposed because it would empower the Railroad and Public Utilities Commission to make the assessments instead of relying on book values as provided in TVA power contracts. The session ended without either of these bills coming to a vote.

TVA in 1952 found that "only 11 municipal power systems in Tennessee made payments in lieu of taxes to the counties in which they held property. Chattanooga, Knoxville, and Nashville each made such county payments—but not Memphis."[96] That year marked the beginning of pressures from county leaders to enlist TVA on their side. Over the ensuing decade delegations and individuals representing county interests pursued this objective with little success. TVA has adhered generally to the following policy position stated in almost identical letters written by TVA's general counsel in 1952 to county officials, in response to their requests for such intervention by TVA:

> TVA feels that the governing bodies of the local taxing jurisdictions in which the municipal electric systems operate are in the best position to assure equitable distribution of the tax equivalents. For that reason the power contracts between TVA and the municipal distributors leave the distribution of tax equivalents to local determination by negotiation among the local units of government. We believe that this policy is consistent with the provisions of the TVA act. . . . TVA encourages efforts toward reasonable distribution wherever possible, and will have no objection to any solution of the problem acceptable to the City and County within the limits of the aggregate payments in lieu of taxes permitted by the power contract.[97]

---

[95] *Nashville Tennessean,* Feb. 2, 1941.

[96] Memorandum from Lawrence L. Durisch, chief, Government Research Branch, to Robert H. Marquis, assistant general counsel, June 3, 1952 (in the files of TVA).

[97] Letters from Joseph C. Swidler to: W. D. Hudson, county judge of Montgomery County, March 5, 1952, and Noble Freemon, county attorney of Lawrence County, March 6, 1952 (in the files of TVA).

The 1954 revision of TVA's power contract introduced for the first time a reference to the intent of Congress as expressed in the 1940 amendment to Section 13 of the TVA Act: "It shall be the responsibility of Municipality to provide for such distribution as may be required by law or as it deems appropriate under the provisions of section 13 of the TVA Act to the State, counties and any other municipal corporations in which it operates of any tax equivalents so collected by Municipality in lieu of State, county, and other municipal taxes."

Early in 1954 the Tennessee County Judges Association instructed its directors and executive secretary "to make a study of the possibilities of obtaining tax revenues for counties from municipal electric systems." The motion also called upon the association "to take a more aggressive position, seeking legislation if necessary, to cure a situation in which . . . the counties are failing to get revenue to which they are entitled."[98] Two professors of The University of Tennessee, Lee S. Greene and Charles P. White, were engaged to make the study, and in November, 1954, they submitted a report which included a finding that forty-four of the fifty-seven municipal systems in Tennessee were taking tax equivalents calculated by using county tax rates but were not paying any of these amounts to the counties.

No serious effort was made by the judges to secure the enactment of legislation in the 1955 session, possibly partly because the professors' report had indicated that the counties did not have a clear-cut case. The element of subsidy by city consumers to extend uniform low rates to rural customers was mentioned, as well as the fact that county taxpayers within cities pay a good portion of county property taxes used for financing services to outside-city residents. The report cautioned against a "temptation to treat tax equivalents and in-lieu payments as an isolated problem. . . . Interwoven into the facets of this matter are many other issues basic to the purse of the commonwealth." It also foresaw the possibility "that a forceful attempt by counties to exact tax payments from electric power distributors could create unrest among

[98] *Knoxville Journal*, Jan. 28, 1954.

other public service enterprises. Upsetting the ethical principle of exempting public property from general taxation could tend to retard necessary expansion of services which generally are provided entirely by public utilities."[99]

In 1956 Rutherford County filed suit against the city of Murfreesboro for $222,170 claimed to have been paid to the city since 1940, based on application of the county tax rates. The Tennessee Supreme Court in 1957, adopting the opinion of the chancellor, ruled against the county on grounds that the formula should be construed "as merely stating a criterion by which the amount in lieu of taxes is to be measured, rather than as creating any rights in any subdivision of government whose tax rate happens to be used as the yardstick." The court noted that Section 9 of the contract defined "the use of the amount in lieu of taxes to be 'for any permissible municipal purpose'" and held that payment of the money to the county "clearly . . . would not be for a municipal purpose."[100]

Rutherford County had argued that the 1940 amendment to the TVA Act, declaring the intention of Congress, required TVA in its contracts to compel the distribution of tax equivalents calculated by using the tax rates of counties. To this the court replied: "if the amendment has the effect contended for by complainant, it is not merely declaratory of existing law, but materially changes the law as it existed prior to its enactment. Furthermore, by imposing new duties on the city and depriving it of that to which it was previously entitled under the terms of its contract, it impairs the obligation of the contract between the city and T.V.A."[101]

Taking its cue from this reference to the contract made prior to the 1940 amendment, Rutherford County filed another suit soon after the city of Murfreesboro entered into a new contract in 1957. This time, in a decision handed down in 1959, the Tennessee Supreme Court held that the 1940 amendment to

[99] Memorandum from Lee S. Greene and C. P. White to Robert A. Everett, County Services Association, Subject: Tax Equivalent Payments on Publicly Owned Electric Properties in Tennessee (duplicated; undated; in TVA Technical Library).

[100] *Rutherford County* v. *City of Murfreesboro*, 202 Tenn. 455, 461, 304 S. W. 2d 635 (1957).

[101] *Ibid.*, p. 464.

the TVA Act and the contract provision declaring the city's responsibility respecting distribution under this amendment had the effect of making the distribution mandatory. The court's opinion took note of the city's argument that the "interpretation by the TVA officials in making this contract . . . is contrary to what we have herein above stated" and dismissed it by saying, "if so, we think theirs is erroneous."[102] TVA's interpretation had been stated on numerous occasions, in substantially the same terms as the following:

> We do not construe the provision of Section 13 of the TVA Act . . . as requiring TVA to enforce distribution of tax equivalent payments to the counties by its municipal distributors, but consider it rather an authorization to TVA to include such a requirement in its municipal power contracts. The final clause of the paragraph is in the form of an expression of Congressional intent as to the responsibilities of the municipalities in the respective states in the distribution of tax equivalents. It seems clear to me that this provision is hortatory or advisory rather than self-executing, and this interpretation is consistent with the traditional reluctance of Congress to interfere in local relationships.[103]

This decision caused great alarm in cities that had been following the practice of taking tax equivalents based on county tax rates. TVA estimated that the aggregate, cumulative liability of all Tennessee cities on this basis, from 1941 to 1959, was $6,843,200. The liability for 1959 alone was $1,738,000, almost a doubling of the 1958 figure, and the trend indicated further increases. TVA also reported that in 1959, there were forty-one municipal systems in Tennessee that made no payments to counties.[104] The U. S. Supreme Court refused to grant the city's request for a writ of certiorari; some municipal officials and lawyers thought that a stronger stand by TVA might have induced the court to grant the writ.[105] However, the view of

[102] *Rutherford County v. City of Murfreesboro*, 205 Tenn. 362, 370, 326 S. W. 2d 653 (1959).
[103] Letter from Joseph C. Swidler, general counsel, to A. B. Huddleston, city attorney of Murfreesboro, July 27, 1956 (in the files of TVA).
[104] Letter from Paul L. Evans to Herbert J. Bingham, March 10, 1960 (in the files of the Tennessee Municipal League).
[105] The memorandum filed with the court by TVA began with: "The Tennessee Valley Authority takes no position as to whether the writ should

TVA's lawyers was that the Murfreesboro case would not present an adequate record for appellate review, as the point at issue was the overruling of a demurrer, and that a better course of action would be to commence another suit in the federal courts. That the cities won the next round (the Tullahoma case) by a 2-to-1 vote in the federal circuit court may be regarded as a vindication of their judgment.

Several cities filed suits in federal district courts aimed at overturning the Tennessee Supreme Court's decision. The case initially regarded by municipal officials as the test case, filed by the city of Jackson, proved to be a dud when the city settled out of court. A case from Tullahoma finally found its way to the U. S. Supreme Court. In this case the district court held for the county, though more equivocally than had the Tennessee Supreme Court.[106] The circuit court of appeals, by a 2-to-1 vote, overruled the district court and accepted TVA's interpretation,[107] and the U. S. Supreme Court, after requesting the Solicitor General to file briefs expressing the views of the United States, declined to accept the case for review.[108]

TVA has not wavered from its interpretation of the law, and it appears that this interpretation will finally prevail. The TVA board chairman restated the TVA position in 1962 in a letter to a county official: "TVA's consistent position has been that the distribution by a municipality of the tax equivalent actually paid by the municipal electric system is a local matter and one which should be resolved on the local level. However, TVA has encouraged the municipalities to make equitable distribution of such payments in lieu of taxes among the respective taxing jurisdictions and a number of municipalities have done so."[109]

In 1961, of the fifty-eight municipal distributors in Tennessee, forty failed to make any payments to counties in lieu of taxes. By 1964 the number not making such payments had been

---

be granted." However, it also pointed out that the Tennessee Supreme Court's interpretation was contrary to that which had been placed on the provision by TVA.

[106] *City of Tullahoma* v. *Coffee County*, 204 F. Supp. 794 (1962).
[107] *City of Tullahoma* v. *Coffee County*, 328 F. 2d 683 (1964).
[108] *Coffee County* v. *City of Tullahoma*, 85 S. C. 698 (1965).
[109] Letter from A. J. Wagner to Fred L. Key, manager of McMinn County, July 9, 1962 (in the files of TVA).

reduced to twenty-five, primarily as a result of agreements precipitated by the counties' temporary victory in the state courts.

Soon after the first Murfreesboro decision against the counties, the Tennessee County Services Association (TCSA) launched another move for state legislation to require tax-equivalent payments to counties. Judge Hudson of Montgomery County, reporting on a visit with TVA Directors Herbert Vogel and Arnold Jones, said: "They were very understanding of our problems, but they told us they couldn't solve them for us. There has to be some enabling legislation from the state first."[110]

Municipal forces were hard put to turn back the counties' bid in the 1959 session of the Tennessee legislature, but they did so, mainly on grounds that to enact such a law would breach the concept of intergovernmental tax immunity. The executive secretary of the Tennessee Municipal League argued that "the present provision in the TVA Act expressing an intent of Congress that municipal electric systems should pay taxes (or in-lieu taxes) is completely contrary to the principle of intergovernmental tax immunity" and commended TVA for its policy of "leaving this matter for local decision, taking into account the overall equities of the relationships between city electric users and taxpayers and rural electric users and taxpayers. . . ." He asserted that "the only defense against federal, state and local taxation of publicly-owned utility and similar operations is the basic principle of intergovernmental immunity" and observed that if this defense should be breached it might follow that the federal government would impose payments in lieu of federal income taxes on TVA and the municipal systems.[111]

A NEW TAX-EQUIVALENT FORMULA

The adverse court decision in the second Murfreesboro case and increasing pressures in the state legislature caused municipal officials to think of compromise. A number of cities and

[110] *Nashville Tennessean,* Oct. 27, 1957.
[111] Letter from Herbert J. Bingham to A. J. Wagner, TVA general manager, Feb. 10, 1959 (in the files of the league).

counties entered into agreements for sharing tax equivalents. Since the Tennessee Supreme Court had based its decision on the use of county tax rates in calculating tax equivalents, municipal leaders thought it would be desirable to establish a new formula not tied to tax rates. TVA personnel were receptive because the wide variations in tax rates and levels of assessments resulted in unequal tax contributions by electric systems and made possible, in their view, excessive tax equivalents in jurisdictions with high tax rates and low levels of assessment. County officials were interested because any amount would be better than nothing, and they realized that the federal courts might reverse the Tennessee decision.

Negotiations on this issue commenced in 1959 and finally ended with a legislative solution in 1969. TVA was unavoidably in the middle, and it undertook to work out "some equitable formula . . . to satisfy both the towns and the counties."[112] The Authority's officials met many times with representatives of the counties and the cities, acting as intermediaries in the dispute.

The Municipal League at first took a position that no new state legislation would be required but subsequently acceded to TVA's point of view that legislation would be desirable in order to give TVA justification for contracts at variance from its contracts with distributors in other states. In 1960 the league retained Joseph C. Swidler, formerly TVA general counsel, as its chief negotiator. His determined effort over most of 1960 to persuade the Authority to adopt a percentage of revenues was unsuccessful. TVA, through James E. Watson, assistant manager of power, countered with a proposal that the tax equivalent be a percentage of the net plant (book) value (4 per cent was suggested): "the TVA board was firm in its unwillingness to approve a tax equivalent system which did not have some flexibility in relation to the level of ad valorem taxes, which was not somehow related to the city's taxing procedures, and which purported to specify how the overall tax equivalent should be divided."[113]

---

[112] Charles McCarthy, TVA general counsel, quoted in the *Knoxville Journal*, Dec. 12, 1959.

[113] Memorandum to file by Swidler, Dec. 12, 1960 (in the files of the Tennessee Municipal League).

City-county negotiations on this issue were helped along by Governor Buford Ellington, who asked selected county and city officials to work with state officials on matters that might require action in the next session of the legislature. At a meeting of this group in the governor's office in April, 1960, a program was agreed upon which included the matter of electric system tax equivalents. This group, designated as the "Governor's Intergovernmental Committee" and reorganized in 1961 as the "Intergovernmental Committee" without state officials, has continued to develop legislative programs on matters of joint concern to cities and counties.

The league in December, 1960, submitted a formal proposal to the counties, through the Governor's Intergovernmental Committee, that municipal systems pay to counties a percentage of total tax equivalents received, in the range of 15 to 20 per cent, provided TVA would agree to permit cities to compute tax equivalents as a percentage of gross revenues. If this was acceptable to county officials, the league suggested that they urge TVA to offer such contract amendments to cities to put the proposal into effect. According to a memorandum filed by Swidler, most county officials on the committee seemed to favor the league's proposal, and there was an excellent chance of securing support of the counties for the proposal if it were combined with a pledge to pay to the counties a specified share of the overall tax equivalents.[114]

In March, 1961, municipalities involved were advised that negotiations were being carried on directly with TCSA instead of through the Governor's Intergovernmental Committee. TCSA, at a meeting the following month in Knoxville, approved a counterproposal calling for 25 per cent of an amount calculated by applying the county tax rate to the book value of a municipal power system in the county in the first year, 28 per cent in the second year, and an increase thereafter of 3 per cent per year until a maximum of 40 per cent would be reached. Also, no county was to receive less than the highest dollar amount it had received in any year nor a lesser percentage of total tax equivalents than the highest percentage that it had received in any

[114] *Ibid.*

year. The proposal reserved to the counties the right to sue for recovery of amounts due for past years, under the Murfreesboro decision, if the cities failed to accept the proposal. This proposal was rejected as totally unacceptable by the cities.

In June, 1961, the league's Electric System Committee met with TVA personnel. At this meeting Watson made some proposals which he said were subject to approval by the TVA board and concurrence of the Tennessee Public Power Association. He said that a primary consideration underlying these proposals was that existing maximum tax equivalents not be exceeded. The need for a new formula to meet the cities' problem of disposing of county tax equivalents was recognized, but a percentage of revenues was unsatisfactory because any such percentage was essentially arbitrary. He proposed a uniform percentage of book values of electric plants (5 per cent was suggested) as the most practicable way to determine a new maximum. He suggested that a city be limited to 80 per cent of the total, with at least 20 per cent to be paid to counties and other cities; however, TVA would not require payments to counties or other cities. Such changes would be approved by TVA only if the counties and cities, or at least most of them involved in the controversy, agreed that it would settle their dispute. The 80 and 20 per cent division had been selected because it appeared to be one that cities and counties might agree to, but TVA would accept any other division mutually acceptable to the two parties.

This proposal was favorably received by the league's committee. Executive Secretary Herbert J. Bingham suggested that the league formally request TVA to provide a contract revision on this basis and that the cities and counties should join in sponsoring state legislation that would require the cities to accept such contract amendments when offered by TVA. At a subsequent meeting of city officials Bingham recommended that the cities attempt to reach a fair settlement with the counties, pointing out that cooperation with them was necessary to attain a number of important goals for local governments in Tennessee and that it would be difficult to fight with them on this matter and try to cooperate with them on others.[115]

[115] I attended these conferences, and this summary is based on my notes.

TVA reported in August, 1961, that reactions of municipal power system personnel to its proposal had been generally favorable and that an effort would be made soon to sell the proposal to county officials. It was recognized that the percentage of net plant to be used might give some difficulty because of variations in property tax rates among the Valley states.[116] Watson subsequently reported to the league's Electric System Committee that discussions had been held with TVPPA "since their agreements really are with the distributors," and that TVPPA did not favor legislation because "they have been free of state control and regulation in the past." He insisted that such payments be kept permissive—"if it is compulsory for a city to take 5 per cent of book value then this becomes a part of the operating expense and it would react unfavorably on marketing bonds"—but he anticipated "that a larger percentage than now would be taken in many cases, so as to minimize the loss to cities. . . . TVA wouldn't object to anyone taking the maximum tax equivalent." He also reported a favorable reaction from TCSA.[117] The league promptly submitted the TVA proposal to TCSA, but there was no response. There is also no record of any discussion or tentative agreement on this matter at a meeting of the Intergovernmental Committee shortly thereafter. Apparently, county representatives thought that things were going their way and there was no need to compromise at that time.

A meeting of TVA, county, and city representatives in May, 1962, failed to produce any concrete proposals for settlement. There was a new development in that "TVA modified its previous position by emphasizing the need for legislation in the 1963 General Assembly providing for a maximum tax equivalent based upon approximately five per cent of the depreciated book value of electric systems, with a statutory requirement for division of the monies between municipality and county."[118] Sev-

[116] Memorandum to the files by Herbert J. Bingham, on conversation with Paul Button, Aug. 16, 1961 (in the files of the Tennessee Municipal League).

[117] Minutes of a meeting in Oct., 1961, prepared by Herbert J. Bingham; the quotations are his summarizations of the comments made (in the files of the Tennessee Municipal League).

[118] Special bulletin of the Tennessee Municipal League, June 1, 1962 (in the files of the league).

eral tables prepared by TVA were passed out at this meeting, including one that showed the effects for each municipal system of paying to counties 20 and 25 per cent of the new proposed maximum formula of 5 per cent of net plant value.[119]

City representatives went into a meeting in August, 1962, with TVA and county representatives, prepared to offer the counties 22 per cent of the tax equivalent. The counties proposed 22½ per cent, providing that no county would receive less than it was then receiving. Representatives of the cities agreed to recommend acceptance of this proposal, provided that all back liability would be eliminated, that the distribution would become effective whenever a city and county executed an agreement, that no existing contract would be affected, and that the city and county organizations would jointly sponsor legislation to confirm such agreements. A county spokesman raised a question about the coercive effect of such legislation, to which Bingham responded that this would be necessary to insure that all counties received their shares. Bingham also raised a question as to whether the percentage should be higher than 5 per cent, to which Watson responded that it would be most difficult to get the TVA board to approve any higher figure. Watson seemingly abandoned TVA's insistence that new legislation require sharing with counties by suggesting that local distribution would be left to local agreement.

The following month brought approval by TCSA and the league of an agreement which included these points: (1) a recommendation that each affected city and county sign an agreement providing that 22½ per cent of the total tax equivalents paid by municipal distributors within the respective counties would go to the counties, but existing contracts, private acts, or understandings should not be disturbed; (2) such agreements should absolve municipalities of any back liability; (3) the two organizations would sponsor legislation recommended by their legal counsel and TVA; (4) with the cooperative assistance of TCSA, the league would seek a revision of the power contracts by TVA to provide for maximum permissible tax equivalents on

[119] TVA personnel, having conferred separately with both parties, were reflecting their relative positions in using the 20 and 25 per cent bases; a report about a month later indicated that the cities were offering 20 per cent and the counties were asking for 25 per cent.

the basis of a percentage of net plant value calculated by the following method: "The state total of maximum tax equivalents for 1962 allowed under present TVA contracts, computed by applying respective city and county tax rates to net plant value, divided by the state total of net plant value; provided, however, that no tax equivalent shall be less than the highest actual amount paid in any of the three preceding years; but in no case shall said percentage be less than 5 per cent."[120]

In January, 1963, TVA finished a draft bill which would have written into state law the standard provisions of TVA power contracts on disposition of revenues and the new tax-equivalent formula based on 5 per cent of net plant value. The bill followed the lines of the city-county agreement; it required distribution of 22½ per cent of the total tax equivalent to a county or counties, and minimum tax equivalents to any other cities served equal to 2 per cent of the net plant value in any such city, unless a private act or contractual agreement provided otherwise. However, the bill was not even introduced in the 1963 session of the legislature, primarily because the league was holding out for a higher percentage than 5 per cent.

Although a federal circuit court held for the cities in the Tullahoma case in February, 1964, the league's Electric System Committee, at a meeting the following month, reaffirmed its position that legislation should be sought to put into effect TVA's proposal and the requirement of a division with the counties. It also reaffirmed the city-county agreement that the percentage should equal the statewide average under the existing tax-rate formula, because TVA statistical reports showed an increase in this average to 5.3 per cent in 1963 (subsequently 5.5 per cent was reported for 1964). This position of the committee was ratified by representatives of affected cities at the annual convention of the league in June, and the proposal was included in the 1965 Local Government Platform approved by the league and TCSA.[121]

After negotiations with personnel in the TVA Office of Power over a period of several months failed to modify their position

[120] Duplicated copy of the agreement (in the files of the Tennessee Municipal League).
[121] *Tennessee Town & City*, XV, No. 6 (June, 1964), 9.

that 5 per cent of net plant value would be the maximum tax equivalent under any new formula, the matter was appealed to the TVA board of directors.[122] City and county representatives met with the TVA board and other TVA officials in February, 1965, and presented their case for a 5.5 per cent level on a basis that this was the statewide average in 1964. The TVA board chairman stated that the board had previously reviewed and approved the 5 per cent proposal, and the board refused to change its position. The board's justification was based on data introduced by Office of Power personnel purporting to show that municipal electric systems in Tennessee were paying a "fair share of the cost of government." At this meeting a municipal preference was expressed for a bill that would incorporate by reference the provisions of TVA's power contracts. The TVA general counsel indicated that it might be unconstitutional to delegate to TVA "the power to write state policy" in this respect, but attorneys for the league did not consider this a problem.[123]

A bill was drafted which required distribution of 22½ per cent to counties and 2 per cent to any other city served, out of aggregate tax equivalents that could not exceed "the maximum amount provided for in the wholesale power contract of the municipality with the Tennessee Valley Authority, and such transfers to the municipality's general funds shall be subject to the terms, conditions and limitations specified in said wholesale power contract." The provision in TVA's draft to give a power board and a municipal governing body joint power to determine the amounts of tax equivalents was deleted; the effect of this change was to make such determinations subject to other laws, general or private, under which the various municipal systems are organized. This bill was introduced late in the 1965 session of the legislature and was approved in the Senate with little opposition. The first vote in the House, on the next-to-last day of the session, was 49 for and 13 against,

---

[122] Although these negotiations were officially carried on by representatives of the Tennessee Municipal League and the Tennessee County Services Association, the main burden fell on officials of the former organization, especially its executive secretary, Herbert J. Bingham.

[123] Relying on *Memphis Power & Light Co. v. City of Memphis*, 172 Tenn. 346, 112 S. W. 2d 817 (1937). According to Bingham, TVA attorneys later concurred in this legal opinion.

one vote short of the required constitutional majority of 50, and a second try on the last day garnered only 46 votes for it. Contributing to its defeat were amendments on the floor of the House which exempted seven municipal systems from its provisions.[124] At least three power managers of these systems were reported to have encouraged opposition to the bill because they feared that it would result in pressure for increased tax equivalents from their systems.

A bill introduced late in the 1967 session of the General Assembly differed in some respects from the 1965 bill: a maximum of 5 per cent of plant value was fixed; instead of incorporating TVA power contracts by reference, detailed provisions were included for calculation and disposition of tax equivalents, paralleling the provisions of TVA power contracts; and it provided that "the total amount to be actually transferred to municipality's general funds for each fiscal year . . . shall be determined by municipality's governing body." The bill failed to reach the floor of either house before the end of the session principally because TVA opposed the 5 per cent maximum, justifying the reversal of its previous commitment on grounds that the 1966 railroad tax cases[125] had established overassessment of utilities and property tax rates would soon be lowered by reassessments ordered by a 1967 law.

The recessed session reconvened in February, 1968. After an unsuccessful effort to persuade TVA to stand by its previous commitment, the league, seeing no hope for a bill opposed by TVA, abandoned the 1967 bill and secured introduction late in the 1968 session of a bill virtually the same as the 1965 bill which incorporated by reference the provisions of TVA power contracts. To make it more attractive to TVA, the stipulation of the 1967 bill that tax-equivalent amounts would be determined

---

[124] The executive director of the Tennessee County Services Association told me on June 7, 1965, that he was glad that the bill did not pass in the amended form. The systems exempted by these amendments were Bristol, Chattanooga, Harriman, Milan, Rockwood, Springfield, and Tullahoma.

[125] A *de facto* classification of property was declared invalid by a federal district court and the Tennessee Supreme Court. *Louisville and Nashville Railroad Co. v. Public Service Commission and State Board of Equalization*, 249 F. Supp. 894 (1966). *Southern Railway Company v. Frank G. Clement, Governor, et al.*, 415 S. W. 2d 146 (1967).

by municipal governing bodies was also omitted. TVA approved this bill. It passed unanimously in the Senate (32-0), but the vote of 34 for and 22 against in the House fell short of the constitutional minimum of 50 affirmative votes.[126]

At the end of 1968 the situation appeared to favor TVA and the municipal power systems. In the absence of an amendment to classify property that might result from a constitutional convention called by a referendum in November, 1968, to meet in August, 1971, the reassessment of all property in the state at 50 per cent of full value, to be completed by 1973, will lower tax rates in most taxing jurisdictions, thereby lowering electric system tax equivalents under the tax-rates formula. TVA and the municipal power systems could afford to wait it out and persistently refused to accept proposals made by municipal officials based on TVA's prior commitment to 5 per cent of book value. The resulting frustrations of municipal officials finally brought a threat of drastic action, in a resolution adopted by the league at its 1968 annual conference recommending "that the Tennessee General Assembly and the Congress of the United States thoroughly examine the tax equivalent policies which are now being pursued by the Tennessee Valley Authority." This resolution was also incorporated into the 1968 and 1969 Local Government Platforms as joint declarations of the league and TCSA.

Municipal officials made known their intentions to seek enactment of new legislation, even though opposed by TVA and the municipal power systems, and continued to talk of a legislative investigation of TVA's tax-equivalent policies by the Tennessee legislature or Congress. State officials became concerned about the possible effects of this controversy on the state's property reassessment program and determined that their intercession might help to resolve it. Governor Ellington arranged for a meeting of two top state officials, William R. Snodgrass, comptroller of the treasury, and S. H. Roberts, executive administrator, office of the governor, with the TVA board of directors on December 16, 1968. At this meeting it was agreed that staff personnel of TVA and the State should try to bring about a renewal of negotiations. This precipitated a series of meetings

[126] Only Coffee County (Tullahoma) was exempted by an amendment in the House.

and negotiating sessions over the next four months in which the primary participants were municipal officials, TVA staff personnel, and a committee of municipal power managers. Having served as catalysts to reactivate meaningful negotiations, the two state officials sent representatives to act as observers. The power side offered a proposal that would have approximated 3.3 per cent of net plant value, which was promptly rejected by the cities. A second proposal was made by TVA and the power managers, which they estimated would initially produce an average of 4.8 per cent of net plant value for municipal power systems except the four large city systems (Memphis, Nashville, Knoxville, and Chattanooga, which by this time had been excluded from consideration) as a result of minimum payments for some systems to avoid sudden reductions; without the minimum payments it was estimated to produce an average of 3.8 per cent of net plant value.

On April 21 the league's negotiators accepted this proposal after wringing a few additional concessions from the power side: a slight increase in the base amount used for calculating the minimum payment; the book value of materials and supplies to be subject to effective tax rates; and a provision that the amount would be determined by "the municipality's governing body, after consultation with the municipality's supervisory body [power board]" instead of TVA's proposal to make this a joint determination of the two bodies. A bill previously drafted by TVA was hastily modified and introduced just before the deadline for introducing new bills; in the closing days of the 1969 session it passed in the Senate by a 25 to 0 vote and in the House by a vote of 74 to 0.[127]

The new act exempts the four large city systems and any city subject to a private act for tax equivalents; all other cities are required to execute a contract amendment when tendered by TVA providing for the following basis of calculating maximum tax-equivalent payments (as of July 1 each year for the ensuing fiscal year ending June 30): (a) one and one-half times the *effective tax rate* of each city and county taxing jurisdiction (actual property tax rate multiplied by the weighted average ratio of assessed to market value determined by dividing the

[127] *Public Acts of Tennessee, 1969*, ch. 237.

total actual assessed valuation of all classes of taxable real property by the total value of the same classes of taxable real property) applied to the net plant value of the power system and the book value of materials and supplies within the taxing jurisdiction; plus (b) 2½ per cent of the adjusted plant value within city taxing jurisdictions (net plant value less the value of underground plant in service and lines and equipment in service designed for operation in excess of 26,000 volts); plus (c) 1½ per cent of the adjusted plant value outside city taxing jurisdictions. Until this formula produces a higher amount, a power system may pay the following minimum: (a) the highest total annual amount paid from the power system's funds, prior to April 1, 1969, for any one of the three consecutive calendar years ending with calendar year 1968, increased by the same percentage as that by which the system's net plant value increased from December 31, 1968, through June 30, 1969; plus (b) the amount by which the calculation under (a) of the tax-equivalent formula (applying effective tax rates) exceeds the result of such a calculation for the year ending with June 30, 1969.

The new act permits tax-equivalent payments to be made "only from current electric system revenues remaining after" payment of or provision for operating expenses, debt service, and "reasonable reserves for renewals, replacements, and contingencies and for cash working capital." Municipal negotiators argued that the concept of payments in lieu of taxes, which enjoy the highest priority against privately owned property, should place these tax equivalents in at least third priority position, ahead of reserves, but TVA personnel adamantly refused to make this concession.

Counties are to receive 22½ per cent of a power system's total tax equivalent unless a private act or contract provides otherwise (shared proportionately to net plant values in two or more counties). This escape route was a factor in the unanimous vote of approval in the legislature, as a number of private acts[128] providing for such exemption were concurrently adopted

---

[128] The acts for Harriman, Loudon and Rockwood require payment of all tax equivalents to the respective cities. Counties are to share for the other systems as follows: Dyersburg—county tax rate applied to net plant value outside cities, or minimum of $15,000; Union City—county tax rate

to satisfy some municipalities opposed to sharing with counties. Payments to cities other than the owner-city are required at a rate of one and one-half times the effective tax rate of the other city applied to the system's net plant value in that city.

The 1969 act represents a true compromise—its terms fell short of the expectations of all of the parties. Municipal officials, after narrowly missing a maximum of 5 per cent of net plant value that TVA had proposed and supported for five years or so, thought that the settlement was too low, and TVA personnel and municipal power system managers thought it was too high. All parties, however, breathed great sighs of relief that an accord had finally been reached to eliminate the unsettled conditions of the past decade. A noticeable change of attitude on the part of TVA personnel in the 1969 round of negotiations was evident. Their flexibility and willingness to compromise at a level which they considered to be too high was probably the major factor in reaching the compromise agreement. We can only guess as to the reasons for moderation of their viewpoint. Alienation of municipal officials, who in the past have been among TVA's strongest supporters, prospects of adverse effects on municipal systems resulting from continued opposition of power managers against municipal officials at the local level, the league's threat of a legislative investigation, and statistical data showing tax equivalents on TVA power to be low in comparison to taxes on the consumers of private power companies, were some elements of the situation that probably helped to induce this change.

---

applied to 50 per cent of net plant value outside cities, or minimum of $1,740; Humboldt, Milan and Trenton—10 per cent of the total tax equivalent; Tullahoma—5 per cent of the total tax equivalent.

7 SUMMING UP

THE TVA POWER PROGRAM has been a success story that provides an outstanding example of government in action for the benefit of people, despite the criticisms we have noted. Even chronic critics of government might be disposed to give the Authority a good score on the basis of its performance in carrying out those purposes assigned to it by Congress. After sixteen years of fairly close association with TVA personnel and observation of its program and results, this author believes that the Authority merits a high rating for efficiency in accomplishing its primary objectives. Rarely indeed, if at all, has TVA been charged with bureaucratic inefficiency, the charge so often made against governmental agencies. Though it has not attained perfection, and of course no man-made institution ever will, its personnel in the main have maintained sufficiently objective and self-critical viewpoints to accomplish corrective action as needed in fairly timely fashion. Some aspects of the power program, however, have become somewhat rigid and less amenable to change by self-scrutiny.

TVA's power program has contributed significantly to the lowering of electric rates and to the spread of rural electrification in areas other than the Valley; yet the private utilities continue to make good profits and their stocks command good prices in the market. Although the "yardstick" concept is subject to criticism because it has not included all elements of cost, it has had the salutary effect of causing the private companies to adopt the high-use, low-cost theory that has been so beneficial to power consumers. Viewed another way, the TVA power program is in part a governmental device for regulating private monopolies, which in many cases have been inadequately regulated by the states.

THE UNITED FRONT AND MUNICIPAL AUTONOMY

TVA, because of its expertise, prestige, and aggressive defense of its power interests, has played a dominant role in shaping Tennessee laws respecting power distribution. These laws make each municipality virtually a free agent in the process of contract negotiations, subject only to statutes largely reflecting TVA policies. In this process TVA has a great advantage over a single municipality, and observers have noted a need for more concerted action by the cities. Sporadically, on special issues, such as levels and disposition of tax equivalents, the Tennessee Municipal League has performed such a role. The Tennessee Valley Public Power Association, an organization made up of managerial personnel of the municipal and cooperative power systems, also has represented distributors on such issues as rates and direct service by TVA to large industries. The league is generally inclined to take an independent stance and to represent the interests of municipal governments, but TVPPA is strongly oriented toward TVA.

In the main, TVA has adhered to a standard power contract when contracting with its distributors, but at any one time all of the contracts in force have not been standard in all respects. This has come about partially from the historical evolution of contractual provisions to meet new situations, because of staggered renewals of contracts, but it also partially reflects exceptions and special provisions insisted upon by distributors. The effort to standardize creates a fundamental dilemma for TVA: how can the Authority treat all distributors alike and at the same time "negotiate" contracts with individual distributors? TVA clearly prefers standardization but continues to talk in terms of negotiation.

The illusion of negotiation is helped along by the fact that most members of municipal governing bodies and power boards are seldom involved in the approval of contracts—the twenty-year term means that it is a once-in-a-lifetime experience for most of them, except for an occasional amendment. However, municipal officials are becoming increasingly aware that virtually nothing is negotiable. TVA might be in a more tenable position, under its present policies, simply to present the standard power contract as the conditions for sale of power and to drop the pretense of negotiation.

Although some of TVA's activities may be viewed as intervention in local affairs, another view is that TVA personnel are simply following through to make sure that the Authority's mission is accomplished. In this perspective, the extent of local irritation might be regarded as a rough measure of the persistence and thoroughness practiced by TVA in enforcing contractual provisions. It can be argued that its distributors know what these provisions are before signing the contracts, that they should expect to hew to the letter of the contract, and that restrictions are to be expected along with the benefits of such contracts. However, this line of argument may oversimplify the situation. It presumes that cities are free agents and voluntarily assume the burdens of the contracts, when as a matter of fact they have no real choice, because their only source of power is TVA—they must take the power on TVA's terms, and there is no practicable alternative. (Even Memphis, big enough to construct a large generating plant, found that its costs were higher than TVA's wholesale charges.) The contractual arrangements, then, are not the result of bargaining between fairly equal parties but represent the impositions of superior federal power safely grounded in the urgent necessity of electric power (although an occasional "short circuit" does cause some "sparks"!). In reality, the contractual relationships between TVA and its municipal distributors fail to meet the partnership test laid down by Board Chairman Gordon R. Clapp: "A true partnership implies freedom to disagree. It accords the people of a region not only a choice among certain courses of action but the right to reject assistance or, if they choose, to do nothing at all."[1]

The idea that TVA and the municipalities are partners tends to break down under scrutiny. The guidelines and limitations laid down in the comprehensive power contracts leave small room for the exercise of significant discretion by local power systems. Local personnel weigh their decisions carefully, for they know that they will be called to account. Years ago Board Chairman Clapp indicated that the determination of retail rates was within the realm of local discretion (see p. 98), but TVA in recent

[1] Gordon R. Clapp, *The TVA: An Approach to the Development of a Region* (Chicago: University of Chicago Press, 1955), p. 91.

years has coerced several distributors to make rate reductions. Although TVA may win the economic argument as to whether such reductions should be made, the fact remains that these are decisions dictated from above. TVA by continuous surveillance through its field staff closely checks the decisions that are made and the manner of operation of the local systems. We see here something less than centralized administration but also considerably less than decentralized administration; the comment of a power board member, "We are just the lackey of TVA," has some foundation.

For people in the Valley who object to TVA power decisions and policies, the channels and procedures for disinterested review have been very poor. Except in a few cases that found their way into the courts, resort has been limited to the Authority's officials who made or approved the decisions initially. An example is the hearing accorded by the TVA board of directors to municipal and county leaders on February 24, 1965 (which the author attended), on the issue of a new tax-equivalent formula. On that occasion the chairman of the board assumed the principal burden of defending TVA's position and announced at the outset that the board had approved the formula prior to its public release by personnel of the Office of Power. Only rarely has there been recourse to presidential or congressional review; pressure by counties in 1940 to secure direct TVA tax-replacement payments was one of the few such instances. This reluctance to carry appeals above the Authority level reflects TVA's independent status and the great prestige that it has usually enjoyed in the legislative and executive branches of the federal government. Perhaps of even more significance is a desire on the part of people in the Valley to keep their differences "within the family," and a feeling that a united front should be presented to the outside because of the perennial battle with private power interests. That these inhibitions are weakening is indicated by the action of the Tennessee Municipal League at its 1968 annual conference, calling for an investigation of TVA's tax-equivalent policies by Congress and the state legislature.

A community of interest between TVA and the municipal and cooperative power systems over the years has developed into a very effective power lobby on state legislative issues. This lobby was successful in blocking the 1950 move to place a tax on utility bills and in exempting sales of electricity from the 1963 local-option sales tax act. However, they failed in a half-hearted attempt to keep the 1963 legislature from extending the state sales tax to apply to electricity sales; a TVA director stated that a more determined effort would have been made if such taxes had not already been levied in neighboring states. If the legislatures of the other states, where TVA's influence is not so dominant, had not previously acted, it is entirely possible that the power lobby's effort in 1963 would have succeeded. Other actual and incipient issues also have involved conflicts of interests with representatives of general municipal governments (the municipal lobby) of the state.

It is worth noting that generally the power lobby has prevailed, infrequently after a direct confrontation but generally because the municipal lobby has elected the route of compromise or concession rather than engagement in a direct conflict. Municipal officials have been heard to say, "We can't beat the power lobby." The unusual aspect of this state of affairs is that the group of elected officials, who would be presumed to have a considerable amount of political support, in the give-and-take of legislative maneuvering seem to come out second-best in contests with appointive officials, who would normally be expected to have a poor political base. TVA has aggressively courted public favor as an example of nonpolitical administration and has carried on an effective information program which has made the people of the state aware of the many advantages of low-cost power. Its information program has disparaged the municipal official as a politician, in contrast to the nonpolitical power system official. These factors no doubt have influenced people's attitudes.

A corollary to TVA's objective of lowest possible rates is its concern that electric revenues not be diverted to nonelectric uses. Its contracts are carefully written to plug any loophole that might permit a municipality to take from the electric system more than a tax equivalent, and the Authority has exerted persuasive efforts, often successfully, to keep tax equivalents below the amounts authorized by the contracts. Although a small number of municipal officials still express feelings that their electric systems should provide more financial support for general municipal activities, the policy of nondiversion has attained wide acceptance. However, there is continuing widespread feeling among municipal officials that TVA's policy and practice is to hold tax equivalents at a low level.

Differences of opinion and contentions that we have noted here are largely the inevitable consequences of TVA's initial decision to place the distribution function in the hands of local agencies. Certain elements of conflict are inherent in this arrangement, such as feelings of local autonomy versus TVA's oversight to insure contract compliance, and conservative pay-as-you-go financing with higher rates (often favored locally) versus TVA's push for lower rates and bond financing of extensions and improvements. TVA has accomplished a major feat of public administration by welding together 108 municipal systems, 50 cooperative distributors, and two private companies[2] into a single utility system, but this has produced some local resentment against the controls applied to achieve this objective. On balance, however, TVA's decision to decentralize the distribution function was probably sound, because it involved the local agencies actively in support of the TVA power program. One seasoned Valley observer expressed the view that if it had assumed the distribution function the Authority would not have survived. Some validity attaches to TVA's claim that its contractual strictures are necessary to carry out the intent of Congress as embodied in the TVA Act. TVA cannot use this argument for all of its policies, however, because the act vests in the Authority considerable discretion and its language delegates broad powers of policy-making.

POWER BOARDS AND LOCAL DEMOCRACY

An important part of TVA doctrine holds that municipalities should place their electric systems under power boards, thereby

[2] These totals changed in 1969 to 110 municipal systems and one private company, with the addition of Smithville, Tennessee, and acquisition by the city of Franklin of the Franklin Power and Light Company. Hickman, Ky., will enter the system in April, 1970.

removing them from political[3] and other undesirable influences emanating from municipal governments. Little doubt exists that such power boards generally are more amenable to TVA's control and that they develop a greater affinity for TVA's methods of operations than would be the case under a departmental form of organization. If one takes a narrow view, as TVA does, of efficiency in a local power system, the power board form of organization would probably get the higher rating. However, if one considers a whole municipal government and what integration of an electric system into it can mean, the departmental form may warrant the better score. The latter is more likely to bring about greater efficiency for the entire government resulting from such factors as economies of scale, joint operations with other similar enterprises, joint occupancy of buildings, and modernized accounting systems and equipment. The departmental form also wins if the primary criterion is responsible, representative government subject to democratic control. The typical appointive power board, composed of members serving rather long, staggered terms, is not very responsive to democratic pressures. Of course it is conceded by proponents of the power board—in fact, it is their principal argument—that the power board will not be sensitive to political considerations. However, experience in the nine Tennessee cities without power boards indicates that a creditable performance can be attained under the departmental form.

In summing up his study of TVA, Pritchett writes, "Fundamentally, its contribution has been the basis it has supplied for faith in democratic institutions."[4] As his study dealt with TVA as a federal agency and encompassed the entire scope of its multiple-purpose program, Pritchett presumably had in mind primarily the example set by the Authority at the federal level. In the light of the comments and information presented here, it may be worthwhile to consider whether such a conclusion

---

[3] TVA's use of the term is in a derogatory sense, as customarily used by reformers. My use of the term subsumes the processes essential to the operation of a democratic government.

[4] C. Herman Pritchett, *The Tennessee Valley Authority: A Study in Public Administration* (Chapel Hill: The University of North Carolina Press, 1943), p. 323.

would be justified with respect to the municipal level of government. Is the independent power board, insulated as it is from the full range of broad questions and conflicts we call "politics," a democratic institution that should be emulated by other branches of municipal government? Should the municipal power board be hailed as a "striking demonstration that public control is compatible with efficiency"[5] when local public control is virtually eliminated by the device of the power board under the tight strictures of a power contract?

Even under the doubtful assumption that the foregoing questions can be answered affirmatively, should this organizational device be extended to other municipal functions? Would the application of the theory ultimately result in the popular election of officials whose sole public duty would be the appointment of boards and commissions to carry on the activities of municipal government? Or is there something to be said for making elective officials quite directly responsible for public functions and accountable to the electorate for their stewardship? Is it true, as TVA power personnel seem to believe, that it is virtually hopeless to expect that elective officials (aided by competent personnel of their selection) might in time discharge public functions in as efficient a manner as independent power boards? Are they so lacking in faith in the processes of education and reform that they are unwilling to participate in such an effort? If TVA efforts to encourage good management practices were directed toward elective officials instead of members of appointive boards responsible for specialized functions, would the good examples have more of an impact on municipal government generally?

In the view of many people, however, the arguments for independent boards outweigh those for integrated government under elective stewards. Among the benefits typically claimed are elimination of personalized or narrowly partisan politics, the enlistment of especially well-qualified people who would not stand for elective public offices, and treatment of utility services as municipal business enterprises. It is understandable that TVA would have such an outlook, headed as it is by an appointive board. But the question persists: are these objectives unattain-

[5] *Ibid.*

able under elective officials? Most observers and critics, even those who roundly condemn public officials, seem to believe that government *can be* better. Is it truly impossible to achieve a highly efficient utility operation as a part of a general municipal government, or is it just not worth the effort?

This is a much-studied and much-debated aspect of public administration, and the issue cannot be definitively resolved in the context of TVA-municipal relationships. In the final analysis, one's preference may depend upon the basic premises and values that he considers to be more important—whether improvements should be sought within the framework of our traditional forms of local representative democracy, or whether the quick and easy route to efficiency through appointive power boards should be followed. TVA's early leaders issued many pronouncements about their desire to foster democratic concepts at the local government level and to work with local officials. One might wonder how these can be reconciled with later statements casting the politician in a very bad role and the Authority's long-standing insistence on administration by power boards, thoroughly insulated from the politicians and dealing at arm's length with other agencies of municipal government.

IS TVA TOO INFLEXIBLE?

In TVA's prescription and administration of the contractual arrangements with its distributors, an unyielding characteristic exists that some observers may regard as commendable. Others may view this aspect as poor policy in the long run for an agency that operates in a political environment, holding that there should be room within the Authority's policies for a little more give-and-take.

TVA personnel are thoroughly dedicated to the cause of low power rates, but some observers question whether this goal has been elevated unduly above all other considerations. The Authority has interpreted the TVA Act to give it a simple mandate of lowest possible rates, which is a distortion of a provision directing that sales of power to industries shall be handled in such a manner as to give the lowest possible rates to domestic and rural consumers. An element of judgment is also involved in the priority of this objective over competing demands, such as full tax equivalents, payment of nondiscriminatory sales taxes levied by popular referenda, and participation in community service projects. With rates in the Valley about 50 per cent below those being charged by neighboring private utilities, can there be a justification for giving other considerations more weight?

A partial explanation for the rigidity of this policy may be found in the emphasis on nonpolitical administration, which, after more than thirty years, has attained the status of an important tradition. Also of significance is the fact that engineers, with their training and conditioning for exact standards and inflexibility, have been dominant in the administration of the power program. From the beginning, the key policy-making positions in the Office of Power have been held by engineers, and it is at this level that power policies are effectively made; rarely has the TVA board of directors reversed or significantly modified policies recommended by the Office of Power. The Authority's attorneys also play important roles in policy formulation and their influence probably ranks with that of the engineers. Contrary to the recent trend of law to become more of a social science, flexible and adaptable to the social and economic environment, the lawyers usually take a hard line, viewing compromise or concession as a possible opening wedge to break down the TVA control system.

Here again one's judgment on this inflexibility of TVA is colored by his own observations, conditioning, and values. Some would regard it as very beneficial that TVA can operate in a nonpolitical manner in a political environment; others would say that it is undesirable in an agency that must deal with political leaders. Historians may record that the indispensability of the Authority's product—electric power—and the strong appeal of low electric rates to the mass of people enabled TVA to base its political support directly on power consumers and to ignore the considerations and compromises that customarily accompany conduct of public business.

TAX EQUIVALENTS

TVA has gradually moved from an early standard of tax equivalents equal to taxes that would be paid by private utilities to a policy of holding the line at a level that represents "a fair share of the cost of government" (the language used in power contracts with cities). The latter nebulous standard is much more adaptable to the Authority's efforts to lower tax equivalents as part of its low-cost power program. As may be expected, there is not always agreement on what constitutes "a fair share of the cost of government."

In addition to the "fair share" concept, until 1969 the standard contract authorized the application of county and city property tax rates to the book values of electric system properties. Through its field staff TVA has undertaken to keep the amounts paid below this level, using as a standard the statewide average of tax equivalents actually paid. Excluding the four largest cities, the Tennessee average of actual payments increased from 3.7 per cent of net plant value in 1964 to 4.3 per cent in 1968. The authorized level in these years, based on application of property tax rates, was 5.8 per cent in 1964 and 6.1 per cent in 1968, excluding the four largest cities. In 1968 half of Tennessee's fifty-nine municipal systems paid 90 per cent or more of authorized amounts, about a third paid from 50 to 89 per cent, and a fifth paid from 11 to 49 per cent. Another factor tending to lower the level of tax equivalents has been the prevailing view in many cities that the determination of amounts to be paid is the sole prerogative of power boards, although this was probably not a correct interpretation of the law.

In following such a policy, TVA apparently was aiming at a measure of statewide equalization of tax equivalents, which admittedly have been at widely varying levels in relation to property taxes generally because of variations in local property assessment levels and tax rates. There is justification for an equalization program of some sort. For a while it appeared that this would be accomplished at 5 per cent of net plant values, the level that TVA proposed in 1962 and supported until 1966. Municipal officials held out for 5.5 per cent, the statewide average in 1964; after unsuccessfully trying to get TVA to agree to this level, they accepted 5 per cent but a bill introduced late in the 1965 session narrowly failed of passage (one vote short of a constitutional majority in the House). Following court rulings in 1966 that utilities generally were over-assessed, TVA withdrew support of the 5 per cent level, despite intense efforts by municipal leaders to hold the Authority to its previous commitment. Moderation on both sides, after State officials reactivated stalled negotiations, finally led to a legislative compromise in 1969 at an estimated level of 4.8 per cent of net plant values with the minimum payments authorized and at 3.8 per cent without such payments; since minimum payments are to be gradually phased out, the ultimate level is likely to be near the latter percentage.

TVA in the past has consistently opposed new taxes on its power product, as a part of its lowest-possible-rates policy. In 1963 it successfully lobbied an exemption from a local sales tax act (competing fuels had to be exempted also) that is depriving local governments of some $4.5 million annually; if the trend to increase the rate of this tax from 1 per cent to 1½ per cent continues the annual loss will exceed $6 million. A slight thaw occurred in 1969 when TVA included removal of this exemption in a proposed package settlement of the tax-equivalent problem. Although the remainder of the package became law, no bill was introduced for removal of the exemption because of a no-new-taxes climate in the state capitol—perhaps anticipated by TVA. Whether payments will actually be made at the authorized levels is uncertain. Although the 1969 law gives the governing body of a municipality power to make the final determination, some power boards will probably succeed in persuading these bodies to accept lower amounts. And the qualification that such payments have a lower priority on current revenues after all other expenses and reserve funds gives to TVA the potential power to hold the payments down—by depressing rate levels the Authority can make revenues insufficient to pay the full amounts. This cannot be viewed as an unlikely occurrence, in the light of TVA's past record.

An undeveloped issue that has evoked comment from some municipal leaders is whether the tax-equivalent loading on the power bills of directly served large industries (5 per cent of power costs excluding facilities rental charges) should be increased to the level paid by customers of TVA's municipal and cooperative distributors (averaged 8.1 per cent of gross power revenues in 1967 and 7.9 per cent in 1968). It has even been suggested that federal agencies should be subjected to the same requirement. Corporate taxes on utility companies in other states are included in the charges for power to federal agencies. For example, the tax-exempt Atomic Energy Commission pays only Tennessee's 1 per cent industrial sales tax on power delivered to its contractors in this state, which compares with state and local taxes of 3.3 and 4.2 per cent paid by AEC in 1967 on comparable power supplied by two companies in other states.[6]

A FINAL WORD

TVA, in combination with its distributors, has a going enterprise that has been, and no doubt will continue to be, very successful in selling electric power at very low rates. However, widespread feeling is evident among municipal officials, and even among some power board officials, that they are not full partners in this enterprise. If the status of full partnership is ever to be attained, considerably more give-and-take than has been manifested by TVA in the past will be needed. This is not likely to come about because of the Authority's fears that concessions will place in jeopardy its primary objective of lowest possible rates. Concentration on this objective could be tempered with a little more concern for the problems of municipal governments.

[6] Letter from S. R. Sapirie, manager, Oak Ridge Operations, Atomic Energy Commission, to me, Feb. 24, 1969 (in the files of the Municipal Technical Advisory Service, The University of Tennessee, Knoxville). The two companies are Electric Energy, Inc., and Ohio Valley Electric Corporation.

APPENDIX 1

POWER SALES BY TVA AND DISTRIBUTORS, IN MILLIONS OF KILOWATT-HOURS AND PERCENTAGES OF TOTALS, BY MAJOR CATEGORIES, 1950–1968

Year ended June 30	Total sales	Direct sales by TVA							Sales by municipal and cooperative systems					
		Fed. agencies		Large industry		Other		Residential		Com. & ind.		Outdoor light	
		kwh.	%	kwh.	%	kwh.	%	kwh.	%	kwh.	%	kwh.	%
1950	13,482	1,969	14.6	3,687	27.4	1,242	9.2	2,796	20.7	3,736	27.7	52	0.4
1951	15,722	2,191	13.9	4,452	28.3	1,051	6.7	3,595	22.9	4,375	27.8	58	0.4
1952	19,303	4,919	25.5	4,830	25.0	652	3.4	4,122	21.4	4,714	24.4	66	0.3
1953	22,728	6,967	30.7	5,109	22.5	642	2.8	4,767	21.0	5,169	22.7	74	0.3
1954	29,057	11,800	40.6	5,544	19.1	650	2.2	5,453	18.8	5,526	19.0	84	0.3
1955	40,971	21,770	53.2	6,031	14.7	687	1.7	6,240	15.2	6,144	15.0	99	0.2
1956	52,616	30,512	58.0	7,228	13.7	595	1.1	7,149	13.6	7,019	13.4	113	0.2
1957	55,816	31,667	56.7	8,007	14.4	587	1.1	7,649	13.7	7,777	13.9	129	0.2
1958	55,319	28,897	52.2	8,362	15.1	556	1.0	9,382	17.0	7,977	14.4	145	0.3
1959	55,864	28,012	50.2	9,518	17.0	1,917	3.4	9,381*	16.8	6,902*	12.4	134*	0.2
1960	57,874	28,284	48.9	10,364	17.9	650	1.1	10,802	18.7	7,629	13.2	145	0.2
1961	58,562	28,209	48.2	10,077	17.2	641	1.1	11,606	19.8	7,866	13.4	163	0.3
1962	58,684	25,891	44.1	10,951	18.7	664	1.1	12,465	21.3	8,525	14.5	188	0.3
1963	61,993	25,211	40.7	12,228	19.7	848	1.3	14,000	22.6	9,479	15.3	227	0.4
1964	66,535	25,362	38.1	14,077	21.2	1,162	1.7	15,040	22.6	10,619	16.0	275	0.4
1965	67,760	20,392	30.1	15,774	23.3	1,534	2.3	16,471	24.3	13,240	19.5	349	0.5
1966	74,734	20,638	27.6	16,765	22.4	1,919	2.6	18,704	25.0	16,290	21.8	418	0.6
1967	79,408	20,226	25.5	18,590	23.4	2,565	3.2	19,912	25.1	17,652	22.2	463	0.6
1968	81,989	18,802	22.9	19,213	23.4	2,130	2.6	22,140	27.0	19,197	23.4	507	0.6

* Reductions resulted from withdrawal of Memphis. The city re-entered the tva system in Jan., 1965.

Sources: TVA Annual Reports, 1950–1968; Operations Municipal and Cooperative Distributors of TVA Power, Annual Reports 1959 and 1968. "Total sales" in this table through 1959 are reconcilable to the totals in TVA Annual Reports by adding "distribution losses" reported in the 1959 distributors operations report; after 1959 such losses were reported in percentages only, but it has been verified that these likewise account for comparable differences in 1960–1968 totals.

APPENDIX 2

YEARS IN WHICH VARIOUS PROVISIONS OF STREET LIGHTING RATE SCHEDULES BECAME EFFECTIVE FOR TENNESSEE OWNER-CITIES

Municipality	Energy charges B5-1 B-5 OLB	Energy charges SL OL	Energy charges SL-1 OL-1	Lamp mnt. chg.[a]	Investment charges 12%	Investment charges 11%	Investment charges 10%	Investment charges 9%	Investment charges 8%	Glassware replacement Cost	Glassware replacement Excess
Alcoa	1955	1957	—	—	1955*	1957	—	—	—	1955	—
Athens	1939	—	—	—	1939	—	1955	—	1962	1939	1955
Bolivar	1935	1961	—	1935	1939	—	—	—	1951	1939	1951
Bristol	1943	1964	—	—	1943	1950	—	1951	—	1943	1950
Brownsville	1938	1947	1964	—	1938	1947	1950	—	—	1938	1950
Chattanooga	1937	1963†	—	1937	—	—	—	—	1963†	—	1963†
Clarksville	1938	—	1946	1938	1944	—	1946*	—	1949	1944	1949
Cleveland	1939	1956	—	—	1939	—	—	—	1950	1939	1950
Clinton	1939	1956	—	—	1939	1956	—	1962	—	1939	1962
Columbia	1938	1957	—	1938	1939	—	—	1955	—	1939	1955
Cookeville	1944	1951	1958	—	1944	1951	1958	1964	—	1944	1964
Covington	1958	—	—	—	1958	—	—	—	—	1958	—
Dayton	1941	1955	—	—	1941	1955	—	—	—	1941	—
Dickson (U)	1935	1946	—	1935	—	1946	—	—	1956	1946	1956
Dickson (R)	1935	1965	—	1935	1951	—	—	—	1956	1951	1956
Dyersburg	1956	—	—	—	1956	—	1969	—	—	1956	1969
Elizabethton	1944	1958	1963	—	1944	—	—	—	1954	1944	1954
Erwin	1945	1963	1965	—	1945	1963	1965	—	—	1945	—
Etowah	1938	1956	—	1938	1940*	1956	—	—	—	1940	—
Fayetteville (U)	1938	—	1946	1938	1939	—	1946	—	—	1939	—

City											
Fayetteville (R)[b]	1935	—	—	1935	1939*	—	1951	—	—	1939	1951
Gallatin	1939	1946	1957	—	1939	1946	1957	1960	1969	1939	1960
Greeneville	1945	1965	—	—	1945	—	1955	—	—	1945	1955
Harriman	1939	1951	—	—	1939	1951	—	—	1957	1939	1957
Humboldt	1938	1947	1957	—	1938	1947	—	1950	—	1938	1950
Jackson	1935	1947[c]	1956	1935	1944	1947	1956	—	—	1944	—
Jellico	1940	—	—	—	1940	—	—	—	1969	1940	—
Johnson City	1945	1958	1965	—	1945	—	—	1957	—	1945	1957
Knoxville	1936	—	—	1936	1963	1969	—	—	—	1963	—
LaFollette	1939	1958	—	—	1939	1958	—	1969	1963	1939	1963
Lawrenceburg	1939	1963	—	—	1939	—	—	—	1961	1939	1961
Lebanon	1941	1946	1963	—	1941	1946	—	—	1953	1941	1953
Lenoir City	1938	1950	—	1938	1941	—	—	—	1950	1941	1950
Lewisburg	1938	—	1945	1938	—	—	1945	1962	—	1945	1959
Lexington	1939	—	—	—	1939	—	1959	—	—	1939	1959
Loudon	1939	1951	—	—	1939	1951	—	1954	—[d]	1939	1954
Maryville	1939	—	1946	—	1939	—	1946	—	—	1939	—
McMinnville	1939	1951	1959	—	1939	1951	—	—	1956	1939	1956
Memphis	1965	—	—	—	1965	—	1969	—	—	1965	—
Milan	1935	1957	1966	1935	1941	1957	—	—	1964	1941	1964

* Indicated percentage again effective under 1969 rate adjustments.
† Power contract terms, but power system has continued prior basis of fixed annual charges varying according to size of lamps.
a Monthly lamp maintenance charges ranged from 80 cents for a 1,000 lumen or 100-watt multiple lamp to $2.15 for a 10,000 lumen or 500-watt multiple lamp, but there were no investment or glassware replacement charges.
b Until 1963 the Lincoln County Electric Membership Corporation.
c In 1954 applied an SLA schedule which included no energy charges and was based on fixtures used: monthly charges from 70 cents for a 2,500 lumen lamp to $3.30 for a 15,000 lumen mercury vapor lamp.
d Lowered to 7 per cent in 1969.

APPENDIX 2 (*Continued*)

Municipality	Energy charges B5-1 B-5 OLB	SL OL	SL-1 OL-1	Lamp mnt. chg.	Investment charges 12%	11%	10%	9%	8%	Glassware replacement Cost	Excess
Morristown	1949	1950	1966	–	1949	1950	1966	–	–	1949	–
Mt. Pleasant	1939	1948	1959	–	1939	1948	–	1969	1957	1939	1957
Murfreesboro	1939	1946	1951	–	1939	1946	1951	1959	1964	1939	1956
Nashville	1939	–	–	–	1939	–	–	–	1953	1939	1953
Newbern	1938	1950	1955	1938	–	1950	1955	–	1958	1950	1958
Newport	1939	1959	1962	–	1939	1959	–	–	1960	1939	1960
Oak Ridge	1960	1961	–	–	1960	1961	–	–	–	1960	–
Paris	1937	1958	–	–	1937	–	1957	–	–	1937	1957
Pulaski	1939	–	–	1939	1947	–	–	–	–	1947	–
Ripley	1938	1947	1964	–	1938	1947	–	1962	–	1938	1962
Rockwood	1939	–	–	–	1939	1969	–	–	–	1939	–
Sevierville	1939	1963	–	–	1939	–	–	1958	–	1939	1958
Shelbyville	1939	1951	1959	–	1939	1951	–	1954	–	1939	1954
Somerville	1935	1963	–	1935	1939	–	–	–	1955	1939	1955
Sparta	–	–	1960	–	–	–	–	–	1960[e]	–	1960
Springfield	1940	1946	1957	–	1940	1946	1957	1960	–	1940	1960
Sweetwater	1939	1964	–	–	1939	–	–	–	1958	1939	1958
Trenton	1937	–	1957	1937	–	–	1957	–	–	1957	–
Tullahoma	–	1947	1962	–	–	1947	1961	1969	–	1947	1961
Union City	1950	1963	–	–	1950*	–	1962	–	–	1950	1962
Winchester	1939	1957	–	–	1939	1957	1969	–	–	1939	1969

* Indicated percentage again effective under 1969 rate adjustments.
[e] Lowered to 6 per cent in 1969.

APPENDIX 3

TVA WHOLESALE POWER RATE—SCHEDULE A

(Revision of February 1969)

Availability

Firm power available under long-term contracts with, and for resale by, States, counties, municipalities, and cooperative organizations of citizens or farmers.

Rate

Demand Charge:
One dollar and five cents per month per kilowatt of demand

Energy Charge:

First	100,000	kilowatt-hours per month at	4.1 mills per kwh
Next	200,000	" " " " "	3.6 " " "
Next	700,000	" " " " "	3.1 " " "
Excess over	1,000,000	" " " " "	2.6 " " "

The final block of the energy charge will be decreased by 0.05 mill per kwh until the first month in which a demand over 5,000 kw is established by any consumer served by Distributor irrespective of the delivery point through which the power is obtained from TVA. If this decrease becomes ineffective, it will be reinstated at the expiration of any period of 36 consecutive months during which no consumer served by Distributor has established a demand of over 5,000 kw; provided, however, if Distributor's only consumer requiring more than 5,000 kw becomes a consumer TVA is entitled to serve directly in accordance with the provisions of the power contract, such reinstatement will be effective as of the same date that the consumer is transferred to TVA. Any such reinstated decrease shall be subject to the same limitation as to duration as the initial decrease.

Adjustments

1. The bill for each month will be increased or decreased by 0.01 mill per kwh for each 0.01 mill or major fraction thereof by which TVA's fossil and nuclear fuel expense per kwh sold by TVA as determined by TVA from its records exceeded or was less than 1.45 mills, respectively, during the most recently completed fiscal year ending with June 30. Each adjustment made pursuant to this paragraph 1 shall be effective for 12 consecutive monthly billings beginning with the first bill rendered from meter readings

taken after August 1 of the calendar year in which each such fiscal year ends.

2. The bill for each month will be increased or decreased by 1 cent per kw of billing demand for each 1 cent or major fraction thereof by which the sum of (a) TVA's interest charges to operations during the most recently completed fiscal year ending with June 30 and (b) the return on the appropriation investment that TVA is obligated to pay for the fiscal year immediately following said most recently completed fiscal year, divided by the sum of the monthly billing demands of power sold by TVA in said most recently completed fiscal year as determined by TVA from its records exceeded or was less than 40 cents, respectively. Each adjustment made pursuant to this paragraph 2 shall be effective for 12 consecutive monthly billings beginning with the first bill rendered from meter readings taken after August 1 of the calendar year in which each such fiscal year ends.

3. There will be added to the bill each month 10 cents per kw and 0.20 mill per kwh for power and energy sold by Distributor in the preceding month to consumers using more than 10,000 kw or 5 million kwh each (herein referred to as large loads), except that such charge will not apply to that portion of a large load up to the following amounts: 10,000 kw plus the amount (not in excess of 20,000 kw) equal to Distributor's demand at the TVA delivery point in excess of the sum of the billing demands of large loads; 5 million kwh plus an amount (not in excess of 15 million kwh) equal to Distributor's purchases of energy at the TVA delivery point in excess of the energy resold to large loads.

4. The bill for each month will be decreased by an amount equal to 0.05 mill per kwh for each 25 kw or major fraction thereof by which the load density in the area served by Distributor was less than 100 kw per square mile. The load density shall be computed by dividing the highest sum of the billing demands established at the point or points of delivery to the Distributor in any month of the latest 12 consecutive month period by the total number of square miles in the entire area supplied by Distributor at the beginning of the month in which such highest sum of the billing demands was established.

Determination of Demand

The demand for any month shall be the highest average during any 60 consecutive minute period of the month of (a) the load measured in kilowatts or (b) 85 percent of the load in kva plus 10 percent of the excess over 5,000 kva of the maximum kva demand for the month for each individual consumer, whichever is the higher.

Facilities Rental

This schedule is designed for a delivery voltage of not less than 161 kv. For delivery at less than 161 kv Distributor will pay to TVA, in addition to other rates and charges including minimum charges, a facilities rental charge of 15 cents per kw per month for the first 10,000 kw of the highest billing demand established at each delivery point during the latest 12 consecutive month period and 5 cents per kw per month for the portion of such demand which is in excess of 10,000 kw except that, for delivery at less than 46 kv, 20 cents shall apply in lieu of 15 cents in the first portion of said facilities rental charge.

Minimum Bill

The minimum bill for demand and energy for any month, exclusive of Adjustments, shall equal 85 percent of the highest demand charge during the previous 36 months; provided, however, that, at Distributor's request, in lieu of such minimum bill being applied individually in the case of two or more delivery points through each of which less than half of the energy taken by Distributor is resold to large lighting and power consumers (defined as consumers with demands of 50 kw or more), the minimum bill for demand and energy for any month, exclusive of Adjustments, for such delivery points, considered together, shall equal the sum of the minimum bills which would otherwise have been applicable to such delivery points for such month; and, provided further, that a special minimum bill shall be applied for any delivery point through which more than 75 percent of the energy taken by Distributor is resold to large lighting and power consumers.

Single-Point Delivery

The above rates are based upon the supply of service through a single delivery and metering point, and at a single voltage. Separate supply for Distributor at other points of delivery, or at different voltage, shall be separately metered and billed.

APPENDIX 4

FUNCTIONS OF THE TVA DISTRIBUTORS ACCOUNTING SECTION[1]

The TVA power program does not terminate with the wholesale delivery of power to municipalities and cooperatives for retail distribution. The TVA Act directs the Board to give preference in the sale of power to municipalities and cooperatives not organized or doing business for profit, to assure the widest possible distribution at the most economical prices without discrimination between consumers, and to provide for a complete accounting of the costs of producing and distributing power. Compliance with these directives obviously requires working very closely with the independent agencies through which power is delivered to the ultimate consumers.

Provisions of the power contracts which are designed to carry out the policy stated in the Act are basically unchanged since the first contracts were negotiated. The parties mutually agree on the purpose—that the distributor is in a nonprofit business operated primarily for the benefit of its consumers through the fullest and widest use at the lowest possible cost. Only through adequate bookkeeping and financial control and reporting can measurement be made of how well the purpose is carried out. Many other provisions in the contracts require watching, which can best be done by persons familiar with accounting records and local office routines. Commingling of funds or accounts is prohibited. Benefits to municipal general funds are limited, usually to payments in lieu of taxes measured by a formula dependent on proper plant accounting for uniform application. Retail rate schedules are of course prescribed and discriminatory application forbidden. Provision is made for changes in rates, dependent on results of operations which in turn depend on accuracy of accounting. Priorities in the use of cash are prescribed. Proper allocations of joint costs are required so that the electric consumer receives a share in the benefits. Administration of these and other provisions falls naturally within the broad field of accounting.

The need for experienced assistance to the distributors in organizing their office work, including billing, collecting, and the several branches of accounting, and in obtaining adequate personnel for such jobs was apparently anticipated by TVA management before the first power contracts were negotiated with municipalities and cooperatives. Also obvious was the need for personnel familiar with utility accounting and records to assist TVA management in the administration of policies designed to satis-

[1] MS furnished by Gifford Cruze, TVA comptroller, May 6, 1965.

factorily carry out the statutory responsibilities of TVA. The first TVA power contract (Tupelo) required the city to keep electric system accounts according to a system prescribed by TVA and stated that the "Authority agrees, at its own expense, to render advisory accounting service in the setting up and administering of such accounts." The same provision has appeared, with minor changes in wording, in every power contract negotiated since 1933 with municipalities and cooperatives.

The first full-time field accountant was hired in June 1934, by which time power service was being supplied to four distributors, and several other contracts were in various stages of negotiation. As contracts became effective during 1935 and 1936 with about 25 additional municipalities and cooperatives, the field staff was increased accordingly, and thereafter additions were made as necessary, more or less in proportion to the number of new distributors. The TEPCO acquisition early in the fiscal year 1940 resulted in additional staff requirements, and for administrative reasons a separate organizational unit, now titled the Distributors Accounting Section, was created early in fiscal year 1941.

Numerical analysis of the staff of the section can be misleading without explanation. There have been as many as 23 employees. Currently there are 15 employees, including a trainee for replacement of a man soon to retire. However, in the earlier years there was a substantial amount of non-repetitive work, mainly in the field of plant accounting. As close as can be estimated, the number of employees engaged in activities similar to those now being carried out has decreased slightly since 1941. While there has been but a small reduction numerically in staff requirements for services comparable to those rendered currently, the service area has grown tremendously. When the section was organized there were 114 distributors serving about 444,000 customers from facilities costing in the neighborhood of $100 million. In 1955, 148 distributors served almost 1,400,000 customers from facilities costing about $500 million. The responsibilities and problems of the Distributors Accounting Section have not grown in direct proportion to the above statistics, but they have increased steadily and have been assimilated with no increase in personnel. Always geared (1) to the needs of Power management for reasonably accurate financial, statistical, and other information in order to adequately administer power contracts and the over-all power program, and (2) to the needs of the distributors in order to avoid the administrative chaos which inevitably results from the lack of a responsible office and accounting organization, further reductions will be made in the future if possible.

The current number of employees (15) is the lowest number since the section was organized in 1941. Ten accountants are located in the field, two in each district, with the district office as headquarters. The balance of the staff is located in Chattanooga, with the supervisor of the section spending most of his time in the field. Activities of the field accountants are so diversified as to defy accurate classification. Studies we have made indicate that approximately 50 percent of their time is spent in what might be called contract administration, primarily for TVA's benefit, and about 50 percent performing various services for the distributors, which could be described narrowly as primarily for the benefit of the distributors. However, there is such an interlocking and intermingling of functions and work that any firm estimate is hazardous.

By contract administration we mean primarily assistance to the Office of Power in distributor contractual relationships. As previously mentioned, the power contracts have a great many provisions related in one way or another to the office routines and accounting performance of the distributors; the field accountants, by training and experience, are able (1) to make such reviews and inspections as to satisfy them that the accounting procedures and policies are functioning reasonably well, and (2) to determine whether or not there have been any transactions which might be considered contract violations. We think of contract administration as primarily for TVA's benefit; however, it would be unusual during the process of review if something did not occur which would remove a portion of the time from such general classification. There is a wide difference between distributors in the amount of time spent in this general activity, depending mainly on the quality of management and the adequacy of the office personnel; some must be watched much more closely than others. As a general rule a visit at least once each month has proved repeatedly to be good policy but is often not possible; much of the benefit to TVA of contract administration activities arises from the prevention of undesirable actions, and extensive inattention too frequently has proved inadvisable.

The activities other than contract administration are much more difficult to describe because of the very wide variety, and to catalog them generally as "primarily for the benefit of the distributor" is debatable. Perhaps the heaviest time consumer in this broad classification is that of training personnel. Training is usually limited to the individual in charge of the office, known under various titles as office manager, treasurer, accountant, etc., but frequently may involve anyone exposed to office problems from the manager to cashiers. Normally the distributors fill the more important jobs by promotion, but in numerous instances that has not been possible. While training results usually from the acquisition of new personnel, there is some training going on constantly among even well-qualified office help. During training, some actual work, such as bookkeeping, plant accounting, billing, etc., is usually and inevitably performed for the distributor (but as little as possible), and contract administration activities are naturally a byproduct. The amount of time required for training activities has decreased substantially as the years have passed, or this section would have needed additional field accountants.

Another category of service results from requests by local management for assistance in some phase of accounting or office work. These are so numerous and varied as to preclude complete enumeration. Reasonable allocation of time of employees engaged in joint activities (the distributors are getting more and more into operations jointly with other municipal departments) and of other joint expenses is a common problem requiring frequent review. More and more branch offices for collecting and for servicing activities are being found necessary, and related accounting problems, mainly in the field of internal control over cash and materials, are requiring management attention and reliance on the field accountants. Construction contracts of various types require close attention, especially when sections of old property are being rebuilt; assistance from TVA accountants is almost always sought in such cases, and obviously the benefit of giving assistance does not accrue solely to the distributor inasmuch as proper accounting benefits the entire power program. Accounting for plant replacements requires constant attention. Devising and revising forms and modernizing office procedures which, because of rapid growth, soon become obsolete are common undertakings. Assistance with reporting, financial and otherwise, in such forms as will be more comprehensible to boards, city councils, and the public, is frequently given. While it is outside the direct responsibility of the field accountants, they have found it advisable under certain circumstances to assist to a very limited extent in the gas department or water department accounting insofar as it involves a definite relationship to electric operations because of joint management or operation. Assistance is given in budgeting and in reporting to REA, FPC, state and tax commissions, and others.

Specific requests for information from many sources, principally TVA management at various levels, require a varying but substantial amount of time, and only the field accountants are in the peculiar position of being able to obtain such data promptly and easily, with their access to the records and knowledge of where to look. Local managers, superintendents, mayors, and board members frequently rely on the field accountants for information about their own operations which they seem unable to obtain more directly or do not wish to obtain in any other way.

As time permits, the field accountants make statistical studies of the reserves for depreciation under the close supervision of the Chattanooga office. The process is designed to furnish an approximation of the reserve requirement against the dollar amount of the plant investment remaining at a given date, and from the results the need for depreciation rate changes can be determined so as to gradually bring the actual reserves into line. This is a long-range program of great importance inasmuch as provisions for depreciation are, except for the cost of purchased power, the greatest single operating expense of the distributors, and the reliability of financial statements and operating results as well as the adequacy of rates for power and energy depend, of course, on a reasonably accurate accounting for costs.

The field accountants have been instrumental in organizing district associations of key accounting personnel. The meetings, usually quarterly, are a means of bringing together personnel with mutual problems and interests. At the request of local managers and where time permits, the field accountants attend meetings of District Managers' associations, board, or city council meetings.

Another area of activity involves actual work assistance, usually in some phase of bookkeeping or report preparation. The field accountants are sometimes called upon for assistance during emergencies, such as the sudden illness or death of a key employee. Then, a few of the distributors have never been able to employ or retain a fully responsible office manager and rely for some assistance on the field accountant; usually some phase of plant accounting is involved, as the unitization of unusual jobs, or closing construction into classified plant accounts, or properly pricing certain retirements, etc. It is in this area that the question of billing for services rendered frequently arises, but where small amounts are involved the conclusion has usually been that the good will created is far more important than the amount of money involved.

In summary, it is evident that usefulness of the field accountants goes far beyond the usual concept of accounting. Perhaps their main value lies in the fact that their familiarity with the distributors' accounts, personnel, office procedures, etc., enables them to act as the eyes and ears of TVA's District Managers. To do so requires not only technical ability but also tact, diplomacy, and a personality which fits into widely varying situations so that they become accepted by each distributor as virtually a part of the local organization. Having reached that status, TVA can be reasonably sure of getting all of the information that is needed.

INDEX

Accounting standards, 167–69
   utility billings, consolidated, 169
Acquisition of private companies, 10–12, 14–15, 27–29, 34, 112
   state action proposed, 27–29, 34
Alabama Power Company, largest TVA customer in early years, 9
Annexation of cooperatives' service areas, 119–22
   arbitration by TVA, 122
   cooperatives object, 119–20
   municipalities defend, 120
"Arm's length" policy, TVA's, 38, 158, 163
Ashwander v. *TVA*, 12–13

Bristol, rate reduction in, 96–97
Browning's acquisition of private companies proposal, 27–29, 34

"Captive cities" under TVA's power contracts, 66
Chattanooga
   contract non-renewal threatened by TVA, 71
   delays rate reduction, 93
   desires diversion of power revenues, 145
   fails to exercise right to build dam, 5
   opposes TVA over service to war production plant, 133–35
   power provisions of charter upheld, 25–26
Citizens for TVA, TVA approves contributions to, 155–56
City, *see* Municipal; Municipalities
Cleveland suburban competition with cooperative, 127–28
Coffee County, Tullahoma v., 217
Congressional opposition to acquisition of private companies, 15
Consumers favored by TVA, 74
Contracts between TVA and municipalities, *see* Power contracts
Contributions
   approved for Citizens for TVA, 155–56
   prohibited by power contracts, 153–56
Controls by TVA over distributors, 20–21, 50–51, 55, 60–61, 145–49, 169–71, 233–34, 239–40, 252–56
   accounting field staff, 169–71

258   Index

Controls by TVA over distributors (*cont.*)
   accounting services, GAO recommends changes in, 170
   accounting standards, 167–69
   inflexibility of TVA, 239–40
   Kentucky court criticizes, 20–21
   municipal officials estimate TVA pressures, 55
   revenues, use of, 145–49
   review procedures, 234
Coolidge vetoes Muscle Shoals bill, 7
Cooperatives, *see* Annexation of cooperatives' service areas; Municipalities vs. cooperatives in suburban areas
County tax equivalents, *see* Tax equivalents for counties
Court cases involving municipal power systems in Tennessee, 24–27
Criticism of TVA
   by courts of Kentucky, 20–21; of Mississippi, 21
   questionnaire answers, 51–53, 55
Crossville objects to acquisition terms, 113

Debt reduction, TVA changes policies on premature, 95
Debt-free Tennessee municipal power systems, 94
Decentralization
   objectives of TVA not attained, 35
   preferred by TVA for power distribution, 32–35
Decentralized distribution under TVA control, 50–51, 236
Direct service by TVA to large industries, *see* Industries
Distribution, decentralization of power, 32–35, 50–51, 236
Distribution systems, *see* Municipal power systems
Distributors
   contracts, *see* Power contracts
   power supply, TVA sole source of, 65–66
   revenues, *see* Revenues
   under TVA controls, *see* Controls by TVA over distributors
District offices, TVA, functions of, 36–37
Diversion of power revenues, *see* Revenues
"Dividends" by TVA actually interest payments, 80–81
Dixon-Yates controversy, 16–17, 66

Electric Home and Farm Authority, 102

Favorable remarks about TVA on questionnaires, 52–53
Federal agencies given preference by TVA, 62–64
Formula for tax equivalents; *see* Tax equivalents, municipal
Franklin Power and Light Company
   circumscribed by TVA, 124–25
   wins court suit by cooperative, 125–27
Fringe areas, *see* Municipalities vs. cooperatives in suburban areas

"Gray Book" of distributors on TVA service to industries, 142–43
"Green Book" issued by TVA on direct service to industries, 140

Hales Bar dam, 5
Hoover vetoes Muscle Shoals bill, 8

Industries, TVA direct service to, 132–44
   dispute with distributors, 138–44
   "Gray Book," distributors', 142–43
   "Green Book," TVA's, 140
   TVA policy evolves, 135–36
   Volunteer Cooperative sues TVA, 136–38
Inflexibility of TVA administration, 239–40
Influence of TVA
   on municipal governments, 54–60, 58–59, 236–39
   on state legislation, 21–23, 234–35
Interest
   costs increase TVA's rates, 80–82
   subsidy to TVA, 80–81, 177
Investment return, *see* Municipal investment, return on

Johnson City criticized for lack of rural service, 118
Joint operations of power systems and other municipal agencies, 158–65, 169
   allocations of expenses, 160–61
   buildings shared with other municipal agencies, 161–64
      municipal officials' views, 163–64
   industrial promotion, 158–59
   meter reading and billing, 164–65
   miscellaneous, 164–65
   utilities, with other, 159–61
   utility billings, consolidated, 169

Kentucky court critical of TVA controls, 20–21
Knoxville
   charter construed to authorize power operation, 25
   power board created, 42–43
   tries to buy private company, 11–12

Laws of Tennessee
   controlling municipal power systems, 23–24
   TVA's influence on, 21–23, 47–50
Legislation influenced by power lobby, 234–35
Legislative Council Committee studies suburban competition issue, 129
Litigation in Tennessee, 24–27
Local distribution systems, *see* Decentralization preferred by TVA; Municipal power systems

Memphis
   Dixon-Yates controversy, 16–17, 66
   leaves TVA system, 66

260 *Index*

Memphis (*cont.*)
   power board subject to some controls by municipal government, 45–46
   power contract sustained by courts, 25
   private company acquired by, 15
   re-entry into TVA system, 209
   rural service criticized, 118–19
   surcharges in power rates, 90–91
Metropolitan government enabling act, TVA influences, 47–50
Middlesboro, Ky., tries to get TVA power, 20–21
Mississippi court critical of TVA, 21
Municipal annexation of cooperatives' service areas, 119–20
Municipal Electric Plant Law of 1935, 23–24
Municipal governments
   non-TVA influences on, 58–60
   TVA favors strong, 56–57
   TVA's influence on, 54–60, 236–39
   vs. power board control of power system, *see* Power boards
Municipal investment, return on, 151, 165–67
   early policy permitting increases, 151, 166
   eliminated by TVA, 166
   Oak Ridge, received by, 166–67
Municipal officials
   estimate TVA's influence, 54–55
   feelings of pressure from TVA, 55
   object to TVA's "arm's length" advocacy, 38–39
   reject Browning's proposal, 28
Municipal power boards, *see* Power boards
Municipal power contracts, *see* Power contracts
Municipal power revenues, *see* Revenues
Municipal power systems
   acquisition terms, disagreements on, 112–13
   cooperative activities with other municipal agencies, *see* Joint operations
   debt-free, 94
   promoted by TVA, 10–11
   rural service by, 117–19
   Tennessee laws controlling, 23–24
   TVA's role in allocating, 110–12
   urban and rural divisions, 100–102
Municipalities
   contracting agents for, 69–71
   favored by TVA for distribution, 32–33
   power supply, TVA sole source of, 65–66
   preference on power supply given to, 61–62
   rural service by, 117–19
   TVA's role in allocating power systems to, 110–12

Index   261

Municipalities (cont.)
  weak in contracting with TVA, 30, 71, 233
Municipalities vs. cooperatives in suburban areas, 119–32
  Cleveland wins in court, 127–28
  consolidation proposed as solution, 131–32
  cooperatives favored by TVA, 124–25, 128–29, 131
  legislative action, 128–31
  Legislative Council Committee, study by, 129
Murfreesboro, Rutherford County v., 215–16
Muscle Shoals
  Commission appointed by Hoover, 8
  developments after World War I, 5–9
  early work, 3–4
  Inquiry Commission, 7
  private power development authorized, 4
  World War I developments, 5

Nashville
  legislation cleared with TVA, 22–23
  objects to TVA's acquisition terms, 12, 112
  rate reductions discussed, 94
  surcharges tried, 91
Negotiation of power contracts, 30, 71–73, 232–33
Norris, Senator George W., sponsors Muscle Shoals bills, 6–7

Oak Ridge receives return on municipal investment, 166–67
"One owner" concept of TVA, 54
Organization, TVA, 35–36

Partnership theory, TVA's, 32–35, 38, 233–34, 243
Political influences, TVA condemns, 38–39
Power, organization of TVA Office of, 35–36
Power boards
  abolition of, 46–47
  adverse effects on municipal governments, 44
  autonomy limited in Memphis, 45–46
  autonomy of, 40–41, 44–47, 54
  composition of, 41–43, 45
    controversies over, 41–43
  experience in municipalities with and without, 57–58
  favored by TVA, 38, 40–41, 57, 236–37
  legal powers of, 44–45
  municipal officials' preferences, 43–44
  number in Tennessee, 43
  protection by metropolitan government enabling act, 47–50
  Smithville pressured by TVA to establish, 115
  vs. municipal government control of power system, 55–59, 236–39
Power consumption by classes of customers, 18–19

262 Index

Power contracts between TVA and municipalities, 29–31, 60–73, 153–56, 232–33
    administration, *see* Controls by TVA over distributors
    contract mandatory under statutory conditions, 115–17
    contracting agents for municipalities, 69–71
    contributions prohibited, 153–56
    lowest possible rates, primacy of, 74
    miscellaneous provisions, 67–69
    negotiation of, 30, 71–73, 232–33
        Tupelo, Miss., wins a round, 72
    rules and regulations, 68–69
    sole supplier of power, TVA as, 65–66
    standard contract and variations, 232
        revision not given municipal review, 73
    state law, subject to, 29
    Tennessee state officials choose neutral role, 30–31
    term of, 66–67
    termination of, 67
Power distribution, decentralization of; *see* Distribution
Power generation, TVA facilities for, 16–17
Power lobby effective in Tennessee, 234–35
Power program, TVA's, 3, 16–18, 176–77
    priority in relation to other programs, 3, 16–18
    subsidy to, 176–77
Power rates, TVA
    comparisons
        commercial and industrial, 77–78
        residential, 77
    congressional mandate modified, 75–76
    discrimination prohibited within classes of consumers, 88
    high use leads to lower rates, 77
    interest costs increase, 80–82
    "lowest possible" concept, 74–77
    municipal governments, charged to, 88
    retail rates, 25–27, 87–91, 100–102, 152–53, 233–34
        amortization charges, 89–90
        control by TVA, 86–89, 233–34
        courts sustain TVA control, 25–27
        increases authorized, 152–53
        sufficiency for tax equivalents not assured, 152–53
        supervision by TVA, 88–89
        surcharges, 90–91
        uniform rates in urban and rural areas; exceptions, 100–102
    retail rate reductions, 91–99
        arguments for, 93–94
        Bristol resists, 96–97
        Chattanooga delays until debt-free, 93

Power rates, TVA (*cont.*)
    early guideline not followed by TVA, 97–98
    municipalities object, 91–97
    Nashville discusses, 94
    statistical summary, 99
    TVA's methods of obtaining, 95–97
    rural rates, 99–102
    state agencies make early effort to regulate, 19–20
    street lighting, 104–109, 246–48
        municipal officials not informed, 107–108
        procedure to lower, 106
        variations in, 108–109
    wholesale rates, 78–86, 249–51
        adjustments in 1967 and 1969, 79–86
        facilities rental charges, 82–84
        fuel costs adjustment, 81–82
        interest costs adjustment, 82
        interests costs increase, 80–81
        load density credit, 81
        minimum bills, 84–86
        schedule, 249–51
    "yardstick" concept, 231
Power revenues, *see* Revenues
Power sales
    major categories, 1950–1968, 245
    promotional activities, 102–104
    promotional assistance, TVA charges distributors for, 103
    to private companies, 9
Power supply, TVA sole source of, 65–66
Preference of federal needs vs. claims of distributors, 62–64
Preference on TVA power, public agencies given statutory, 9, 61–62
Private acts regulate some municipal systems, 24
Private companies
    acquisition of, 10–12, 14–15, 112
        congressional opposition, 15
    favored by Senator Underwood's bill, 6–7
    power purchases from TVA, 9
    sale to TVA opposed in courts, 12–14
Program priorities of TVA, 3, 16–18

Questionnaires
    remarks critical of TVA, 51–53, 55
    remarks favorable about TVA, 52–53

Rates, *see* Power rates
Regulation of TVA attempted by state agencies, 19–20
Retail rates, *see* Power rates
Return on municipal investment, *see* Municipal investment

Revenue Bond Law of 1935, 24
Revenues, diversion of power, 145-49, 156-58, 235-36
  debt service, 156-58
  Lenoir City case, 156-58
  municipal officials' viewpoints, 146-47
Revenues, priorities in use of, 148-53
  contract provisions, 151-52
  power boards sometimes distort, 151
  surplus revenues, use of, 152
  tax equivalents, 149-52
Roosevelt, President Theodore, action on power bills, 4-5
Rural Electrification Administration queries TVA re statute requiring power contract, 115-17
Rural service, 99-100, 110-11, 117-19
  Johnson City delays, 118
  Memphis delays, 118-19
  municipal officials' views, 118
  municipalities, by
    declined by some, 110-11
    others provide, 117-19
    TVA encourages, 117
  TVA pioneers in, 99-100
Rutherford County v. Murfreesboro, 215-16

Sales of power, *see* Power sales
Service areas, 122-32, 138
  agreements between distributors, 122-23
  law of 1968 fixes, 130-31
  TVA argues cooperatives have none, 138
  TVA protects cooperative, 124-25
Smithville secures TVA power contract, 114-15
Sole supplier of power, TVA must be, 65-66
South Fulton fails to get TVA power contract, 115
Sparta secures TVA power contract, 113-14
State of Tennessee
  acquisition of private companies proposal, 27-29, 34
  agencies in early conflicts with TVA, 19-20
  chooses neutral role, 30-31
  law controls TVA-distributor contracts, 29
  laws reflect TVA's influence, 21-23, 234-35
  power policy, 30-31
States, relative use of TVA power by, 15
Steam plants in TVA system, 16
Street lighting rates, *see* Power rates
Subsidy to TVA power program, 176-77
Suburban competition, *see* Municipalities vs. cooperatives in suburban areas

Index 265

Tax equivalents
  counties guaranteed minimum payments from TVA, 179–80, 211
  industries directly served by TVA pay less, 188–89, 242–43
  policy
    early TVA, 173–75
    pre-TVA, 172–73
    shifts in TVA, 175–77, 179–80, 189–91, 203, 230, 240–41
    state, 178
  power rate calculations, included in, 177
  private companies' taxes as a standard, 173–77
  private companies' taxes, compared with, 186–88
    gross revenues comparison, weakness of, 187–88
  TVA, paid by, 180
Tax equivalents for counties, 210–19, 229–30
  congressional intent, 211–12
  controversy leads to new formula, 219
  county officials seek legislative requirement, 211–14, 218
  court suits by cities, 217; by counties, 215–17
  law of 1969 requires, 229–30
  municipal power systems, paid by some, 217–18
  TVA policy, 213, 216–17
  university professors study, 214–15
Tax equivalents, municipal, 189–230
  authorized amounts, less than, 190–91, 204–10, 241–42
    Alcoa, 206–207
    Greeneville, 206
    Jellico, 208–209
    Memphis, 209–10
    Nashville, 207–208
  authorized amounts used by TVA in pre-contract discussions, 206
  base for calculating, 196–200
  book value base, 196–97
    effects of depreciation on, 198–99
  determination, which body makes, 192–95
  "fair share of cost of government," 196
  federal sales tax, for, 201
  formula
    legislative approval of change, 228
    negotiations on change, 219–28, 241–42
  governing body empowered to determine by 1969 law, 195
  Harriman retroactive payments challenged by TVA, 203–204
  law governing determination of, 192–95
  materials and supplies
    excluded from base, 197
    included in base, 198
  minimums, TVA grants exceptional, 200–201
  offsets for other taxes, 201–202

Tax equivalents, municipal (*cont.*)
  power boards
    given effective control by TVA bill draft, 195
    violate power contracts, 206–208
  power rates, relation to, 87–88, 152–53
  priority high in Kentucky, 150
  priority low in Tennessee, 149–51
  private companies taxes, compared with, 190–91
  property taxes only as standard, 191–92
    Cleveland, 191–92
    Knoxville, 192
    Newbern, 191
  rates: authorized, 200; frozen by TVA, 200
  retroactive payments prohibited, 202–204
Taxes
  opposition by TVA, 180–86, 242
  power sales exemption from local sales tax, 183–86
    fiscal results of, 184–85
    municipal officials' views, 185–86
    removal proposed by TVA, 184, 242
  sales tax (state) applied to power sales, 182
Tennessee
  area served by TVA power, 15
  cities enter TVA system, 9–12
  cities vote for TVA power, 11, 15
  Electric Power Company
    builds Hales Bar dam, 5
    loses in federal court, 26–27
  legislator criticizes TVA, 71–72
  Municipal Electric Plant Law of 1935, 23–24
  municipal power systems under private acts, 24
  Revenue Bond Law of 1935, 24
  River studied by Corps of Engineers, 7–8
  State of, *see* State of Tennessee
Tullahoma votes against municipal generating plant, 146
Tullahoma v. Coffee County, 217
Tupelo, Miss., wins in contract negotiations, 72
TVA Act, Congress enacts, 9
  section 13 amendment, 178–80

Volunteer Cooperative sues TVA over service to industry, 136–38

Wholesale power rates, TVA; *see* Power rates, TVA
Wilson Dam, power wasted at, 8

"Yardstick," TVA power rates as, 231

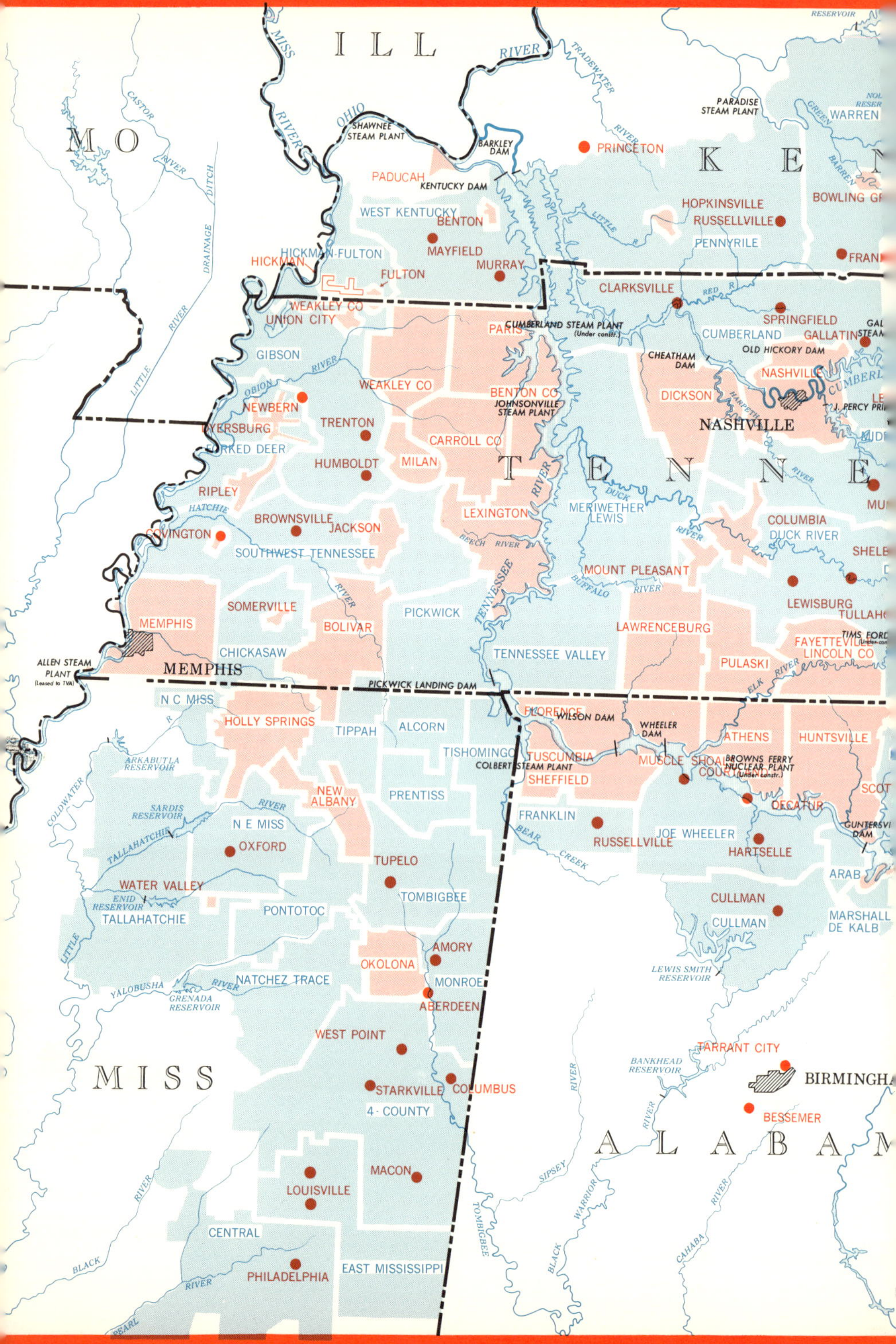
ILL
MO
KEN
TENNE
MISS
ALABAM
MISS RIVER
OHIO RIVER
TRADEWATER RIVER
GREEN RIVER
BARREN RIVER
CUMBERLAND
TENNESSEE RIVER
DUCK RIVER
BUFFALO RIVER
ELK RIVER
HATCHIE
OBION RIVER
FORKED DEER
BEECH RIVER
CASTOR RIVER
DRAINAGE DITCH
LITTLE RIVER
COLDWATER
TALLAHATCHIE
YALOBUSHA
PEARL RIVER
BLACK RIVER
TOMBIGBEE
SIPSEY RIVER
BLACK WARRIOR
CAHABA RIVER
BEAR CREEK
HARPETH
RED R
SHAWNEE STEAM PLANT
BARKLEY DAM
KENTUCKY DAM
PARADISE STEAM PLANT
CUMBERLAND STEAM PLANT (Under constr.)
CHEATHAM DAM
OLD HICKORY DAM
JOHNSONVILLE STEAM PLANT
J. PERCY PRIEST
ALLEN STEAM PLANT (Leased to TVA)
PICKWICK LANDING DAM
WILSON DAM
WHEELER DAM
COLBERT STEAM PLANT
BROWNS FERRY NUCLEAR PLANT (Under constr.)
GUNTERSVILLE DAM
TIMS FORD
ARKABUTLA RESERVOIR
SARDIS RESERVOIR
ENID RESERVOIR
GRENADA RESERVOIR
LEWIS SMITH RESERVOIR
BANKHEAD RESERVOIR
PADUCAH
PRINCETON
WARREN
WEST KENTUCKY
BENTON
MAYFIELD
MURRAY
HOPKINSVILLE
RUSSELLVILLE
PENNYRILE
BOWLING GR
FRAN
HICKMAN
HICKMAN-FULTON
FULTON
WEAKLEY CO
UNION CITY
CLARKSVILLE
SPRINGFIELD
CUMBERLAND
GALLATIN
PARIS
GIBSON
NEWBERN
DYERSBURG
TRENTON
WEAKLEY CO
BENTON CO
CARROLL CO
DICKSON
NASHVILLE
MILAN
HUMBOLDT
FORKED DEER
RIPLEY
BROWNSVILLE
JACKSON
LEXINGTON
MERIWETHER LEWIS
COLUMBIA
DUCK RIVER
COVINGTON
SOUTHWEST TENNESSEE
MOUNT PLEASANT
SOMERVILLE
BOLIVAR
PICKWICK
LEWISBURG
MEMPHIS
CHICKASAW
LAWRENCEBURG
TENNESSEE VALLEY
PULASKI
FAYETTEVILLE
LINCOLN CO
N C MISS
HOLLY SPRINGS
TIPPAH
ALCORN
TISHOMINGO
FLORENCE
TUSCUMBIA
SHEFFIELD
MUSCLE SHOALS
ATHENS
HUNTSVILLE
NEW ALBANY
PRENTISS
FRANKLIN
RUSSELLVILLE
JOE WHEELER
DECATUR
HARTSELLE
N E MISS
OXFORD
TUPELO
TOMBIGBEE
WATER VALLEY
PONTOTOC
TALLAHATCHIE
CULLMAN
MARSHALL DE KALB
ARAB
AMORY
OKOLONA
MONROE
NATCHEZ TRACE
ABERDEEN
WEST POINT
STARKVILLE
COLUMBUS
4-COUNTY
TARRANT CITY
BIRMINGHA
BESSEMER
MACON
LOUISVILLE
CENTRAL
PHILADELPHIA
EAST MISSISSIPPI